New Directions in Econo

To Krystyna, Sonia, Anna and Michał

New Directions in
Econometric Practice

General to Specific Modelling, Cointegration

and Vector Autoregression

Wojciech W. Charemza and Derek F. Deadman

University of Leicester

Edward Elgar

© Wojciech W. Charemza, Derek F. Deadman, 1992

Published by
Edward Elgar Publishing Limited
Gower House
Croft Road
Aldershot
Hants GU11 3HR
England

Edward Elgar Publishing Limited
Old Post Road
Brookfield
Vermont 05036
USA

Reprinted 1993 (twice)

A CIP catalogue record for this book is available from the British Library

Library of Congress Cataloging-in-Publication Data
Charemza, Wojciech.
    New directions in econometric practice : general to specific modelling, cointegration, and vector autoregression / Wojciech W. Charemza and Derek F. Deadman.
        p. cm.
    Includes bibliographical references and indexes.
    1. Econometric models. I. Deadman, Derek. II. Title.
HB141.C473 1992
330'.01'5195—dc20   91-44597
                                                                CIP
ISBN 1 85278 461 X
    1 85278 846 1 (paperback)

Printed and bound in Great Britain at the University Press, Cambridge.

Contents

Foreword by Richard E. Quandt

The present volume represents an innovative approach to teaching econometrics. Most of the existing texts share two basic characteristics: (a) they concentrate on expositing econometric theory and techniques and (b) they cover 'standard' econometric techniques, such as (generalized) regression models, simultaneous equations models, limited dependent variable models, etc. The authors of the present text take a different approach, which practical researchers will find most welcome and which will answer the oft—heard question by students, 'Yes, yes, it's nice to know all these techniques, but if I do some research, how do I know what to do next?'

The volume exposits in detail the process by which empirical research is done. After a brief critique of the Cowles Foundation approach, it starts out with a most welcome chapter on data mining, a subject that is woefully neglected not only in the teaching of econometrics, but, one suspects, often in the practice of it. It then turns to the methodology introduced in the important 1978 paper of Davidson, Hendry, Srba and Yeo. It is a particularly interesting unifying theme of the book that the various techniques that are discussed chapter—by—chapter are nearly always illustrated with reference to the consumption model in that pioneering paper. The volume is thus one in which important techniques and methods are introduced and in which these methods are invariably applied to a concrete case that accompanies the reader from beginning to end.

An excellent discussion of error correction models is followed by a chapter that espouses the general philosophy of going from a general model to a more specific one and does this in the context of autoregressive—distributed lag models. Cointegration, vector autoregressions and Granger causality follow in neat order. The last two chapters deal with the various exogeneity concepts on the one hand and with nonnested models and encompassing on the other. The authors succeed entirely in reaching a happy balance between 'proving things' (although no arduous proofs of any kind are ever presented), providing rationales or explanations, and illustrating the material by working out the appropriate technique or procedure in the context of the consumption function model.

Many of these concepts that are systematically covered here are either completely omitted in standard textbooks or are given only the scantiest mention. It is a *tour de force* to write a book that makes all these concepts completely accessible to students on an intermediate level, i.e. those that have had no more than one course in statistics. It is safe to predict that teachers and students alike will relish the clarity, as well as the concrete orientation of this excellent volume.

Princeton University   RICHARD E. QUANDT

Preface

This book has its origins in a series of undergraduate lectures entitled 'The theory and applications of economic modelling' given over several years by both authors at the University of Leicester. Our experience is that nowadays, when there are so many excellent econometric textbooks and computing packages available, diligent students do not normally encounter particular difficulties in absorbing the principles of econometric theory, or in carrying out the estimation of models. Combining these elements with relevant economic theory to produce a convincing piece of empirical econometric modelling is another matter. Whilst it seems natural and superficially appealing to students to run countless regressions and attempt to choose that which appears to be the 'best' model, this approach has been widely criticized as failing to provide credible results. Unfortunately, descriptions of alternative systematic (and methodologically superior) practices of deriving sound econometric models tend to be available only in abstract and difficult academic articles.

In this book we have attempted to remedy this problem by explaining the basic concepts and computations of contemporary econometric methodologies at a level accessible to non–specialists. The methodologies described include general–to–specific modelling, cointegration and vector autoregressive (VAR) modelling. These are all relevant for time series rather than cross–section econometrics.

The book is intended to be suitable for final year undergraduates, economic practitioners and postgraduates who wish to apply modern econometric techniques as part of essentially non–econometric theses. More advanced readers will need to supplement this book by following up the further reading which is given in each chapter.

It is assumed that the reader has followed an introductory course in mathematical statistics and multiple regression analysis (including basic tests on the General Linear Model), and also has some knowledge of elementary macroeconomics.

For Chapters 6 and 7, an understanding of linear simultaneous equation models would be useful, although a short introduction to this is given.

In order to illustrate the approaches to modelling discussed in this book, we have used a single example throughout. The model of Davidson, Hendry, Srba and Yeo of UK aggregate consumption expenditure, published in 1978, which was a major influence on recent developments in applied econometric analysis is re–examined in the light of these new developments. Whilst it is possible to study particular chapters in isolation, since the basic example is that of the model above, it is advisable that the reader at least glances through Chapter 3 where this model is discussed.

Most chapters are accompanied by a stylized output generated from the use of the computer package *PC–GIVE*. When the book was started, this package provided the most convenient tool for calculating the modern diagnostic tests and procedures necessary to implement the new methodologies (for example, a series of Lagrange Multiplier tests or the Johansen cointegration procedure). Such has been the increase in interest in these new techniques that currently several other packages exist which will perform nearly all of the computations discussed in this book. Examples of such packages are *TSP* version 4.2, *REG–X*, and the 1991 versions of *MICROFIT* and *RATS*.

A special debt is owed by the authors to Richard Quandt who has provided a continuous stream of encouragement and suggestions, and who has generously consented to write a foreword to the book. We were also most fortunate and grateful for comments received from David Hendry which have materially improved the text in many places. In addition we wish to acknowledge the help we have had from both students and colleagues at Leicester, particularly from Francis Green, Peter Jackson, George Norman and Sailesh Tanna who have read the entire text, and Ali Al–Nowaihi and Catherine Price who have commented on various chapters. We also wish to thank Maria Blangiewicz of Gdańsk University who helped greatly in the computation of the tables which appear in the Appendix. Both authors wish to blame the other for any remaining errors.

Chapter 1

Traditional Methodology in Retrospect

1.1   Introduction

It has become common for economists to express or discuss a theory in terms of an equation or a set of equations. Even elementary economics textbooks present postulated relationships between economic variables in an algebraic form, and make inferences by mathematical manipulations. It is then quite natural to attempt to give quantitative measures to these relationships. The most widely used tool of economists to determine empirical forms of theoretical constructs is that of *econometrics*.

The likely originator of the term 'econometrics' defined it as '...the unification of economic theory, statistics, and mathematics...' (Frisch (1936, p.95)). Much of the early empirical work in economics (that is, prior to 1940) was concerned with the measurement of demand elasticities, and the representation of the business cycle. To a great extent, this reflected the activity of economists in developing theory in these areas, and the particular availability of reasonably long runs of statistical data on agricultural commodities, foreign trade and various industries. The later development of national income accounting in conjunction with Keynesian economic theory created new opportunities for the econometric analysis of macroeconomic series, including complete models of economies. These estimated macroeconomic models could be used for economic policy purposes, such as forecasting or simulation.

Reflecting these possibilities, the *objectives* of econometrics have been described by Christ (1966, p.4) as:

...the production of quantitative economic statements that either

1

explain the behaviour of variables we have already seen, or *forecast* (i.e. *predict*) behaviour that we have not yet seen, or both.

Irrespective of which of these objectives is being considered, it is clear that in order to undertake econometric analysis one must have:

1. Economic theory,
2. Statistical data,
3. A method that allows for the expression of the economic theory using the statistical data (in practice, a theory of estimation stemming from econometric theory),
4. A 'know–how', which tells us how to apply the estimation theory to the statistical data, and how to decide whether this application has been successful.

The problem is illustrated by the following example of a Keynesian consumption function. The theory which is further developed in Chapter 3 says that:

a) Real consumption at time t, denoted by C_t , is a 'fairly stable' function of real income (Y_t) in the same period,

$$C_t = f(Y_t) .$$

b) $MPC = dC_t/dY_t < 1$,

where MPC is the marginal propensity to consume.

c) $MPC < APC$ where $APC = C_t/Y_t$,

and APC denotes the average propensity to consume.

d) As real income rises the APC falls.

This is the *economic theory*, that is point (1) above.

Statistical data representing the theoretical constructs can be found in, say, a statistical yearbook to meet point (2). The *theory of estimation* gives rise to a selection of estimation methods (ordinary least squares for example) relevant for point (3). But what about 'know how' ?

One can formulate a practically infinite number of models consistent with this simple form of the Keynesian theory that could be estimated from suitable data, such as:

$$C_t = \alpha_0 + \alpha_1 Y_t + error\ term\ ,$$

$$C_t = \alpha_0 + \alpha_1 Y_t + \alpha_2 Y_{t-1} + error\ term\ ,$$

$$C_t = \alpha_0 + \alpha_1 Y_t + \alpha_2 C_{t-1} + \alpha_3 Z_t + error\ term\ ,$$

where, for example, Z_t could be an interest rate, a measure of wealth, or some consumption rationing measure, and the 'error term' stands for the combined influence of other variables omitted from the equations, none of which are individually important enough to be explicitly included. The problem of 'know how' is to apply an estimation method which combines the statistical data, the economic theory and the statistical theory in such a way as to lead to the 'best' model from the point of view of fulfilling the objectives of econometrics, either in *explaining* consumption, or in *forecasting* it, or both.

Christ (1966, pp. 4–6) discusses six properties that would be considered desirable in an estimated model: relevance, simplicity, theoretical plausibility, explanatory ability, accuracy of coefficients and forecasting ability. A 'good' model will display all of these properties to some degree. However, the existence of a potentially large number of theoretically plausible models which also satisfy some or all of the criteria makes the model choice problem a nontrivial one in practice. 'Know hows' relate to methods of defining 'good' models, and to finding them.

The 'know hows' of econometrics are the subject of this book. We call a 'know how' a *methodology*. A formal definition of methodology is given by Durbin (1988) as the:

> Study or knowledge of the methods or practices used in a scientific or other intellectual discipline, either (a) that part of training which deals explicitly with the "how to's" of a field, e.g. statistical methods and how to apply them; or (b) conscious awareness on the part of a practitioner of the often unconsciously implemented "How to's". The latter sense is particularly important when something has gone wrong and a new beginning or new direction is needed to solve a problem.

However, a more light–hearted view of methodology is that of Leamer (1983a, p.40):

> Methodology, like sex, is better demonstrated than discussed, though often better anticipated than experienced.

In this book, we will discuss and demonstrate some modern methodological approaches to econometric model building. Of course, we hope the experience of reading the book proves rewarding.

1.2   Principles of Traditional Methodology

Morgan (1990, p.11) in her detailed history of econometrics argues that, by the 1940s, theory and practice had developed into a programme which can be recognized as modern econometrics. This programme is widely associated with the Cowles Commission for Research in Economics. The Cowles Commission was founded in Chicago in 1932 by the American businessman Alfred Cowles, originally to undertake work on the determination of stock market prices. In fact, its primary research area became that of econometrics, and to this end it grouped together several of the leading mathematical statisticians and econometricians in the United States at that time (for instance Haavelmo, Hurwicz, Klein, Koopmans and Wald). Simultaneously in Europe, Frisch (who also acted as a research consultant for the Cowles Commission) and Tinbergen were pursuing their work on time series analysis and macrodynamic modelling, though often in disagreement with each other and with those on the Cowles Commission staff. A crucial development and an important link between all these researchers was provided by Haavelmo (a former research assistant to Frisch) whose 1944 paper 'The Probability Approach in Econometrics' formed the basis upon which the Cowles Commission developed the macrodynamic modelling of Tinbergen.

The Haavelmo paper moved the emphasis of econometrics from the measurement of parameters (for example demand elasticities) and the problems of the quality of statistical data, to the testing of theories. The methodology reflecting this new emphasis which is now identified with the Cowles Commission emerged via a series of theoretical monographs published by the Commission, and within empirical work carried out by researchers in the 1940s attempting to implement some of the Commission's ideas. No specific 'know how' was formally presented. Instead, a consensus of opinion grew up as to the assumptions which were appropriate for the building and testing of econometric models. In most cases, these assumptions were 'hidden' rather than explicit, and must be inferred from the published work of that time.

To make these inferences, therefore, we will consider one of the earliest of all econometric textbooks (Tinbergen (1951)). This text surveys a wide range of empirical studies from this crucial period, and also presents what have now become accepted as the central assumptions of the Cowles Commission methodology.

A typical Cowles Commission time series model can be described in the following form:

$$Y_t = \alpha X_t + \theta W_t + error1, \qquad (1.1)$$

which can be accompanied by another equation or equations, say:

$$X_t = \beta Y_t + \gamma Z_t + error2 . \tag{1.2}$$

We will not discuss any assumptions concerning the errors of these equations. This is essentially a problem for estimation theory.

Tinbergen (1951, p.207) tells us that:

> ...the first thing to be done in any particular application is to give a correct economic analysis of the relation to be investigated .... - Two things should be carefully kept in mind: first, the necessity to know exactly what relation one really is interested in and second to know what factors enter into this relation.

In modern parlance, we would say that:

1. *Zero restrictions* on the parameters in equations (1.1) and (1.2) above are known. The parameter on the variable Z_t in equation (1.1) is equal to zero, as is the parameter on W_t in equation (1.2). That is, the theory says that Z_t does not appear in equation (1.1), and W_t does not appear in equation (1.2).

Tinbergen (pp. 19–20) asks: 'What should be the mathematical form of the relation?...A very general mathematical theorem is of advantage in all these cases: namely, that within a small range of variation, nearly every function can be approximated by a *linear* one.' In relation to the parameters of these functions, Tinbergen (p.205) states:

> It is often maintained that the method of multiple correlation is too rigid since it assumes the regression coefficients to be constant. It is very easy, however, to replace those coefficients by functions of other variables which means that they will be variable...On the other hand it may be observed that experience supplies us with cases of a remarkable constancy of regression coefficients.

We can summarize these ideas as:

2. The relations are *invariant in time*. The parameters of the two equation model above, namely α, β, θ and γ, are taken as unchanging for different values of t. Thus, the model repeats itself for each t. It is conditional only on the values of the variables, and not on time.

Also, the previous statement by Tinbergen implies:

3. The parameters are *structurally invariant*, that is they are invariant with respect to changes in the variables of the model. Movements in parameters are permitted to be (at least in part) systematically related to movements in variables which do not appear in the model being investigated, but not to movements of those appearing in the model.

In relation to the variables in a model, Tinbergen says (p.14):

> The problem usually is to explain the changes in the magnitude of a phenomenon, X, from the changes in the size of other phenomena, Y, Z, and so on, which we may call the causes of X.

When more than one relation exists between the variables to be studied (as in the two equation model above), Tinbergen (p.201) tells us:

> ...it is very useful to make a distinction between the simultaneous variables which have to be explained by the set of equations and the so—called "predetermined" variables which may also be found in the equations. Predetermined variables may be either data or lagged values of the simultaneous variables.

Hence, it was assumed that:

4. It is known *a priori* which variable is a *cause*, and which is a *result* of the relation (the *causal ordering* is known). It is known, therefore, which variables in the model are *endogenous* (values determined within the model) and which are *exogenous* (values determined outside the model). Thus, in the two equation model above, it would

be natural to specify X_t and Y_t as endogenous, and W_t and Z_t as exogenous.

Perhaps the most interesting comments made by Tinbergen from the point of view of this book are those relating to the testing of theories in economics. Let x be the variable to be explained, and x' the predicted value of x from the regression equation. Then Tinbergen states (p.195) that

> ...as to the testing of the theory, two extreme cases may present themselves:
>
> (1)   if x and x' are badly correlated, the theory is erroneous or at least incomplete;
>
> (2)   if the correlation between x and x' is complete, the theory does not contradict the facts.

Tinbergen (pp. 84–85) thus explains that:

> The statistician, when testing a relation set up by economic theory, may draw unconditional and conditional conclusions. The *unconditional* conclusions, however, are only *negative*. These conclusions may play a role when the theory is checked. If, namely, the correlation coefficient turns out to be too low (in comparison to the standard set before), the conclusion must be that the relation is incompatible with the facts. In other words, the theory is incorrect, or at least incomplete. The positive conclusions which can be drawn do not appear when the theoretical relation is checked: it cannot be *proved* that a theory is correct. The correlation may be high: other theories, however, may also lead to a high correlation...If we want to draw positive conclusions, additional information is necessary...

Tinbergen concentrates on three additional conditions which he suggests must be present before positive statements or inferences can be made from an estimated regression having a high multiple correlation coefficient (or equivalently, high coefficient of determination). These conditions essentially imply that the estimated relationship is properly specified. Specifically, the first condition is that there should be no significant determining factors omitted from the regression. This reflected the belief at that time that, in practice, errors of omission (specification errors) were more important than errors of measurement (Tinbergen (1951, p.200)). Secondly, any statements made are conditional upon the lag lengths on variables being correct. These lag lengths need not be specified in advance, but can be determined by trial and error to maximize the correlation between the variable to be explained and its predicted values (Tinbergen (1951, p.86)). Finally, and most important to Tinbergen (p.86), estimated regression coefficients should have the signs expected for them from the economic theory being modelled.

Thus, positive conclusions made from an estimated model were *conditional* on the assumed relationship being correct in its choice of variables and length of lags and so on. The additional conditions over and above a high correlation for a model needed to be satisfied before inferences could be made from that estimated model.

In retrospect, given these guidelines, it is not surprising that empirical investigations placed great weight on a combination of the goodness of fit of their models and the consistency of the signs of estimated parameters with the given theory. The theory could be rejected if the data seemed inconsistent with it, as evidenced, for example, by a low multiple correlation coefficient. However, more than one theory could be supported by the data, and any conclusions were conditional upon the relationship being correct. In other words:

5.   The model *cannot be verified directly against 'rival' models*. It can be tested with the use of 'classical' (Neyman-Pearson type) tests against 'nature'. Usually this meant the use of R^2 (the coefficient of determination), Student–t ratios and F tests (see Chapter 2). Tintner (1952, p.187), writing at about the same time, makes this same point explicitly when discussing time series models. He states: 'There is as yet no valid procedure for the choice between various theories and hypotheses.'

With these guidelines for model building and testing established, econometrics entered its mature period. The

1950s and 1960s represented the high—water mark for the profession, with a massive expansion of both theory and empirical studies. The Cowles Commission emphasis on simultaneous equation models was reflected in an increase in both the number and size of estimated macroeconometric models. The pioneering structural multi—equation model is usually recognized as the 24 equation model of the Dutch economy constructed in 1936 by Tinbergen (an English version of this work was published in Tinbergen (1959)). Another widely discussed early model (termed Klein's Model 1) was the six equation model describing the inter—war economy of the USA published by Klein (1950). The tendency was to build larger and larger models. Whilst the Klein and Goldberger (1955) model consisted of 20 equations, the 1965 version of the Brookings model had 160 equations (see Duesenberry *et al.* (1965)), and the Brookings MARK II model about 200 equations (see McCarthy (1972)). Wynn and Holden (1974, pp. 120–172) provide a comparative review of seven models published between 1950 and 1965, and Nerlove (1965) gives a tabular survey of econometric models covering the same period.

For their pioneering work in econometrics, Tinbergen and Frisch were jointly awarded the first Nobel prize in Economics, and the same award went to Klein and Haavelmo, two more members of the Cowles Commission, some years later. A great spirit of optimism and confidence in the future of econometrics existed. Econometric theory as enshrined in standard econometric texts presented a vision of a central core of accepted analysis which was being continuously refined and developed. The assumptions of the Cowles Commission approach outlined above were rarely questioned. Econometrics was viewed as a set of techniques necessary to handle the relaxation of the assumptions of the General Linear Model required because of the special problems faced by economists. Typically a 'true' model was introduced which would exhibit some particular problem (for example, heteroscedastic or serially correlated errors) and the properties of the ordinary least squares estimator for this model were investigated. A 'better' estimator would then be proposed.

1.3 The Failure of Traditional Econometrics

The growing scepticism towards the value of traditional econometric analysis which followed the 'golden age' of econometrics of the 1950s and 1960s may be illustrated by the following two remarks:

> On pessimistic days I doubt that economists have learned any-
> thing from the mountains of computer print—outs that fill their
> offices. On especially pessimistic days, I doubt that they ever will.
> (Leamer (1983b, p.325)),

and:

> Even within the academic profession, one is sensing a doubt as to
> whether the generation of more numbers for their own sake is
> fruitful. The ad hoc approach of many practising econometricians
> to the problem of hypothesis testing and inference is illustrated by
> the popular image of much econometrics as a high R^2 in search of
> a theory. Garbage in — garbage out is how many describe their
> own activity. (Desai (1976, p.vii)).

These views of the value of applied econometric research became increasingly held from the mid 1970s onwards. As noted above, the two preceding decades had been full of optimism for econometrics. Unfortunately the real practical problems of model specification and selection had been rarely addressed, and a gap developed between what theorists were developing 'on the top floor' and what applied econometricians were actually doing with data 'in the basement'.

Not knowing what was an appropriate methodological approach to the building of econometric models in practice, applied workers developed their own. Computing advances removed one major obstacle to routine calculation, which led to the Cowles Commission methodology being systematically abused in ways detailed in Chapter 2 below. Such was the scale of this abuse that eventually in applied research much econometric work became ultimately unconvincing (see

Leamer (1983a, p.37)). By the middle of the 1970s, this disquiet on the progress of applied research was becoming evident, as indicated by Desai's remark above. (See also the further reading at the end of this chapter.)

Moreover, the forecasting performance of several large scale macroeconometric models was found to be poor. Simple mechanistic time series methods provided severe competition to forecasts made using large and expensive models, which supposedly incorporated the knowledge of the working of the economic system built up on the back of extensive econometric research over many years. For instance, Cooper (1972) compared one–step ahead forecasts made with the use of seven structural econometric models of the USA economy with a naive forecast obtained from an autoregressive model. In most cases the naive forecasts were superior to those from the econometric models. Although later studies on the comparison of time series and econometric forecasts have been more favourable to those of econometrics (see Granger and Newbold (1986, pp. 287–292) for a survey), a belief grew up that the simpler and cheaper time series methods could be at least as accurate as those from large scale econometric models.

From the earlier position of self–confidence, self doubt became widespread within the profession. Economists who were willing to say something about applied econometrics were divided into three groups:

1. Those who dismissed econometrics as alchemy;
2. Those who still believed in the traditional approach, pointing at wrong specification and imperfect estimation methods as the principal cause of the crisis in applied econometrics;
3. Those who postulated revisions of the five Cowles Commission assumptions above.

This book will concentrate on the third group who have reacted positively to the deficiencies that they perceived in traditional methodology. A number of alternative methodological approaches have been proposed, and while econometricians do not claim to have all the answers to the problems of model building, there is a new vitality and spirit of enquiry in applied research.

To return to the opening remark of this section, Leamer also states 'But there are optimistic days as well' (Leamer (1983b, p.325)). The remainder of this book will concern itself with an examination of some of the new methodological approaches which have given rise to this optimism, and provide guidelines for the practical analysis of time series data which avoid some of the weaknesses of traditional methodology.

1.4 Suggestions for Further Reading

An examination of the work of the Cowles Commission (renamed the Cowles Foundation for Economic Research in 1955) is to be found in Epstein (1987). Morgan (1990, Chapter 8) contains a detailed discussion of Haavelmo's 1944 paper, and its importance to econometric methodology. Aldrich (1989) also considers this paper, particularly with reference to questions of the structural invariance of models. Discussions of the difficulties in using traditional methodology are to be found in Hendry (1980) and Sims (1980). An interesting overview of the history and methodology of econometrics has been given by Spanos (1986, Chapter 1). Klein (1971b) gives an optimistic view of the results of three decades of econometrics and of its future, whilst Worswick (1972) argued that much less had been learnt from this work than was generally thought. Further, often contradictory comparisons of the predictive performances and policy analyses of structural econometric models can be found in Naylor, Seales and Wichern (1972), McNees (1979), Christ (1975) and Malinvaud (1981). The performance of econometric models in the 1980s are discussed, *inter alia*, in Wallis (1989) for the UK, and in Adams and Klein (1991) for the USA.

Chapter 2

Data Mining

2.1 Model Selection through 'Data Mining'

'Data mining' in its various forms reflects the general problem of not being in a position to conduct controlled experiments. This may lead to procedures which use a fixed data sample in some sequential manner to arrive at the final model specification. Suppose that we define a 'good' model as a specification which exhibits a high coefficient of determination, 'significant' Student–t ratios and possibly a Durbin-Watson statistic close to 2. A tempting and quite common practice is the taking of the widest possible set of variables (called here the 'candidates') which might eventually enter the model, running numerous regressions using as the regressors subsets of the entire set of the 'candidates', and then selecting the 'best' regression, that is that with the highest coefficient of determination or with the highest Student–t ratios.

Imagine that the aim is to model the consumption function. The investigator might prepare a set of potential regressors such as lagged consumption, total personal disposable income, expected income (measured, for instance, as the one–step ahead prediction of income), income adjusted for the stock of liquid assets, total wealth of the last period and total wealth averaged over the last two periods. These variables can in turn be deflated by at least two different price indices: the retail price index and the cost–of–living index. This gives rise to a set of 12 potential explanatory variables and enables the formulation of some sensible looking consumption functions, such as:

1. consumption explained by its own lagged value and current unadjusted income;
2. consumption explained by current and expected income.

14

3. consumption explained by its own lagged value and current adjusted income;
4. consumption explained by current unadjusted income and lagged wealth;

By changing the deflator, another four equations can be formulated. Why not estimate them all and choose the one that has good Student–t ratios and a high R^2 ? If, on these criteria, the 'best' is equation 4 and the 'worst' is equation 2, we may even conclude that the analysis shows the significant impact of current income on consumption and that expected income does not influence current consumption. Would such a conclusion be justified?

Approaches such as these, termed 'data mining', gave rise to published models in the 1960s and early 1970s consisting usually of a lot of equations with convincing statistics and impressive 'goodness–of–fit' measures. Typically, an equation of such a model is presented in the form:

$$y_t = 2.134 + 0.345 \cdot x_t + error ,$$
$$\quad (5.21) \quad (3.02)$$

$$R^2 = 0.956 \quad , \quad DW = 2.10 ,$$

with Student–t values in parentheses below the parameter estimates and with R^2 and DW standing respectively for the coefficient of determination and the Durbin–Watson statistic. It turns out, as we shall show in the remaining sections of this chapter, that neither R^2 nor t–values are very useful as powerful selection criteria precisely because their values can be influenced by, and to some extent are under the control of the experimenter. Exclusive reliance on R^2 and t–statistics as model choice criteria can easily lead to the selection of poor models.

2.2   The R^2 and Student–t Statistic Criteria

(a) The R^2 criterion

First let us regard the coefficient of determination as merely a non–stochastic descriptive measure of a model, namely the square of the correlation coefficient between the dependent variable of an equation and its least squares prediction. It is usually defined for an equation with an intercept and estimated by the ordinary least squares (*OLS*) method as:

$$R^2 = 1 - \frac{\Sigma\, \hat{u}_t^2}{\Sigma(y_t - \bar{y}_t)^2} \, , \text{ or } R^2 = 1 - \frac{S_u^2}{S_y^2} \cdot \frac{T-k}{T} \, ,$$

where the $\hat{u}_t$ are *OLS* residuals, y_t denotes observations on the dependent variable with a mean $\bar{y}$ and variance S_y^2 ($t = 1$, $2,..., T$), and S_u^2 is an unbiased estimate of the error term variance, that is:

$$S_u^2 = \frac{1}{T-k} \Sigma\, \hat{u}_t^2 \, ,$$

where Σ stands for a summation over the entire sample (from $t = 1$ to $t = T$) and k is the number of regressors. Suppose now that we wish to add a new regressor, say z_t , to the already existing set of regressors, $x_{1t}, x_{2t},..., x_{kt}$. As its name implies, the *OLS* method produces estimates of parameters that minimize the sum of the squares of the residuals in the fitted model. If the residual sum of squares in the regression of y_t on $x_{1t}, x_{2t},..., x_{kt}$ is $\Sigma\hat{u}_t^2$, the residual sum of squares in the regression of y_t on all the x_ts and the new variable z_t, say $\Sigma\hat{e}_t^2$, cannot be greater than $\Sigma\hat{u}_t^2$, even if z_t is not significantly correlated with y_t. Consequently, adding a new explanatory variable is always 'good' if one wishes to improve goodness of fit. This problem is partially overcome by using the 'adjusted' R^2 value, which takes into account the number of explanatory variables, that is by computing the adjusted coefficient of determination:

$$\bar{R}^2 = 1 - \frac{T-1}{T-m} \cdot (1 - R^2) \, ,$$

where m is the number of explanatory variables.

The use of either R^2 or $\bar{R}^2$ as a decision variable to choose between models is a dangerous procedure. It has been shown (for example Theil (1971, pp. 543–545), or Johnston (1984, pp. 504–505)) that, *on average*, the $\bar{R}^2$ associated with a 'true' model will exceed that from an incorrectly specified model. But this result holds only 'on average'; it does *not* imply that a 'false' model cannot have an $\bar{R}^2$ greater than that of a 'true' model, and the mechanical choosing of models on the basis of their $\bar{R}^2$ is likely to result in the choice of such 'false' models. Clearly, also, the criterion of maximizing $\bar{R}^2$ is of no use when none of the models considered is a 'true' or 'good' model. Dhrymes (1970b, pp. 177–185) proved that in adding a variable to a model, the $\bar{R}^2$ for this new model will increase if the Student–t value associated with this new variable exceeds unity, which is well below the values normally required for statistical significance at conventional levels of significance.

The R^2 criterion is also not useful for making a selection from regressions having different dependent variables (forms of a model). To see why this is so, consider the *OLS* estimation of the regressions:

$$y_t = \beta_0 + \beta_1 x_{1t} + \beta_2 x_{2t} + error, \qquad (2.1)$$

and:

$$y_t - x_{1t} = \theta_0 + \theta_1 x_{1t} + \theta_2 x_{2t} + error. \qquad (2.2)$$

OLS will force the estimates of the intercepts to be equal, the coefficients on x_{2t} to be equal and the estimates of β_1 and θ_1 to obey the restriction $\theta_1 = \beta_1 - 1$. The residuals will be identical, and thus the residual sums of squares from equations (2.1) and (2.2) will be the same. However, as the left-hand side (dependent) variables in the two equations are different, the total sum of squares to be explained and hence the R^2s in the two models will differ. We may conclude that if the model is merely re—written so that there is a change in the variation of the 'dependent variable', there will be an alteration in the associated coefficient of determination.

When it comes to testing whether the explanatory variables are singly or jointly significant, one always faces the problem reflected in the *Leamer critique* of structural models. This relates to the 'fragility' of statistical inferences made using the non—experimental data typically available to econometricians (see Leamer (1983a)). Suppose that we wish to test whether the reduction in the residual sum of squares obtained by adding a new variable, say x_{k+1}, to the model is significant. The null hypothesis H_0 is then:

$$H_0: \beta_{k+1} = 0,$$

and the appropriate test statistic may be expressed in terms of R^2 as:

$$F = \frac{R^2 - R_0^2}{(1 - R^2)} \cdot (T-k-1) \sim F(1, T-k-1).$$

Here R_0^2 is the coefficient of determination obtained for the restricted model, that is from the estimated model with only k explanatory variables, and R^2 is computed for the model estimated with the full set of $k + 1$ explanatory variables. However, as the sample size T increases, the value of F will tend to increase. Simultaneously, with the increase in the number of degrees of freedom, the critical values for the F test decrease. Consequently, it is easy to finish up with a 'significant' F statistic even for a meaningless increase in R^2. More generally, Leamer (1983a, p.39) states that:

> Diagnostic tests such as goodness—of—fit tests, without explicit alternative hypotheses, are useless since, if the sample size is large enough, any maintained hypothesis will be rejected ... Such tests therefore degenerate into elaborate rituals for measuring the effective sample size.

Although the test above has been written in terms of R^2, that is in terms of the coefficient of determination, it is not a test of the significance of R^2. In the General Linear Model where the explanatory variables are taken as non—stochastic, R^2 is purely a descriptive statistic, as has been stressed by Koerts and Abrahamse (1969). There are severe problems in attempting to use R^2 for statistical inference in the General Linear Model, and in particular as a test statistic in the determination of the correct specification of an economic model. To be used as a test statistic, it would be necessary to be able to determine the sampling distribution or distribution function of R^2. Koerts and Abrahamse (1969, Chapter 8) show that the distribution function of R^2 depends on both the unknown error variance and the particular values taken by the explanatory variables in the model (to which the distribution function of R^2 is particularly sensitive). Hence, values of R^2 belonging to different models (for example with different explanatory variables) cannot be compared in any straightforward way as they may have quite different distribution functions. In particular, this result gives no support to the practice of choosing a final specification on the grounds of the highest coefficient of determination.

(b) The Student–*t* criterion

A potential misuse of the Student–*t* statistic criterion is illustrated below by a simple example. Suppose that we have a set of four potential explanatory variables and the problem is to model aggregate consumption:

C_t – aggregate consumption,

Y_t – national income,

M_t – a measure of the stock of money,

P_t – consumers' price index,

PD_t – retail price index.

Suppose that we adopt a level of significance of $\alpha = 0.05$, and the number of observations is 25. Four OLS regressions have been run, giving the following *t*–values:

Regression 1:	C on	Y, (1.3)	P, (2.0)	
Regression 2:	C on	M, (1.1)	P, (1.5)	
Regression 3:	C on	Y, (1.7)	PD, (2.0)	
Regression 4:	C on	M, (2.2)	PD. (2.3)	

The Student–*t* ratios for the coefficients on particular

variables are given in brackets and the tabulated critical value of the Student t–test is 2.06. Commonly, regression 4 seems to be preferred, because the t–statistics are the highest. Do the t–statistics mean that the parameters in this regression are statistically significant at the 0.05 level of significance? The answer is: we don't know whether they are significant or not, because the regression result was selected out of four outcomes *conditionally* on the other three results.

Why is this important? Consider the following example. Imagine that there is a 'dependent' variable y_t and 100 'explanatory' variables $x_{1t}, x_{2t}, \dots, x_{100t}$. Assume that the distributions of all these variables are identical and independent. Hence, the explanatory variables are uncorrelated with y_t. Suppose that we have 100 vectors of realizations on these variables (one vector for each variable) and we fit an *OLS* regression of y_t on x_{1t}, then of y_t on x_{2t} and so on. At a significance level of 0.05 we can expect that about five out of these 100 regressions will be 'significant', that is they will have Student–t values lying in the rejection region. If we select these five models and ignore the rest, we will have five 'good' models, despite the fact that the explanatory variables are uncorrelated with y_t.

Consider a further example. Suppose that we wish to fit the 'best' (in terms of the highest Student–t ratio) regression model explaining aggregate consumption expenditure in the United Kingdom for the period 1957–1975. Using quarterly data, we have 76 observations available (this same set of data will be discussed and used extensively in the numerical examples in later chapters). The general form of the model is the following:

$$CONS_t = \alpha_0 y_t + \alpha_1 Q1_t + \alpha_2 Q2_t + \alpha_3 Q3_t + \alpha_4 Q4_t + \epsilon_t ,$$

where $CONS_t$ denotes aggregate consumption expenditure, y_t is an explanatory variable, ϵ_t is an error term and $Q1_t$, $Q2_t$,

$Q3_t$ and $Q4_t$ are seasonal dummy variables (that is, $Q1_t$ is equal to one for the first quarter of each year and zero otherwise, and so on). How do you react to the information that the Student$-t$ value for the parameter α_0 on the variable y_t is 2.48? It definitely looks impressive, being in the critical region of the Student$-t$ test and, according to the traditional interpretation, indicates a significant positive influence on consumption by y_t. But perhaps it would be useful to know what the variable y_t stands for? Well, it is nothing but a series of 76 random numbers generated from the standard normal distribution with zero mean and variance of one. Obviously, it would be rather heroic to argue that random numbers generated by a computer have anything in common with aggregate consumption in the UK. But why did we have such a 'significant' t-value? Quite simply, this is *the highest Student$-t$ value selected out of 100 trials*. One hundred series of 76 normal random numbers were generated and $CONS_t$ was regressed on each of these series. Most of the regression results were, as expected, nonsensical (for instance, for the very first regression the t-value was, quite justifiably, equal to -0.11), but among them there were a few which looked quite sensible. If the best of them were selected, there is 'statistical evidence' for the claim that aggregate consumption in the UK is determined by random numbers !

For the case of orthogonal 'explanatory' variables it is straightforward to evaluate probabilities that regressors not correlated with the dependent variable appear to be significant, that is belong to the conventionally evaluated critical region (see Lovell (1983)). To show this, let us assume that an investigator believes that a dependent variable, y_t, is determined by at most two explanatory variables, but has a list of ten equally plausible explanatory variables to choose from. These 'candidate' variables are denoted as x_{1t}, x_{2t} ...,x_{10t}. In fact and, of course, unknown to the investigator, none of the ten variables is related to y_t. If *a priori* theory could direct or restrict the set of potential explanatory variables to only two of them, say x_{1t} and x_{2t}, then only a single regression of the form:

$$y_t = \beta_0 + \beta_1 x_{1t} + \beta_2 x_{2t} + u_t,$$

would be run. In such a case, the probability of rejecting the null hypothesis that $\beta_1 = \beta_2 = 0$, that is the probability of a Type I error (rejecting the true null hypothesis), is at whatever nominal level of significance the test is conducted. In the text below we denote the nominal (or claimed) level of significance that is conventionally adopted in order to read from tables of critical values of the Student–t distribution for $T - k - 1$ degrees of freedom, by α, while the true probability of the Type I error, the true significance level, is denoted by α^*. Evidently, if we select two explanatory variables out of two candidates, then $\alpha^* = \alpha$.

Suppose, however, that data mining was performed so that the model adopted is the result of selection following exploratory regression analysis. To simplify matters, it is assumed that there is no multicollinearity among the potential regressors so that all the x_{it} variables are orthogonal to each other, and the variance of the error term is known. With orthogonal regressors, the coefficient obtained on x_{it} will be the same whether or not other x_{it} variables appear in an equation fitted by *OLS*. Thus, in order to select the two variables to enter the regression, ten simple regressions can be run and the two explanatory variables with the highest associated Student–t statistic for their estimated coefficients selected. The problem is to determine the actual Type I error involved in this procedure; that is, the probability that the t–statistic in the final selected form will appear to be significant at the nominal significance level.

If the nominal significance level is taken to be 0.05 then, under the given assumptions, when the ten regressions are run the probabilities of obtaining $X = 0, 1, 2,..., 10$ nominally significant t–values are given by the binomial distribution:

$$P(X{=}x) = \frac{10!}{x!\,(10{-}x)!}\, p^{x}\,(1{-}p)^{10-x}\,,$$

where x is the number of 'successes' (significant t–values) in these ten independent trials and p is the probability of a success in any trial.

With $p = 0.05$, then:

$$P(X = 0) = 0.5987$$
$$P(X = 1) = 0.3151$$
$$P(X = 2) = 0.0746$$
$$P(X = 3) = 0.0105$$

$$\begin{matrix} \cdot & & \cdot \\ \cdot & & \cdot \end{matrix}$$

$$P(X = 10) = \text{approximately zero}\,.$$

Thus, in running ten regressions the probability that none will display a significant coefficient is only 0.5987 even when, in fact, no explanatory variable is related to y_t.

The true significance level (α^*) involved in presenting the final selected equation can now be determined. If the two variables with the highest Student–t statistics are selected, then the probability that neither coefficient is found to be statistically significant is:

$P(\text{first not signif.}) \cdot P(\text{second not signif.} \mid \text{first not signif.})\,,$

but as these are independent events, this probability is equal to:

$$(1 - \alpha^*) \cdot (1 - \alpha^*) = (1 - \alpha^*)^2\,.$$

The value of α^* may then be found by equating this probability to the probability given above that no coefficients turn out to be significant when all ten regressions are run, so that:

$$(1 - \alpha^*)^2 = P(X = 0) = 0.5987\,,$$

which gives $\alpha^* = 0.226$. This is considerably above the nominal level of 0.05, at which the coefficients would normally be tested. Thus the nominal significance level understates the probability of incorrectly rejecting the null hypothesis that the regression coefficients are zero when the regressors have been selected on the basis of their Student–t statistics. The difference between the true and nominal level of significance is the essence of 'Lovell bias', which refers to the alteration that needs to be made to the nominal significance level where regressors are selected from a set of 'candidates'. More generally, Lovell's 'rule of thumb' for computing the true significance level α^* when selecting k regressors out of c 'candidates' at a nominal significance level α is:

$$\alpha^* = 1 - (1 - \alpha)^{c/k} ,$$

which can be approximated as:

$$\tilde{\alpha}^* \simeq \frac{c}{k} \cdot \alpha .$$

Again, if $c = k$, then $\alpha^* = \alpha$. That is, the true and nominal significance levels are equal if no data mining is performed. Values of α^*, tabulated for the number of explanatory variables from 2 to 10 and number of 'candidates' equal to 10, 15, ..., 50 are given in Table 1 in the Appendix. They can be used for evaluating the impact of data mining on the significance of the parameters of a finally selected model.

In practice the effect of data mining might be not as devastating as shown by the scale of 'Lovell bias'. The potential explanatory variables are often not orthogonal. For example, the various measures of income in the consumption function are likely to be correlated with each other. This would lead to a reduction in 'Lovell bias'. Unfortunately, the need to estimate the error variance is likely to work in the opposite direction. Lovell (1983) concludes that the 'rule of thumb' above still provides a rough and ready guide to the exaggerated claims of significance that are likely to arise from data mining in these more realistic cases.

2.3   Pretesting and Model Selection

One particular form of sequential model formulation that has been investigated in some detail is termed 'pretesting' and, like typical data mining, relates to model choice following preliminary testing for significance.

Consider the following (true) regression equation (given in deviations from means, so that the intercept term disappears):

$$y_t = \beta_1 x_{1t} + \beta_2 x_{2t} + error .$$

There are at least three straightforward estimates of the parameter β_1:

1. The multiple regression estimate, say $\hat{\beta}_1$, which is generally unbiased with the sample variance $\sigma^2 / \Sigma x_{1t}^2 (1 - r^2)$, where r is the linear correlation coefficient of x_{1t} and x_{2t}, and σ^2 is the variance of the error term.

2. The simple regression estimate, say $\hat{b}_1$, obtained when y_t is regressed on x_{1t} alone, which will generally be biased (unless $\beta_2 = 0$ or x_{1t} and x_{2t} are orthogonal), with a sample variance (generally smaller than that in 1), equal to $\sigma^2 / \Sigma x_{1t}^2$.

3. The 'pretest' estimator, say $\hat{\beta}_1^*$, such as:

$$\hat{\beta}_1^* = \begin{cases} \hat{b}_1 & , \text{if } |t| \leq t_\alpha \\ \hat{\beta}_1 & , \text{if } |t| > t_\alpha \end{cases} ,$$

where t is the calculated Student$-t$ ratio associated with the multiple regression estimate of β_2, which is compared with the tabulated value t_α at the α level of significance. It is assumed that no data mining has preceded the choice of the two regressors, so that α is also the true significance level.

Thus, the pretest estimator in this simple case is the result of a choice between the simple and multiple regression estimate of the coefficient on x_{1t} based on a Student–t test of the significance of the other regression coefficient, β_2. Its statistical properties are complicated. Bancroft (1944) has shown, however, that the pretest estimator is generally biased. If bias were the only criterion, then $\hat{\beta}_1^*$ would be taken to be the multiple regression estimate, $\hat{\beta}_1$. However, the restriction on the model when x_{2t} is omitted may give rise to a more efficient estimator of β_1, and hence one may be prepared to incur some bias in order to achieve greater efficiency. Wallace and Ashar (1972) have considered the three estimators above explicitly on the grounds of a mean square error (*MSE*) criterion (that is sampling variance $+$ $(\text{bias})^2$; see for example Pindyck and Rubinfeld (1991, p.29)), which allows for a comparison to be made between biased and unbiased estimators with different variances.

For the case above, it is easy to show that the mean square errors of the simple and multiple regression estimates of β_1 are:

$$MSE\,(\hat{b}_1) \;=\; \frac{\sigma^2}{\Sigma x_{1t}^2} + \beta_2^2\, r^2\, \frac{\Sigma x_{2t}^2}{\Sigma x_{1t}^2},$$

and:

$$MSE\,(\hat{\beta}_1) \;=\; \frac{\sigma^2}{\Sigma x_{1t}^2 (1 - r^2)}.$$

Then $MSE\,(\hat{b}_1) \leq MSE\,(\hat{\beta}_1)$ if $\quad \dfrac{\beta_2^2}{\text{var}(\hat{\beta}_2)} \leq 1\,,$

where $\text{var}(\hat{\beta}_2)$ is the true (not estimated) sampling variance of the *OLS* estimator of β_2. This ratio bears a superficial resemblance to the (squared) Student–t statistic that would be used to test the statistical significance of β_2. Unfortunately, there is no implied relationship between the finding of a statistically significant coefficient for β_2 using $t = 1$ as the critical value for the Student–t test, and for $MSE\,(\hat{\beta}_1)$ to be lower than $MSE\,(\hat{b}_1)$.

For a given value of $\text{var}(\hat{\beta}_2)$ there is a range of values of β_2 for which the mean square error of the simple regression estimator exceeds that of the multiple regression estimator, and another range where the opposite is true. From the point of view of sequential model building, however, it would be attractive if it could be shown that the pretest estimator $\hat{\beta}_1^*$ had a lower *MSE* than that for either $\hat{b}_1$ or $\hat{\beta}_1$ over the whole range of possible β_2 values. The form and derivation of the *MSE* for the pretest estimator is complicated (see Judge *et al.* (1985, Section 3.1.3) for a general analysis) and is not given here. One of the most interesting findings of Wallace and Ashar, however, was that for a given sample variance of $\hat{\beta}_2$ there is no range of values of β_2 for which the mean square error of the pretest estimator is lower than the mean square errors of both $\hat{\beta}_1$ and $\hat{b}_1$. The implication of this is that leaving the specification of the model to be determined solely by the data will be less successful than a specification based on a strong (and correct) prior belief either that x_{2t} should be included or excluded. The general form of the mean square error function for $\hat{\beta}_1^*$ (that is for the pretest estimator) depends on the level of significance α adopted for the Student–t test on β_2. Weak prior beliefs about the importance of x_{2t} in the regression can be reflected through the choice of a larger value for α. Wallace and Ashar (1972) conclude: 'If we are not sure *a priori* whether a particular variable(s) belongs in a model, pretesting in the sense discussed here or in more elaborate step–wise regression selector programs will, on average, yield estimators that are sure to be worse than least squares estimators derived from an accurate prior specification.'

2.4 Data Mining and the Failure of Traditional Econometrics

We can draw together the implications of data mining for econometric model building by considering the following rather extreme case which may, however, contain elements familiar to any instructor of econometrics. Suppose that a student asks for your comments on the quality of an estimated regression which includes all the standard diagnostic statistics such as Student–t values, a Durbin–Watson statistic and a coefficient of determination. Would it be relevant to ask for details as to how this model was obtained? Would it alter your opinion as to the credibility of the model if the student said that the functional form tested was derived on the basis of careful economic reasoning and was the only regression fitted, as compared with the knowledge that this regression was the outcome of an extensive and unstructured search involving the fitting of many equations? Is the meaning of the test statistics affected by the process by which the model was developed from a fixed data sample?

It is the implication of this chapter that the credibility that can be ascribed to any reported econometric estimate is most assuredly related to the process by which it was generated. Realistically, it is natural that econometricians will wish to use a fixed data sample in some sequential way. The pure case of the reasoned economic argument leading to a well defined model which is estimated and tested just the once from the available data sample conflicts with common sense. Surely the sample evidence contained within estimated models should be useful in the improvement of our understanding of the process which has generated the observed data? That is, in practice, some amount of data mining is inevitable.

However, Section 1.4 noted the disquiet that emerged regarding traditional econometric methodology, undermining the credibility that could be attached to its results. This chapter has indicated that it was not the Cowles Commission framework as such that was the problem (although, as we will see, certain assumptions of this approach are open to discussion). More generally, it was the abuse of the methodological principles implied by the Cowles Commission, and in particular the widespread growth of data mining in its various forms, that are recognized as the central weakness of the prevailing methodology as actually practised. Applied econometrics had singularly failed to provide models that produced satisfactory out-of-sample predictions, or resolved competing economic theories. The important question then is not whether data mining will be involved in the modelling of economic relationships, but how this should be done. It is the contention of the remaining chapters of this book that it is possible to conduct a structured and purposeful approach to econometric model building that avoids the worst aspects of data mining. Because of this, the models that result will simply be that much more convincing.

2.5   Suggestions for Further Reading

The original Lovell (1983) paper was followed by some additional contributions and extensions by Denton (1985) and Caudill (1988). In econometric textbooks, the problems posed by data mining are discussed briefly by Johnston (1984, pp. 501–504), Maddala (1988, pp. 420–421) and Kmenta (1986, pp. 598–600), and more fully by Goldberger (1991, Chapter 24). An important discussion of the place of data mining in the wider context of econometric methodology has been given by Granger (1990, pp. 8–11). The problem of data mining is related to the more general area of *specification searches* which has an extensive literature of its own (see for example Leamer (1978) or Maddala (1981)). An argument against the Leamer critique of the spurious significance tests in large samples is given in Phillips (1988a) in an article which forms part of a symposium on econometric methodology. A useful review of the early pretest literature is given by Wallace (1977) and a discussion of the Wallace and Ashar example is included in Kennedy (1990). A humorous account of data mining is given by Karni and Shapiro (1980).

Chapter 3

Origins of a Modern Methodology: The *DHSY* Consumption Function

3.1   Introduction

It is widely acknowledged that the work of Davidson, Hendry, Srba and Yeo (1978) (*DHSY* hereafter) on modelling aggregate consumption in the UK has had an important influence on the way many econometricians now use time series data to model economic relationships. Some of the strands of their analysis have since received considerable attention which in turn has led to the development of new econometric approaches and ideas. These new developments include general to specific modelling (see Chapter 4), cointegration analysis (see Chapter 5) and encompassing (see Chapter 8).

It will be useful, therefore, to reconsider the original *DHSY* analysis, albeit in a simplified and modified form, in order to outline some of the methodological questions posed by this paper. This chapter will also give an introduction to the theory of consumption modelling, and will explain the notation and meaning of the computer output produced by a modern econometric software package.

3.2   Economic Background

Since econometric modelling deals with the interaction of economic theory and empirical analysis, it will be useful to discuss some economic theory relevant to the formulation of models of aggregate consumption expenditure. Two of the main economic theories of the consumption function are the Absolute Income Hypothesis (Keynes (1936)), and the Permanent Income Hypothesis (Friedman (1957)). Hereafter, these theories will be denoted simply as *AIH* and *PIH*.

Keynes's 'fundamental psychological law' stated that

'men are disposed, as a rule and on the average, to increase their consumption as their income increases, but not by as much as the increase in their income' (Keynes (1936, p.96)). In the terminology that has become standard, the *marginal propensity to consume* is less than unity. Keynes also expected that the proportion of income saved would increase as incomes increased, so that the *average propensity to consume* would decline. Income and consumption were expressed in real terms. As is common with most macroeconomic theory, the theory was presented in terms of individual behaviour, but used to describe aggregate behaviour, despite the well known aggregation problem (for example see Allen (1966, pp. 694–701)). Much attention was given to the differences between short run and long run behaviour of aggregate consumption (a distinction which as will be seen is reflected in the way *DHSY* ultimately formulated their model). The marginal propensity to consume was thought to be sensitive to the money value of wealth, and its short run value was expected to be less than its long run value.

The simplest formulation of a model which captures at least some of these ideas and which could be estimated from time series data is:

$$CONS_t = \alpha + \beta \cdot INC_t + \epsilon_t,\qquad(3.1)$$

where consumption ($CONS_t$) and income (INC_t) are measured in real *per capita* form, and ϵ_t is an error term. Here it is assumed that the intercept α is positive and, according to the *AIH*, the marginal propensity to consume (*MPC*) or β, is greater than zero but less than one.

As the average propensity to consume (*APC*) is the ratio of consumption to income, then:

$$APC = \frac{CONS_t}{INC_t} = \frac{\alpha}{INC_t} + \beta.$$

Hence, as income rises, the *APC* falls. In the long run as

income rises, $APC = MPC$, but for the short run (for example for cyclical data), $MPC < APC$.

The 'stylized history of the early econometrics of the consumption function' has been examined by Thomas (1989) and Spanos (1989). This history is that, initially, short time series were used to estimate equation (3.1) above, with results which at first appeared consistent with the Keynesian postulates. Subsequently, however, long data series became available for the United States which indicated no reduction in the APC over time, and which was therefore inconsistent with this simple formulation. Moreover, the short run function appeared to have an intercept which increased over time, whilst budget (cross section) studies suggested that the average propensity to consume moved cyclically. 'New' theories of aggregate consumption behaviour were put forward to explain these apparent anomalies. Although Thomas and Spanos argue that this is a distortion of the way in which events actually proceeded, by the late 1950s there existed a substantial body of theoretical and empirical work on aggregate consumption behaviour alternative to the Absolute Income Hypothesis (see Farrell (1959) or Ferber (1962)).

Of these 'new' theories, perhaps the most enduring has been that of the Permanent Income Hypothesis. As the name suggests, individuals or consuming units are seen as making consumption decisions on the basis of expected, normal or permanent income, rather than on measured current real income as in the AIH. Permanent income is defined as the maximum amount a consuming unit thinks it could consume while maintaining its wealth position intact. Consumption is defined in a physical rather than a monetary sense, in that expenditure on durable goods in any period is treated as saving (apart from any depreciation of the asset in that period). The difference between measured and permanent (or planned) income is termed transitory income and the difference between measured and permanent consumption is termed transitory consumption. Two of the central assumptions of the PIH are that:

1. permanent consumption $(CONS_t^p)$ is proportional to

permanent income, (INC_t^P),

or: $$CONS_t^P = \alpha_1 \cdot INC_t^P , \qquad (3.2)$$

and:

2. transitory consumption and transitory income are uncorrelated (that is 'windfall gains' are saved or spent on durable goods, rather than spent on nondurables).

This theory gives rise to several implications which can be tested (particularly with the use of cross section data) without the need to measure permanent income or consumption.   Direct estimation of equation (3.2) above requires measures of both these concepts.

Actual consumption expenditure on non–durables $(CONS_t)$ is usually taken to stand for permanent consumption, both on the grounds that the consumer unit has some direct control over actual consumption expenditure, and because any discrepancy between the two (transitory consumption) will appear in the error term of the equation and not pose any particular econometric problems.   Thus, equation (3.2) above could now be written as:

$$CONS_t = \alpha_1 \cdot INC_t^P + \epsilon_t , \qquad (3.3)$$

where ϵ_t is an error term.

Measurement of permanent income can be approached through the use of the adaptive expectations hypothesis, where permanent income (INC_t^P) alters between periods in proportion to the difference between actual income (INC_t) in a period, and permanent income in the previous period.

Thus:

$$INC_t^P - INC_{t-1}^P = (1 - \lambda)(INC_t - INC_{t-1}^P), \qquad (3.4)$$

$$0 < \lambda < 1.$$

With these assumptions about the measurement of permanent consumption and income, equation (3.2) above may now be written in a form suitable for estimation by using the so–called Koyck transformation (for example see Kmenta (1986, pp. 528–529) or Johnston (1984, pp. 346–348)). That is, substitute INC_t^P in (3.3) by $INC_{t-1}^P + (1 - \lambda)(INC_t - INC_{t-1}^P)$ from (3.4), giving:

$$
\begin{aligned}
CONS_t &= \alpha_1[INC_{t-1}^P + (1 - \lambda)INC_t - (1 - \lambda)INC_{t-1}^P] + \epsilon_t \\
&= \alpha_1\lambda INC_{t-1}^P + \alpha_1(1 - \lambda)INC_t + \epsilon_t. \qquad (3.5)
\end{aligned}
$$

Lagging equation (3.3), and multiplying it by λ gives:

$$\lambda CONS_{t-1} = \lambda\alpha_1 INC_{t-1}^P + \lambda\epsilon_{t-1},$$

and subtracting this from (3.5) yields:

$$CONS_t - \lambda CONS_{t-1} = \alpha_1(1 - \lambda)INC_t + (\epsilon_t - \lambda\epsilon_{t-1}).$$

This may be written as:

$$CONS_t = \beta_1 CONS_{t-1} + \beta_2 INC_t + v_t, \qquad (3.6)$$

where:

$$\beta_1 = \lambda, \quad \beta_2 = \alpha_1(1 - \lambda), \text{ and } v_t = \epsilon_t - \lambda\epsilon_{t-1}.$$

The coefficient β_2 in equation (3.6) is the short run marginal propensity to consume. In the long run, if the economy reaches a static equilibrium, consumption and income will be constant from period to period. Long run parameters may then be derived from (3.6) by solving this equation for long run consumption, $CONS^*$, assuming that $CONS^* = CONS_t = CONS_{t-1}$, so that:

$$CONS^* = \frac{\beta_2}{1-\beta_1} \cdot INC_t + \frac{1}{1-\beta_1} \cdot v_t ,$$

where the long run average and marginal propensities to consume are $\frac{\beta_2}{1-\beta_1}$ and the long run income elasticity of consumption is unity.

If a consumption function is estimated using measured consumption and measured income in the form:

$$CONS_t = \delta_0 + \delta_1 \cdot INC_t + \epsilon_t ,$$

then the *PIH* would predict (among other things) that:

1. the marginal propensity to consume (δ_1) will be less than the average propensity to consume;
2. the income elasticity of consumption would tend to rise the longer the time series over which the function is fitted; and
3. the marginal propensity to consume estimated from real *per capita* data would be less than that for undeflated data.

Another rationale for an econometric equation in the form of (3.6) is that of *habit persistence*. A consumer is viewed as having a desired level of consumption, $CONS_t^d$, which is related to current income. When current income alters, inertial factors prevent an immediate movement to the new desired consumption level. Instead, a partial movement is made, so that:

$$CONS_t^d = \alpha + \beta \cdot INC_t \,,$$

with:

$$CONS_t - CONS_{t-1} = (1-\gamma)(CONS_t^d - CONS_{t-1}) + \epsilon_t \,,$$

$$0 < \gamma < 1 \,.$$

This leads to an estimating form:

$$CONS_t = (1-\gamma) \cdot \alpha + \gamma \cdot CONS_{t-1} + (1-\gamma) \cdot \beta \cdot INC_t + \epsilon_t \,,$$

which is similar to equation (3.6), though it has an intercept term. Other aggregate consumption theories also lead to estimating forms similar to equation (3.6).

3.3   Models of Absolute and Permanent Income

Most of the empirical results in this book have been obtained through the use of *PC–GIVE*. *PC–GIVE* is a computer package for econometric data analysis and estimation which may be run on *IBM* and *IBM*–compatible personal computers. *GIVE* stands for Generalised Instrumental Variables Estimators. It is an interactive menu–driven package constructed to reflect aspects of the econometric methodology presented in the Davidson *et al.* (1978) paper, and hence is especially relevant for the analysis of time series data. The use of this package is described in Hendry (1989). However, such has been the growth of interest in the methodological developments in econometric modelling since *DHSY*, that recently several other packages have become available which will perform nearly all the computations in this book. These include *TSP* version 4.2, *REG–X*, and the 1991 versions of *MICROFIT* and *RATS*.

PC–GIVE provides a wide and rich set of descriptive and diagnostic statistics. We will concentrate, however, on only a small part of this potential output, namely the basic statistics available following the estimation of a single equation by ordinary least squares. To illustrate and explain these statistics, consider the estimation of the models for the Absolute and Permanent Income Hypotheses introduced in Section 3.2 above.

To facilitate direct comparison with the *DHSY* model, the data chosen are UK quarterly seasonally unadjusted non–durable consumption expenditure and personal disposable income from the first quarter of 1957 (denoted by 1957(1)), to the fourth quarter of 1975 (1975(4)), in millions of pounds at 1970 prices. The data were taken from Pokorny (1987, p.408), which may differ slightly from the unpublished data used in the Davidson *et al.* (1978) paper (see Pokorny (1987, note 9, p.399)). This accounts for the small differences between the original *DHSY* results and those reported below where direct comparison is possible.

As lagged values of these variables will be required, five observations at the start of the sample are used to create these variables. An important test of any model is how well it predicts out–of–sample periods, so the last 20 observations (1971(1) to 1975(4)) are reserved for this evaluation. Hence, the estimation period (hereafter termed the sample period) becomes 1958(2) to 1970(4), a sample of 51 observations. Figure 3.1 displays the scatter diagram of consumption and income for this sample period.

This figure shows an evident correlation between the two variables. Nevertheless, the dispersion of points seems to increase with the values of consumption and income, which

Fig 3.1: Correlation between consumption and income

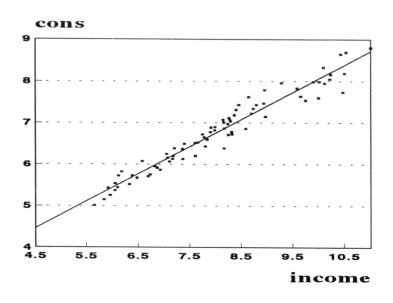

suggests that the appropriate form of the consumption function may not be a simple linear relationship between consumption and income.

For further analysis it will be useful to have some specific
notation for in–sample and out–of–sample (forecast or post
sample) periods.

We will denote the time series as:

$t = 1, 2,..., T, T + 1,...., T^*$, where $T = 51$ and $T^* = 71$,

so that:

$t = 1, 2,..., T$ is the sample period, and
$t = T + 1,..., T^*$ is the forecast or post sample period.

The means and standard deviations of the consumption and
income variables for the sample period are given at the start
of Section 3.7. Also given there is the correlation matrix for

the variables from which it can be seen that the simple correlation coefficient between consumption and income over the sample period is 0.9559.

Consider the estimation of equation (3.1) above, the simplest formulation of the consumption function presented. The computer output for this estimation is presented in Section 3.7 under MODEL 3.1. The parameter estimates for the intercept (INCPT) and income variable (INC) are given in the column headed 'COEF' (the abbreviation 'VARI' stands for 'variable'). The other statistics reported are as follows.

(1)　RSS: the residual (error) sum of squares of the fitted model.

(2)　σ: the estimated standard error of the residuals, calculated as:

$$\sigma = \left(\frac{RSS}{T-k}\right)^{1/2},$$

where k is the number of independent variables in the model, including the intercept. (Here, $k = 2$, and $T = 51$.)

(3)　STD ERR: These are the estimated standard errors of the coefficients, obtained as the square roots of the diagonal elements of the variance–covariance matrix of the *OLS* estimators (for example, see Johnston (1984, p.173)).

(4)　H.C.S.E.: Heteroscedastic Consistent Standard Errors. These are consistent estimates of the standard errors of the regression coefficients if the errors in the model are heteroscedastic. If these values and those for the standard errors in (3) above differ markedly, heteroscedasticity may be inferred. In this case, the H.C.S.E. measure may be preferred. The formulae for their computation are given in White (1980).

(5)　*t*–VALUE: The ratio of the estimated parameter value to its estimated standard error used to test the null hypothesis that the parameter is equal to zero. Under the null hypothesis and additional assumptions about normality for the error term, the ratio has the Student–t distribution with T–k degrees of freedom.

(6) R^2: Coefficient of determination as defined and discussed in Chapter 2.

(7)   F: Statistic used for testing the null hypothesis that all the parameters in the model (apart from the intercept) are jointly equal to zero. It is defined as:

$$F = \frac{ESS/(k-1)}{RSS/(T-k)} = \frac{R^2/(k-1)}{(1-R^2)/(T-k)} \, ,$$

where ESS is the explained sum of squares of the model. Under the null hypothesis, the ratio has the F–distribution with $k - 1$ and $T - k$ degrees of freedom (see Johnston (1984, p.186)). In this case, as there is only one parameter to be tested, the F value is equal to the square of the t–value on this parameter, as may be confirmed.

(8)   DW: Durbin–Watson statistic. This is used to test for autocorrelated errors in the model, and particularly for first order autocorrelation. It is calculated from the residuals of the fitted model. Formally, tests are conducted using the appropriate statistical tables, which are widely available (for example in Johnston (1984, pp. 554–557)). These tables are applicable to models containing an intercept term. Loosely, the hypothesis of no first order autocorrelation in the errors will not be rejected if the DW value is close to 2 (Johnston (1984, p.314)). The test may be misleading if a lagged dependent variable is present among the regressors, as in this case the calculated Durbin–Watson value is biased upwards towards 2 (see Durbin (1970)). Different tables (Farebrother (1980)) should be used when there is no intercept in the regression.

(9) FORECAST χ^2: A test for the constancy of the parameters of the model (including the error variance) in the post sample period compared with its values for the sample period. It is defined as:

$$\text{Forecast } \chi^2 = \frac{\displaystyle\sum_{t=T+1}^{T^*} e_{ft}^2}{\sigma^2} = \frac{(T^* - T) \cdot MSE_f}{\sigma^2} \ ,$$

where $MSE_f = \dfrac{\Sigma e_{ft}^2}{T^* - T}$ and e_{ft} is the forecast error made for period t ($t = T + 1, ..., T^*$) using the post sample data on the independent variables with the vector of estimated model parameters obtained from the sample data. It should be recalled that in the discussion on the choice of sample period, 20 observations were reserved for the evaluation of the model in out–of–sample periods. Under the null hypothesis that all parameter values are unchanged between the sample and post sample periods, this statistic is (asymptotically) distributed as χ^2 with $(T^* - T)$ degrees of freedom. In the computer output, the *Forecast* χ^2 value is divided by its degrees of freedom, that is by the number of observations retained for the forecast period. This allows an immediate *ad hoc* evaluation of the statistic, as this value under the null hypothesis should be below two. Values substantially above this would indicate rejection of the null, and hence imply that at least some parameter values may have altered from the sample period. The test has weak power (that is, the probability that the test will correctly reject a false null hypothesis is low), and should be used as a signal rather than a thorough test.

(10)   CHOW TEST: A model specification test on the constancy of the model's parameters over the entire sample and post sample (forecast) periods. Formally, it is calculated as:

$$CHOW\ TEST = \frac{(RSS^* - RSS)/(T^* - T)}{RSS/(T - k)},$$

where RSS^* is the residual sum of squares from the model estimated using both sample and post sample data. The null hypothesis is the same as that for the *Forecast* χ^2 test in (9) above. Under the null hypothesis, the *Chow Test* has (asymptotically) the F distribution with $T^* - T$ and $T - k$ degrees of freedom. Rejection of the null implies rejection of the model estimated over sample and forecast periods. For a more detailed discussion of this test see Harvey (1990, pp. 183–184).

Two other features of the computer output which will be used in the discussion of various estimated models are as follows:

(11)   *STANDARD ERRORS OF FORECAST*: A graph of actual and forecast values for the post sample data, along with error bars of ($\pm$) two standard errors of forecast (see Johnston (1984, pp. 42–45)) is produced (see for example Figure 3.2). The error bands provide 95% confidence intervals for the forecast, or a range within which forecast values would be expected to lie if the model was performing in the post sample period as it had in the sample period.

(12)   *LAGGED VARIABLES*: In Section 3.7, and in subsequent chapters, lagged variables will be denoted in the computer output in the column headed VARI, by the name of the variable followed by the length of lag. Thus, for example, consumption lagged one period is CONS 1 (MODEL 3.2) and the difference between the logarithms of consumption and income, both lagged four periods, is lc_li 4 (MODEL 3.7).

Fig. 3.2: Prediction from MODEL 3.1

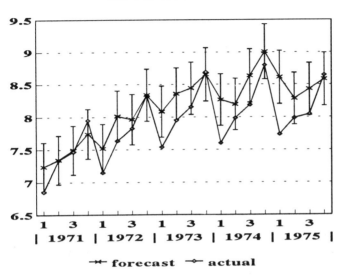

With these diagnostic statistics, we can return to MODEL 3.1 in Section 3.7, in order to comment on the adequacy of equation (3.1) to represent aggregate consumption over the sample and post sample periods. The fit of the model is satisfactory. Both coefficients are statistically significant, a comment that can be made given the acceptable value of the Durbin–Watson statistic. The conventional and heteroscedastic consistent standard errors of the estimated coefficients are not dissimilar so that heteroscedasticity in the errors is not indicated. At the mean values of consumption and income, the *APC* is 0.858. The *MPC* of 0.728 is less than the *APC*. However, the post sample performance of this simple model is far from satisfactory. Figure 3.2 indicates that the forecast values are generally above the realized values, and in some cases the realized values lie outside the confidence limits for the forecast. Both the *Forecast* χ^2 and

Fig. 3.3: Time series of consumption and income

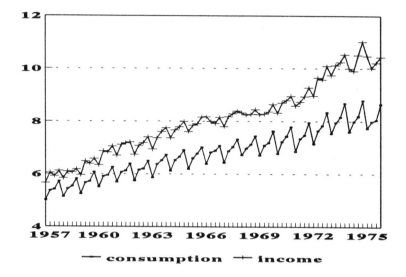

— consumption —+— income

the *Chow* test reject the null hypothesis of no change in the model's parameters between the sample and post sample periods.

Estimation of a simple form of the Permanent Income Hypothesis (equation (3.6), but including an intercept) is no more satisfactory. The computer output for MODEL 3.2 indicates not only the failure of this model to satisfy the forecast tests, but also includes a negative coefficient on the lagged consumption variable, which is inconsistent with the *PIH*.

One reason for the observed weakness of the models estimated to represent the Absolute and Permanent Income Hypotheses might be the lack of attention paid to the time series properties of the data. The graph of the consumption and income data for both sample and post sample periods given in Figure 3.3 shows the marked trends and seasonal patterns exhibited by both series. This suggests that the estimation of the model might be improved if one took account of these features of the data series.

It would be possible to repeat the estimation of the two models above using detrended and deseasonalized data, but this approach is generally not recommended. If series have been seasonally adjusted by different methods, the economic relationship between the series may be distorted (see Wallis (1974)). This can be important as it is not always clear how official statistics have been seasonally adjusted. An alternative way forward is to follow Hendry (1974) and use a combination of trend and seasonal dummy variables to model these effects. It is shown later in the text that using trend and seasonal dummy variables is not the only alternative to using detrended and seasonally adjusted data. Technically (see Chapter 5) the use of such dummy variables corresponds to the assumption that the model is subject to a 'deterministic trend' and 'deterministic seasonality'.

There is also the possibility that there were special effects or events within the sample period which may have distorted the series. Advance warning of possible purchase tax increases in a forthcoming budget may have caused consumers to switch expenditure from the second quarter to the first quarter of 1968. A similar reaction may have occurred between the first two quarters of 1973 relating to the introduction of Value Added Tax. It therefore seems reasonable to include a special dummy variable to allow for the presence of such effects in the periods identified above.

In order to model these trend, seasonal and special effects, define new variables as follows:

$$Q1_t = \begin{cases} 1 \text{ in first quarter} \\ 0 \text{ otherwise} \end{cases},$$

$$Q2_t = \begin{cases} 1 \text{ in second quarter} \\ 0 \text{ otherwise} \end{cases},$$

$$Q3_t = \begin{cases} 1 \text{ in third quarter} \\ 0 \text{ otherwise} \end{cases},$$

$$T = t = 1, 2, 3,..., 51 \quad,$$

$$DT1_t = Q1_t \cdot T \ , \quad DT2_t = Q2_t \cdot T \ , \quad DT3_t = Q3_t \cdot T \ ,$$

$$DO_t = \begin{cases} 1 \text{ for } 1968(1) \text{ and } 1973(1) \\ -1 \text{ for } 1968(2) \text{ and } 1973(2) \ . \\ 0 \text{ otherwise} \end{cases}$$

The variables $Q1_t$, $Q2_t$ and $Q3_t$ are seasonal dummy variables. There is no $Q4_t$ variable as the estimated model will include an intercept term and the joint presence of all four dummy variables and an intercept term would make the model estimation procedure break down (see Johnston (1984, p.226)). The variable T is a time trend. The variables $DT1_t$, $DT2_t$, and $DT3_t$ allow for multiplicative seasonality, where the absolute value of the seasonal effect changes over time. Thus the consecutive values of $DT2_t$ will be 1, 0, 0, 0, 5, 0, 0, 0, 9, 0, 0, 0, *etc.* (recall that the sample period starts at a second quarter of a year). DO_t relates to the special effects that might have caused expenditure switching prior to budget announcements.

The equation to be estimated is now:

$$CONS_t = \beta_0 + \beta_1 INC_t + \beta_2 Q1_t + \beta_3 Q2_t + \beta_4 Q3_t +$$

$$\beta_5 T + \beta_6 DT1_t + \beta_7 DT2_t + \beta_8 DT3_t + \beta_9 DO_t + \epsilon_t \ .$$

The results of estimating this equation are reported in Section 3.7 under MODEL 3.3. The majority of the variables which have now been added to the earlier model of the Absolute Income Hypothesis are statistically significant at conventional levels of significance. The computer output for this extended model also shows, however, that it fails the *Forecast* χ^2 and *Chow* tests. In addition, Figure 3.4 shows that some realizations lie outside the confidence intervals for the forecasts.

Fig. 3.4: Prediction from MODEL 3.3

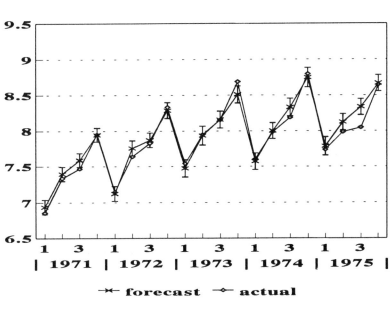

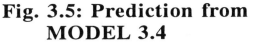

Fig. 3.5: Prediction from MODEL 3.4

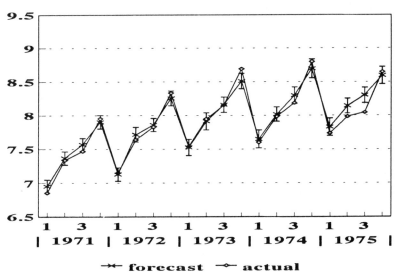

When the new variables are added to the model for Permanent Income (equation (3.6) with an intercept term), the estimated model (MODEL 3.4 in Section 3.7) now has the expected sign for the coefficient on lagged consumption compared with the earlier result in MODEL 3.2. However, MODEL 3.4 fails the forecast tests and, as Figure 3.5 shows, produces confidence intervals for forecasts that do not include the realized values, particularly towards the end of the post sample period.

The implied long run marginal propensity to consume from MODEL 3.4 is $\dfrac{0.225}{1 - 0.273}$ or 0.310 which is very low compared with what would be expected under either the Absolute or Permanent Income Hypotheses. Similarly, the long run income elasticity of consumption calculated at the mean values of consumption and income is only 0.36, well below the value of unity for the theory the model purports to represent.

3.4   The *DHSY* Model

It is not our intention to provide a detailed account of the *DHSY* paper. A good discussion on these lines is to be found in Pokorny (1987, pp. 380–397). Rather, we will concentrate on those points in the *DHSY* analysis which represented substantial methodological departures from what was generally practised in applied econometrics at that time.

The model that will be considered initially and which will eventually lead to a developed *DHSY* model is:

$$\Delta_4 cons_t = \beta_1 \Delta_4 inc_t + \beta_2 \Delta \Delta_4 inc_t + \beta_3 \Delta_4 DO_t + e_t , \quad (3.7)$$

where $cons_t$ and inc_t are the natural logarithms of the consumption and income variables defined in Section 3.3, DO_t is the 'special effects' variable also defined there, e_t is an error term, and the symbols Δ and Δ_4 denote difference operators such that:

$$\Delta x_t = x_t - x_{t-1} \, ,$$

and:

$$\Delta_4 x_t = x_t - x_{t-4} \, .$$

A justification for the use of logarithms and differences will be discussed below.

At first glance, this equation would seem to have very little similarity to either MODEL 3.3 or 3.4 which were the estimated forms of the representations of the Absolute and Permanent Income Hypotheses. However, it was not the intention of *DHSY* to provide a new theory of aggregate consumption, but rather to model this variable within the framework of generally accepted theory. We will see shortly that equation (3.7) does in fact have an interpretation consistent with the Permanent Income Hypothesis.

The use of logarithms in this model rather than the raw data in levels can be justified on grounds of both statistical and economic theory. Figure 3.3 seems to show that the dispersion of the consumption series increases with the level of the series. This may also be true for the income series. MODEL 3.4 allowed for a changing seasonal pattern by the variables $DT1_t$, $DT2_t$ and $DT3_t$. However, if the standard deviation of a series is proportional to its level, then data expressed in terms of logarithms will exhibit approximately constant variance (see Cryer (1986, pp. 94–95)). Chapter 5 will indicate why it is useful to work with data which exhibits a constant variance. In the *DHSY* model, however, such a data transformation is not only a technical matter. As will become evident shortly, the economic model developed by *DHSY* naturally leads to the use of variables in logarithmic form.

The model presented above and estimated as MODEL 3.4 used a time trend variable to model the upward tendency of the data in levels. If logarithms are now used instead of levels, the series will display a linear trend if the raw data display exponential growth. The marked seasonal pattern of the data was modelled in MODEL 3.4 by seasonal dummy variables. The use of time trends and seasonal dummies is not only expensive in terms of degrees of freedom but, as we indicated above, may also be considered to be rather *ad hoc* in nature. Investigators often prefer to try to model trend and seasonal effects simultaneously within an estimated model, rather than introduce special variables in an attempt to eliminate their effect (for example, see Granger and Newbold (1986, p.37)).

In particular, it is common to handle trend and seasonal effects by *differencing* the data. Consider the following artificial example displayed below:

x_t	f_t	z_t	g_t	v_t	l_t	Δl_t
1	0	1	0	—	—	—
2	1	4	3	—	—	—
3	1	9	7	—	—	—
4	8	16	20	—	—	—
5	4	25	24	4	24	—
6	5	36	35	4	32	8
7	5	49	47	4	40	8
8	12	64	68	4	48	8
9	8	81	80	4	56	8
10	9	100	99	4	64	8
11	9	121	119	4	72	8
12	16	144	148	4	80	8

Above, x_t and z_t are linear and quadratic trends respectively. If we take the series as representing three years of quarterly data, new series with additive seasonal effects can be constructed by simply adding seasonal effects of (say) -1, -1, -2 and $+4$ to each appropriate quarterly value. This yields the series f_t (linear trend with additive seasonality) and g_t (quadratic trend with additive seasonality).

The variables v_t and l_t represent the effect of *seasonal differencing*. Thus;

$$v_t = f_t - f_{t-4} = \Delta_4 f_t ,$$

and:

$$l_t = g_t - g_{t-4} = \Delta_4 g_t .$$

A *seasonal difference* is simply the difference between an observation and its value for the corresponding season one year before. If the variables are measured in logarithms, then the seasonal differences can be shown to be measures of the growth rates of the variables (see Cryer (1986, p.95)). One should note, however, that seasonal dummy variables and seasonal differences do not account for precisely the same phenomenon. The difference between deterministic and stochastic seasonality will be discussed in Chapter 5.

It can be seen immediately from the figures above that seasonal differencing converts a linear trend with an additive seasonal effect (f_t) to a constant (that is to a variable with no trend or seasonal pattern). Seasonal differencing of the quadratic trend with additive seasonality (g_t), however, results in a series (l_t) which still contains a trend but with no seasonal pattern. The final column of figures shows that this trend can be modelled by taking the *first differences* of the seasonally differenced series. That is, Δl_t is defined as:

$$\Delta l_t = l_t - l_{t-1} = (g_t - g_{t-4}) - (g_{t-1} - g_{t-5}) ,$$

and this series contains neither trend nor seasonal effects.

From inspection of Figure 3.3 it seems that both consumption and income may be subject to linear trends. Formal tests for this conjecture will be given in Chapter 5. Both variables also display a marked seasonal pattern. From the remarks and example above, it would seem reasonable to re-estimate the models of the Absolute and Permanent Income Hypotheses using logarithms and seasonal differencing of the variables rather than time trends and seasonal dummies. For example, reconsider MODEL 3.3 in Section 3.7

where now the consumption and income variables are measured in natural logarithms and the trend and seasonal dummy variables are omitted:

$$cons_t = \alpha_1 + \alpha_2 inc_t + \alpha_3 DO_t + \epsilon_t, \qquad (3.8)$$

Lagging equation (3.8) by four periods and subtracting the result from equation (3.8) yields:

$$\Delta_4 cons_t = \alpha_2 \Delta_4 inc_t + \alpha_3 \Delta_4 DO_t + \Delta_4 \epsilon_t, \qquad (3.9)$$

This is not quite the same as the initial model presented at the start of this section. This was:

$$\Delta_4 cons_t = \beta_1 \Delta_4 inc_t + \beta_2 \Delta\Delta_4 inc_t + \beta_3 \Delta_4 DO_t + e_t, \quad (3.7)$$

where:

$$\Delta\Delta_4 inc_t = (inc_t - inc_{t-4}) - (inc_{t-1} - inc_{t-5}).$$

Compared with equation (3.9), this equation has an extra term $\Delta\Delta_4 inc_t$. From our discussion above, the term $\Delta\Delta_4 inc_t$ could be an appropriate form for the income variable if income displayed nonlinear growth. Whether on this interpretation it would also be sensible to include the term Δinc_t in the equation is something the reader might like to think about after considering Chapter 5 on *cointegration*.

However, the term $\Delta\Delta_4 inc_t$ may be given an economic rather than a statistical interpretation. Equation (3.7) implies that consumption this quarter is the same as in the corresponding quarter one year before, modified by β_1 times the change in income over this same period. Under the Permanent Income Hypothesis, for β_1 to be positive it must be that some of this increase in income is treated as an increase in permanent income. Suppose that this change in income is larger than the change in income on an annual basis experienced in the previous quarter, that is suppose $\Delta\Delta_4 inc_t$ is positive. Then if the consumer considers this extra rise to be transitory income, the consumer will reduce consumption from the level implied by treating the whole of the income increase as permanent. The converse argument would hold where $\Delta\Delta_4 inc_t$ was negative. Thus, on the grounds of economic theory, β_2 may be expected to be negative.

The results of estimating equation (3.7) are given in Section 3.7 under MODEL 3.5. On statistical grounds, this represents an improvement over both MODELS 3.3 and 3.4 in explaining aggregate consumption. The coefficients on the income variables are statistically significant and carry their expected signs under the Permanent Income Hypothesis. The parameter constancy tests do not signal the problems that were encountered earlier. Figure 3.6 displays the confidence intervals for the forecasts which invariably include the realized values. The seasonal differencing introduced to model the seasonal pattern of the data is at least as successful as the use of seasonal dummy variables. The main statistical qualification to the foregoing is the rather low value for the Durbin–Watson statistic. This implies that caution should be exercised on any statements about statistical significance, and could indicate that some important variables may have been omitted from the analysis.

Equation (3.7) is a restricted or *specific* case of a more *general* model. Equation (3.7) can be written as:

$$cons_t = cons_{t-4} + (\beta_1 + \beta_2)inc_t - (\beta_1 + \beta_2)inc_{t-4} - \beta_2 inc_{t-1} +$$

$$\beta_2 inc_{t-5} + \beta_3 DO_t - \beta_3 DO_{t-4} + e_t .$$

This a restricted form of the general equation:

Fig. 3.6: Prediction from MODEL 3.5

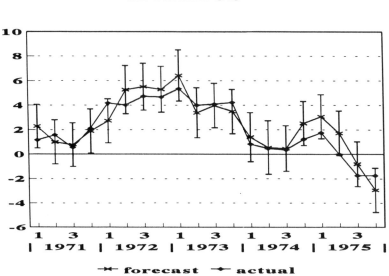

$$cons_t = \theta_1 cons_{t-4} + \theta_2 inc_t + \theta_3 inc_{t-4} + \theta_4 inc_{t-1} + \theta_5 inc_{t-5} +$$

$$\theta_6 DO_t + \theta_7 DO_{t-4} + e_t , \qquad (3.10)$$

with restrictions:

$$\theta_1 = 1 , \ \theta_2 = -\theta_3 , \ \theta_4 = -\theta_5 \text{ and } \theta_6 = -\theta_7 .$$

MODEL 3.6 in Section 3.7 gives the results of fitting the unrestricted equation (3.10). The coefficient on lagged consumption is close to unity. The signs on income and income lagged four periods are approximately equal but opposite in sign, as are the coefficients on income lagged one and five periods, and the special events variable lagged one and four periods. Generally, we may conclude that the unrestricted and restricted estimates are quite close, so that on the grounds of statistical efficiency, equation (3.7) which is the restricted form of equation (3.10) would be preferred. Formal tests for restrictions on models such as these will be presented in Chapter 4.

Apart from the questionable value for the Durbin–Watson statistic noted above, there is a major reason to feel unhappy with equation (3.7). This equation can be rejected on the grounds of economic theory rather than statistical diagnostic testing.

The economic theories considered in Section 3.2 were 'steady state' or long run theories. That is, they related economic variables in situations where any adjustments of the consumer units to positions of disequilibrium were assumed to have been completed. Economic models should have sensible interpretations for both situations of *static equilibrium*, where the variables are assumed to be unchanging between periods, and for *stable equilibrium*, where all variables are changing at some constant rate.

It can be seen immediately that equation (3.7) has no static equilibrium solution. In the long run, the special effects variable DO_t may be ignored. For static equilibrium, $cons_t = cons_{t-4}$ and $inc_t = inc_{t-4}$, so that $\Delta_4 cons_t = \Delta_4 inc_t = \Delta\Delta_4 inc_t = 0$. In this situation, equation (3.7) reduces to the uninformative result:

$$0 = \beta_1 \cdot 0 + \beta_2 \cdot 0 \,,$$

which is not a long run relationship between consumption and income.

In order to consider whether equation (3.7) has a stable equilibrium solution, assume that both consumption and income are growing at a constant rate of $100 \cdot g\%$ *per annum*. Provided g is not bigger than about 0.2, the seasonal differences $\Delta_4 cons_t$ and $\Delta_4 inc_t$ will closely approximate g (see Cryer (1986, p.95)). Thus we may take $\Delta_4 cons_t = \Delta_4 inc_t = g$ so that consequently, $\Delta\Delta_4 inc_t = 0$. The 'long run' version of MODEL 3.5 may be written as:

$$\Delta_4 cons_t = 0.674 \cdot \Delta_4 inc_t \, ,$$

which implies a long run income elasticity of only 0.674, which is well below the unitary value called for by the economic theories considered earlier. It is not possible to solve MODEL 3.5 for a stable equilibrium solution as substituting g into the equation above gives:

$$g = 0.674 \cdot g \, .$$

The conclusion is that the model represented by equation (3.7) and estimated as MODEL 3.5 is useful in reflecting short run behaviour only. This model fails to generate plausible long run properties of the relationship between consumption and income.

DHSY considered that what was needed was a model which would generate a long run unitary income elasticity of consumption. As the economic theories considered earlier suggested a long run proportionality between consumption and income, the long run solution should be of the form:

$$CONS_t = K \cdot INC_t \, ,$$

where K is a constant for any given growth rate, so that the long run ratio of consumption to income (the *APC*) is also constant.

Equation (3.7) explained the current level of consumption expenditure in terms of adjustments made to consumption for the corresponding quarter one year before. Suppose that one year ago the consumer did not experience an *APC* of K. That is, suppose:

$$\frac{CONS_{t-4}}{INC_{t-4}} \neq K \, , \quad \text{or} \quad (cons_{t-4} - inc_{t-4}) \neq \ln K \, .$$

If this ratio was greater than K, then in order to try to get back to a long run equilibrium path, the consumer in period t will reduce its consumption relative to $CONS_{t-4}$ and *vice versa* for a ratio smaller than K. Hence, it is worthwhile considering adding a term $(cons_{t-4} - inc_{t-4})$ to equation (3.7), yielding:

$$\Delta_4 cons_t = \beta_1 \Delta_4 inc_t + \beta_2 \Delta\Delta_4 inc_t + \beta_3 \Delta_4 DO_t +$$

$$\beta_4 (cons_{t-4} - inc_{t-4}) + e_t , \qquad (3.11)$$

where β_4 is expected to be negative.

Through this new term, the consumer is seen as attempting to correct a short run disequilibrium position. Accordingly, equation (3.11) is said to contain an *error correction mechanism*, represented by the term $(cons_{t-4} - inc_{t-4})$.

Equation (3.11) represents a marked theoretical improvement over the models considered earlier in that it has both static and stable equilibrium solutions.

For static equilibrium, the equation solves as:

$$\beta_4 (cons_{t-4} - inc_{t-4}) = 0 ,$$

and as in general, $\beta_4 \neq 0$, then:

$$cons_t = inc_t ,$$

which implies a long run unitary income elasticity of consumption.

For stable equilibrium, where consumption and income are growing at a constant rate g, the model solves as:

$$g = \beta_1 g + \beta_4 (cons_{t-4} - inc_{t-4}) , \text{ or:}$$

$$cons_{t-4} = inc_{t-4} + \frac{g \cdot (1-\beta_1)}{\beta_4} .$$

The long run consumption function can then be written as:

$$CONS_t = \Psi \cdot INC_t , \qquad (3.12)$$

where $\Psi = \exp \left\{ \dfrac{g \cdot (1-\beta_1)}{\beta_4} \right\}$.

Equation (3.12) exhibits a unitary elasticity as required. As $\beta_4 < 0$, the long run *APC* in equation (3.12) is inversely related to the rate of growth, g, a finding consistent with inter–country evidence (Davidson *et al.* (1978, p.681)).

The results of fitting equation (3.11) are given under MODEL 3.7 in Section 3.7. All coefficients are statistically significant and carry their expected signs under the theory outlined above. However, the model fails the tests of parameter constancy at the 1% level of significance, and some realizations lie outside the confidence intervals for forecasts, especially towards the end of the forecast period as can be seen in Figure 3.7. As the Durbin–Watson statistic lies in the indeterminate range (5% level), all statements regarding statistical significance must be treated with caution.

Compared with the sample period, the post sample period experienced much higher rates of inflation. *DHSY* considered that the continuing relatively poor performance of their model in the forecast or post sample period might have been due to the omission of inflation effects. As the model is estimated using variables measured in real terms, what is envisaged are possible effects of price changes not seen as being immediately reflected in money income changes. Such effects could work either to increase or reduce real consumption from what it otherwise would have been.

There could be a 'money illusion' effect (Branson and Klevorick (1969)) if consumers do not notice the increase in

Fig. 3.7: Prediction from
MODEL 3.7

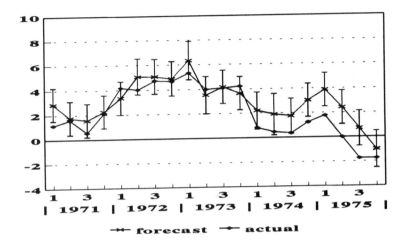

prices, but interpret a rise in money income as an increase in real income. This would imply a positive coefficient on a price change variable introduced into equation (3.11).

Alternatively, Deaton (1977) has argued that inflation is often unanticipated, with consumers interpreting the price rises of goods they typically purchase as relative price increases rather than as a general rise in the aggregate price level. This may be the case particularly when inflation is accelerating. The response of consumers to unanticipated inflation viewed in this way would be to reduce their real consumption, leading to what Deaton has termed 'involuntary saving through unanticipated inflation'.

To allow for these potential inflation effects, and to be consistent with the terms already in equation (3.11), Davidson *et al.*(1978) estimated an equation of the form:

Fig. 3.8: Prediction from MODEL 3.8

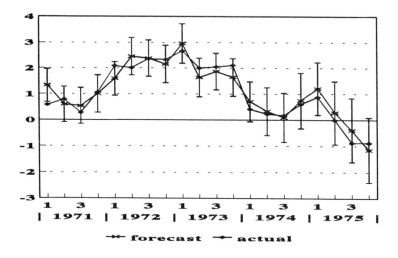

$$\Delta_4\, cons_t = \beta_1 \Delta_4 inc_t + \beta_2 \Delta\Delta_4 inc_t + \beta_3 \Delta_4 DO_t + \beta_4 (cons_{t-4} -$$

$$inc_{t-4}) + \beta_5 inf_t + \beta_6 \Delta inf_t + e_t, \qquad (3.13)$$

where the rate of inflation is approximated by $inf_t = \Delta_4 p_t$, and where p_t is the natural logarithm of the implicit price deflator used to construct the series on $CONS_t$. This is the final form of the *DHSY* model for aggregate consumption expenditure that we shall consider. Under the Deaton hypothesis , if inflation is unanticipated β_5 will be negative, and if inflation is both accelerating and unanticipated, then β_6 will also be negative.

MODEL 3.8 in Section 3.7 reports the estimation of equation (3.13) for the sample period. The Durbin–Watson statistic has increased in value compared with MODEL 3.7, and is now above the upper bound value for the test. Both parameter constancy tests now imply that the null hypothesis of no parameter value changes between the sample and post sample periods cannot be rejected. Figure 3.8 shows that there is good agreement between model forecasts and realizations, with the realizations falling within the 95% confidence limits for the forecasts. With a constant rate of growth of real income and a constant rate of inflation, the model has a stable equilibrium solution of the required form.

3.5 Methodological Aspects of *DHSY* Modelling

One of the implications of data mining was that an investigator would almost certainly end up with a model that, superficially at least, seemed consistent with the theory postulated and which received support from the data. The corollary is that for any widely researched area, the potential exists for the coexistence of many such alternative models. This is clearly unfortunate. Though not linking the large number of alternative empirical models of aggregate consumption expenditure specifically to data mining, *DHSY* did regard the existence of a 'plethora of substantially different quarterly equations' (Davidson *et al.* (1978, p.661)) estimated from essentially the same data sets and reflecting similar theories as representing a serious weakness of traditional methodology.

They suggested that a minimal requirement of any new model should be that it could explain why previous researchers got their results, as well as providing some explanation of something that previous models did not. New models should be interpretable within an explicit (economic) theoretical framework, and be consistent with the properties of the observed data. The major innovation here is the requirement to be able to explain, or incorporate, previous research findings. This is not a trivial task. In the *DHSY* study, this problem was approached by first standardizing three rival models so that they reflected common data sets, methods of seasonal adjustment and other data transformations, and functional forms.   Second, a general model was constructed which contained the three alternative models as special cases. Technically, the three models were *nested* within a general model, so that each individual model was a specific or special case of this general model.   Statistical tests were then used to determine whether the constraints on the general model necessary to give rise to a specific model are supported by the data.   The initial *DHSY* model considered above (equation (3.7)) was the result of just this procedure.   The idea that one should start with a general model and progressively simplify it by means of significance tests is also central to the *DHSY* approach to building a particular model, as well as the model choice or selection problem outlined above.

When one model can explain or account for the behaviour or performance of another rival model, the former model is said to *encompass* the latter.   Clearly, a general model should encompass a restricted or nested form of the model.   However, if the restrictions cannot be rejected, the 'parsimonious' or restricted model would be preferred because data limitations favour the estimation of the simplest acceptable model. The encompassing principle is not limited to the case of nested models.   Procedures exist which allow separate rival models to be compared where neither model can be obtained as a special case of the other.   Chapter 8 will explore the encompassing principle in more detail, and consider some tests proposed for non—nested models.

Economic theorists have tended to concentrate on developing theories that explain static or long run relationships between economic variables.   In Section 3.4 above, for example, it was considered important that from the point of view of established theory, an estimated consumption function should exhibit a long run unitary income elasticity of consumption.   *Cointegration* analysis is concerned with the development of tests relevant for investigating long run relationships, and will be discussed in detail in Chapter 5.

Theorists are normally silent on the short run dynamics of their models, such as the lag lengths appropriate for each of the variables.   An approach to modelling short run dynamics was proposed in Davidson *et al.* (1978, p.680) and has been developed by Hendry (1979).   An 'overparameterized' model is defined which contains more lags than are expected to be necessary. The model is then reduced in scale by a sequence of statistical tests. One advantage of this approach is that the significance level for the sequence of tests is known (see Section 4.5 below). This is in contrast with approaches which start with 'simple' models that are successively made more complicated by the addition of new variables or longer lag lengths on existing variables in response to various diagnostic tests. In the Davidson *et al.* (1978) paper, these short run dynamics were modelled through an error correction mechanism, which allowed consumption to return to its long run growth path following a disturbance which took it from this path.

Starting with a general model and subjecting it to a sequence of tests of restrictions to determine if there is an acceptable specific model is termed *general to specific* modelling. A simple example was given in Section 3.4 where restricted and unrestricted versions of equation (3.10) were compared. Further applications of this principle to the *DHSY* model will be considered in Chapter 4.

It would be wrong to see the *DHSY* model as representing a complete break from the Cowles Commission methodology considered in Chapter 1. There we listed and explained five assumptions of this methodology, namely

1. *A priori* restrictions;
2. Time invariance of parameters;
3. Parameter invariance with respect to changes in variables;
4. Known causal ordering;
5. No verification against rival models.

Only in respect of the fifth of these assumptions did Davidson *et al.* (1978) attempt to move away from the Cowles Commission framework. The paper contained several ideas which have subsequently been developed and represented an example of what 'best practice' econometrics could achieve within the confines of traditional methodology. The *DHSY* model is not entirely free from data mining, as the inflation effects were added to correct for an observed weakness of that model. Some data mining is inevitable in any applied study. However, in this case, the development of the model was the outcome of a systematic and directed testing of a sequence of models constrained throughout by the requirements of what was considered to be a relevant economic theory. In so far as this approach was decidedly uncommon, the results carried conviction.

3.6   Testing for Parameter Constancy

Two important assumptions of the Cowles Commission methodology were that the parameters in any model formulated to describe an economic relationship should be constant over time and should be invariant to alterations in the distribution of the variables that make up the model. Chapter 7 will introduce the concept of *structural invariance* which is concerned with the second of these questions.

With respect to the time constancy of parameters, we have already introduced the *Forecast* χ^2 and *Chow* tests to compare the performance of a model between the sample and post sample (or forecast) periods. Whilst these are useful guides to parameter constancy, it would also be advantageous to consider the stability of the parameters in the sample period, and to be able to identify specific points within the sample and/or post sample periods where a structural break in the model may have occurred. Three diagnostic tools relevant for such inquiries are the plots of *recursive least squares coefficients*, *one–step residuals* and *scaled recursive Chow test statistics*.

(a) Recursive Least Squares Coefficients

As interest is on the behaviour of the parameters of the model over time, an obvious starting point would be to plot each estimated coefficient against time. That is, starting from the small sub sample of $t = 1, 2, ..., n$, where $n \geq k$, estimate the k parameters of the model by ordinary least squares. Then extend the sample period by one observation to $t = 1, 2, ..., n+1$, and re–estimate the model. Continue this procedure until the estimation period is the complete sample $t = 1, 2,...,$ T. For each regression, the values of the coefficients may be plotted against the latest time period in the sample used for the estimation of that regression.

Formally, let X_t represent the $t \times k$ matrix of observations on the k independent variables, and x_t be the t–th row of X_t (that is, the observations on the independent variables at time t). Let y_t^* be the $t \times 1$ vector of observations and y_t be the observation at time t, on the dependent variable. Then the *OLS* estimator of the $k \times 1$ vector of parameters, β_t, in the relation:

$$y_t = x_t' \cdot \beta_t + u_t \quad , \quad t \geq n ,$$

is:

$$\hat{\beta}_t = (X_t' \cdot X_t)^{-1} \cdot X_t' \cdot y_t^* .$$

This vector of estimated coefficients is calculated sequentially for $t = n$, then $t = n + 1$, up to $t = T$, by rolling forward the data admitted to the sample one period at a time. Updating (or *recursive*) formulae exist which allow for the re–estimation of $\hat{\beta}_t$ when a new period is added to the sample without the need to recompute the inverse of $(X_t' \cdot X_t)$ each time. Hence, these least squares estimates are called *recursive least squares* coefficients.

As an illustration, consider the recursive least squares estimation of the coefficients of the concluding *DHSY* model (equation (3.13)) considered in Section 3.5, using the same sample period, 1958(2) to 1970(4). For computational reasons, the variable DO_t will be omitted from the analysis. (Students should try to work out why this is necessary.)

Time paths of the coefficients in the model are presented in Figures 3.9 to 3.13. The initial instability of the parameter estimates for all the variables simply reflects the small number of observations used to estimate them at the start of the

RLS Coefficients: Model 3.8

Fig. 3.9 *d4li*

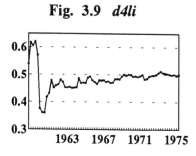

Fig. 3.10 *dd4li*

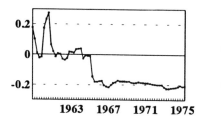

Fig. 3.11 *lc_li 4*

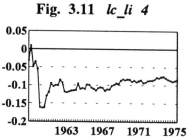

Fig. 3.12 *inf*

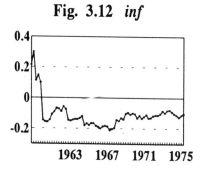

Fig. 3.13 *dinf*

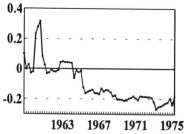

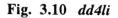

recursions. As can be seen, the coefficients on $\Delta_4 inc_t$, $(cons_{t-4} - inc_{t-4})$ and inf_t remain relatively stable over the sample period. The coefficients for both $\Delta\Delta_4 inc_t$ and Δinf_t are less stable, however, taking positive values around 1963/64 before becoming negative. MODEL 3.9 in Section 3.7 gives the *OLS* estimates for the last recursion, using the full sample data. MODEL 3.9 is thus the same as MODEL 3.8 but with the variable DO_t omitted. There is little difference between the parameter estimates of these two equations. For future reference, MODEL 3.10 gives the results when the entire sample and post sample data are used.

(b) One–Step Residuals

At each recursion, an *OLS* residual for the last period in the sample, $\tilde{v}_t$, can be obtained as:

$$\tilde{v}_t = y_t - x_t' \cdot \hat{\beta}_t .$$

From the set of such residuals available at time t, the standard error of the regression, $\hat{\sigma}_t = \left[\dfrac{\Sigma \tilde{v}_t^2}{t-k} \right]^{1/2}$, may be calculated.

Suppose that there is a structural break somewhere within the sample period. Then the coefficients of the model should be relatively stable for successive recursions until that point is reached. Similarly, the residual calculated for the last period in each sample used in a recursion should be of the same order of magnitude as those that preceded it. Once the break point is reached, however, the residual calculated for this period is likely to appear abnormal compared with the other residuals, as the model will provide a poor fit for the break period.

Thus another guide to parameter constancy in a model is provided by plotting the residual for the last period in the

Fig. 3.14: One-step residuals:
MODEL 3.9

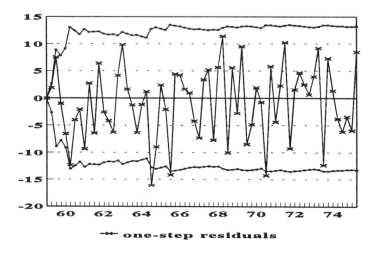

sample used for the recursion against time. This residual is termed a *one–step residual*. The plot also includes error bands of $\pm 2 \cdot \hat{\sigma}_t$ around zero. Values of one–step residuals which lie outside these bands are suggestive of either 'outlier' (or exceptional) values for y_t or of some alteration in the structural parameters of the model.

Figure 3.14 shows the plot of the one–step residuals for MODEL 3.9. It can be seen, for example, that there may have been a structural break in the model in the first quarter of 1965 as for this period, the recursive one–step residual lies outside the error band. There are similar breaks in the first quarters of 1966 and 1971.

(c) Scaled Recursive Chow Test

A test for the statistical significance of a possible break is provided by a *recursive Chow test*. If the residual sum of squares for the model fitted by *OLS* up to and including period *t–1* is *RSS*, and if the corresponding residual sum of squares for the model fitted up to and including period *t* is *RSS** , then the Chow test statistic is calculated as:

$$Chow_t = \frac{(\,RSS^* - RSS\,)}{RSS/(t-k)}.$$

Under the null hypothesis that there has been no structural change in the model between periods $t - 1$ and t, this statistic has the F distribution with 1 and $t - k$ degrees of freedom. This statistic can be calculated for each recursion and plotted against time. As the statistic and the critical values of F are functions of t, it is useful to divide the *Chow* value by its 5% critical value from the tables of F to yield a *scaled recursive Chow test* for each recursion. Hence, the statistic plotted is:

$$\frac{Chow_t}{F_{0.05}(1,t-k)},$$

which under the null hypothesis should be less than unity. Values of this statistic greater than unity imply that the null of no structural change between periods $t - 1$ and t would be rejected at the 5% level of significance.

Figure 3.15 indicates that the earlier suggestion of a structural break in the model in the first quarter of 1965 is supported by a statistically significant scaled *Chow* test value. There are also significant values for the first quarters of 1966 and 1971 which clearly correspond to the substantial negative values of the one–step residuals for these periods shown in Figure 3.14.

Many books and articles use a further set of residuals to test for parameter constancy. It is important not to confuse the tests above with those based on what are called *Recursive*

Fig. 3.15: Scaled recursive Chow test
MODEL 3.9

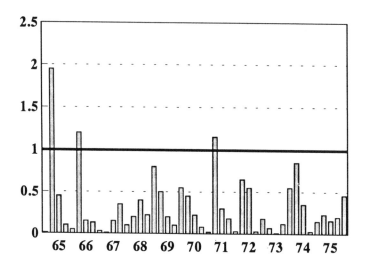

Residuals. From any recursion, one could calculate a *one–step ahead prediction error* (or *innovation*) for period t as:

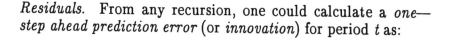

$$v_t = y_t - x'_t \cdot \hat{\beta}_{t-1} \, ,$$

by using the parameter vector estimated from the data up to and including $t - 1$. These residuals can be shown to be unbiased and uncorrelated, but heteroscedastic. When each residual is divided by a term proportional to the square root of its variance, the result is termed a *standardized innovation* or *recursive residual.*

3.7   Stylized Computer Output (*PC–GIVE*)

Present Sample Dates are 1958 (2) to 1975 (4) less 20 Forecasts

MEANS OF VARIABLES

CONS	INCPT	INC
6490.1765	1.0000	7563.3333

STANDARD DEVIATIONS OF VARIABLES

CONS	INCPT	INC
609.6314	.0000	800.0422

CORRELATION MATRIX

	CONS	INCPT	INC
CONS	1.000		
INCPT	.0000	1.000	
INC	.9559	.0000	1.000

Simple form of Absolute Income Hypothesis

MODEL 3.1: Modelling CONS by OLS (equation (3.1) in text)

The Sample is 1958 (2) to 1975 (4) less 20 Forecasts

VARI	COEF	STD ERR	H.C.S.E.	t–VALUE
INCPT	981.08	243.12	249.81	4.03530
INC	.72840	.03197	.03388	22.7836

$R^2 = .9137$ $\sigma = 180.86$ $F(1, 49) = 519.09$ $DW = 2.242$
$RSS = 1602807.86$ For 2 Variables and 51 Observations

Tests Of Parameter CONSTANCY Over : 1971 $1 - 1975$ 4

Forecast $\chi^2(20)/20$	=	4.23
CHOW TEST(20, 49)	=	2.46

Simple form of Permanent Income Hypothesis

MODEL 3.2: Modelling CONS by OLS (equation (3.6) in text with intercept)

The Sample is 1958 (2) to 1975 (4) less 20 Forecasts

VARI	COEF	STD ERR	H.C.S.E.	t–VALUE
CONS 1	−.2072	.08030	.06804	−2.5814
INCPT	1277.8	257.30	289.88	4.96645
INC	.86561	.06117	.04809	14.1512

R^2 = .924 σ = 171.234 F(2, 48) = 292.88 DW = 1.837
RSS = 1407420.329 For 3 Variables and 51 Observations
Tests Of Parameter CONSTANCY Over : 1971 1 − 1975 4

Forecast $\chi^2(20)/20$	=	4.68
CHOW TEST(20, 48)	=	2.23

Absolute Income Hypothesis with trend and dummies

MODEL 3.3: Modelling CONS by OLS

The Sample is 1958 (2) to 1975 (4) less 20 Forecasts

VARI	COEF	STD ERR	H.C.S.E.	t–VALUE
INCPT	3748.79	222.28	260.41	16.8644
INC	.300855	.03625	.04222	8.29855
Q1	−397.90	43.209	41.116	−9.2104
Q2	−208.86	37.684	40.569	−5.5424
Q3	−182.84	38.183	32.611	−4.7886
TREND	23.4166	2.0494	2.3114	11.4258
DT1	−5.8447	1.1828	1.0186	−4.9413
DT2	−2.2434	1.1094	1.3196	−2.0222
DT3	−.84485	1.0913	.93466	−.77411
DO	48.0869	32.654	26.179	1.47261

R^2 = .9961 σ = 41.6105 F(9, 41) = 1187.93 DW = 1.811
RSS = 70989.1018 For 10 Variables and 51 Observations

Tests Of Parameter CONSTANCY Over : 1971 1 — 1975 4

Forecast $\chi^2(20)/20$	=	6.09
CHOW TEST(20, 41)	=	3.59

Permanent Income Hypothesis with trend and dummies

MODEL 3.4: Modelling CONS by OLS

The Sample is 1958 (2) to 1975 (4) less 20 Forecasts

VARI	COEF	STD ERR	H.C.S.E.	t–VALUE
CONS 1	.27267	.12608	.13621	2.16261
INCPT	2755.2	506.38	544.57	5.44098
INC	.22526	.04927	.05185	4.57171
Q1	−486.7	58.279	62.883	−8.3511
Q2	−118.9	55.061	62.547	−2.1603
Q3	−190.2	36.738	35.244	−5.1788
TREND	17.024	3.5485	3.9378	4.79749
DT1	−6.041	1.1367	1.1273	−5.3143
DT2	−1.619	1.1011	1.3214	−1.4710
DT3	−.2894	1.0765	1.0960	−.26883
DO	75.543	33.759	20.425	2.23767

R^2 = .9965 σ = 39.86 F(10, 40) = 1165.49 DW = 2.088
RSS = 63557.7913 For 11 Variables and 51 Observations

Tests Of Parameter CONSTANCY Over : 1971 1 — 1975 4

Forecast $\chi^2(20)/20$	=	6.25
CHOW TEST(20, 40)	=	3.28

Introducing logarithms and differences

MODEL 3.5: Modelling d4lc by OLS (equation (3.7) in text)

The Sample is 1958 (2) to 1975 (4) less 20 Forecasts

VARI	COEF	STD ERR	H.C.S.E.	t–VALUE
d4li	.67400	.03396	.03089	19.8455
dd4li	−.2658	.05935	.06603	−4.4790
d4DO	.00769	.00475	.00389	1.61924

$\sigma = .00886$ $F(2, 48) = 201.01$ $DW = 1.026$
$RSS = .00377$ For 3 Variables and 51 Observations

Tests Of Parameter CONSTANCY Over : 1971 1 − 1975 4

Forecast $\chi^2(20)/20$	=	1.11
CHOW TEST(20, 48)	=	1.01

Unrestricted version of MODEL 3.5

MODEL 3.6: Modelling lc by OLS (equation (3.10) in text)

The Sample is 1958 (2) to 1975 (4) less 20 Forecasts

VARI	COEF	STD ERR	H.C.S.E.	t–VALUE
lc 4	.99912	.03238	.03305	30.8548
li	.30299	.05415	.06780	5.59569
li 1	.14818	.04924	.04970	3.00960
li 4	−.2805	.05311	.07350	−5.2817
li 5	−.1686	.04868	.04556	−3.4645
DO	.00943	.00504	.00301	1.87166
DO 4	−.0077	.00466	.00370	−1.6555

$\sigma = .0064$ $F(7, 44) = $ (very large) $DW = 1.683$
$RSS = .00184$ For 7 Variables and 51 Observations

Tests Of Parameter CONSTANCY Over: 1971 1 − 1975 4

Forecast $\chi^2(20)/20$	=	2.99
CHOW TEST(20, 44)	=	2.24

Error–correction model

MODEL 3.7: Modelling d4lc by OLS (equation (3.11) in text)

The Sample is 1958 (2) to 1975 (4) less 20 Forecasts

VARI	COEF	STD ERR	H.C.S.E.	t–VALUE
d4li	.50748	.03679	.03864	13.7948
dd4li	−.1745	.04667	.04012	−3.7397
lc_li 4	−.0561	.00898	.00871	−6.2496
d4DO	.00827	.00355	.00182	2.32986

$\sigma = .00662$ F(3, 47) = 253.27 DW = 1.575
RSS = .0020618 For 4 Variables and 51 Observations

Tests Of Parameter CONSTANCY Over : 1971 1 − 1975 4

Forecast $\chi^2(20)/20$ = 3.81
CHOW TEST(20, 47) = 2.79

Error–correction and inflation

MODEL 3.8: Modelling d4lc by OLS (equation (3.13) in text)

The Sample is 1958 (2) TO 1975 (4) less 20 Forecasts

VARI	COEF	STD ERR	H.C.S.E.	t–VALUE
d4li	.49638	.04014	.03437	12.3668
dd4li	−.2141	.05106	.03747	−4.1944
lc_li 4	−.0843	.02303	.01972	−3.6610
d4DO	.00756	.00333	.00145	2.26929
inf	−.1013	.07281	.06757	−1.3921
dinf	−.1934	.11498	.10404	−1.6821

$\sigma = .0062$ F(5, 45) = 175.04 DW = 1.743
RSS = .00173 For 6 Variables and 51 Observations

Tests Of Parameter CONSTANCY Over : 1971 1 − 1975 4

Forecast $\chi^2(20)/20$ = 1.16
CHOW TEST(20, 45) = 1.08

Testing for parameter constancy: recursive least squares

Variable DO omitted, Sample 1958 (2) – 1970 (4)

MODEL 3.9: Modelling d4lc by OLS

The Sample is 1958 (2) to 1975 (4) less 20 Forecasts

VARI	COEF	STD ERR	H.C.S.E.	t–VALUE
d4li	.49916	.04189	.03824	11.9159
dinf	−.2082	.11986	.11256	−1.7378
lc_li 4	−.0845	.02405	.02234	−3.5175
inf	−.1043	.07601	.07244	−1.3723
dd4li	−.1864	.05177	.04488	−3.6021

$\sigma = .0064$ $F(4, 46) = 199.51$ $DW = 1.964$
$RSS = .001928$ For 5 Variables and 51 Observations

Tests Of Parameter CONSTANCY Over : 1971 1 − 1975 4

Forecast $\chi^2(20)/20$ =   1.19
CHOW TEST$(20, 46)$ =   1.15

As model 3.9 but estimated for the entire sample: 1958:2 − 1975:4

MODEL 3.10: Modelling d4lc by OLS

The Sample is 1958 (2) to 1975 (4) less 0 Forecasts

VARI	COEF	STD ERR	H.C.S.E.	t–VALUE
d4li	.49489	.03130	.02777	15.8097
dinf	−.2357	.09325	.10345	−2.5278
lc_li 4	−.0870	.01305	.01230	−6.6754
in f	−.1126	.02433	.02208	−4.6278
dd4li	−.2107	.04177	.03403	−5.0455

$\sigma = .00661$ $F(4, 66) = 286.77$ $DW = 2.218$
$RSS = .002889$ For 5 Variables and 71 Observations

3.8   Suggestions for Further Reading

The economic theory which underlies the Absolute and Permanent Income Hypotheses is discussed in various macroeconomic textbooks (for example Levačić and Rebmann (1982) or Gapinski (1982). More advanced theoretical and empirical analysis on the Permanent Income Hypothesis is given in Hall (1978), Flavin (1981), Christious, Eichenbaum and Marshall (1991), and Campbell and Mankiw (1990, 1991).

The literature on the *DHSY* model and its predecessors and followers is quite voluminous. The *DHSY* model itself represented the development of an earlier model of aggregate demand by Hendry (1974). Among later works, that of Hendry and von Ungern–Sternberg (1980) which developed the *DHSY* model with a redefined income variable should be mentioned. Patterson (1986) has presented an analogue to the *DHSY* model based on annual rather than quarterly data, and investigated its structural stability through tests based on recursive residuals. Finally, Hendry, Muellbauer and Murphy (1990) have reconsidered the *DHSY* model from the perspective of ten years advancement in econometrics.

Recursive least squares estimation and inference into stability testing, developed originally by Brown, Durbin and Evans (1975), is now included in most contemporary econometric textbooks. Particularly popular are the CUSUM and CUSUMSQ tests (for example see Johnston (1984, pp. 384–392), or Harvey (1990, pp. 153–154)). An example of the use of these tests is Deadman and Ghatak (1981). A generalization of the CUSUM test to include models containing lagged dependent variables has been given by Kramer, Ploberger and Alt (1988). These tests can be regarded as analogous to the scaled recursive Chow test presented in this chapter. Pesaran, Smith and Yeo (1985) give a review of various tests of structural stability. Examples of the use of recursive estimation analysis are Charemza (1990a), Charemza and Ghatak (1990), and especially Hendry and Ericsson (1991).

Chapter 4

General to Specific Modelling

4.1 Autoregressive Distributed Lag Modelling

One of the main methodological innovations of the Davidson *et al.* (1978) approach to modelling consumption (see Chapter 3) was that a 'good' empirical econometric model could be developed by starting from a relatively large, general model and by gradually reducing its size and transforming the variables through the testing of various linear and nonlinear restrictions. Let us reconsider equations (3.7) and (3.10) from Chapter 3. We said that equation (3.10) was a *general* one, without any restrictions on parameters and (3.7) was a *specific* one. That is, equation (3.7) could be derived from equation (3.10) by imposing various restrictions on the parameters in equation (3.10). After estimation, we compared the results for (3.10) (MODEL 3.6 in Section 3.7) with that for (3.7) (MODEL 3.5) and concluded that because the unrestricted estimates seemed quite close to those implied by the restrictions, the specific model was a valid one, in that it did not contradict the general model.

In this chapter we present a detailed discussion of *general to specific* modelling. By general to specific modelling we mean the formulation of a fairly unrestricted dynamic model, herewith called a general model, which is subsequently tested, transformed and reduced in size by performing a number of tests for restrictions. A general model in a convenient notation is presented and sets of restrictions on this model which would eventually lead to economically interpretable models are discussed. We also describe how the validity of the restrictions imposed may be tested statistically, as the procedure applied in Chapter 3 (namely judging intuitively whether the restricted and unrestricted coefficients are 'close' or 'remote' from each other) is not statistically rigorous.

The general model is usually described in an *autoregressive distributed lag (ADL)* form. This means that a dependent variable y_t is expressed as a function of its own lagged values, and the current and lagged values of all explanatory variables. A straightforward notation for an *ADL* model uses the *lag operator L^r*, defined for a variable x_t as:

$$L^r x_t = x_{t-r} \, .$$

It is also convenient to use *scalar polynomials* in L:

$$\alpha(L) = \sum_{i=m}^{n} \alpha_i L^i \, ,$$

so that:

$$\alpha(L)x_t = \sum_{i=m}^{n} \alpha_i L^i x_t = \alpha_m x_{t-m} + \alpha_{m+1} x_{t-m-1} + \ldots + \alpha_n x_{t-n} \, .$$

That is, $\alpha(L)x_t$ is a weighted sum of lagged values of a variable x_t up to the level of n. Normally m is zero or one but it may be negative if the notation is to be used for a model which includes leads as well as lags.

The simple first order autoregressive model:

$$y_t = \alpha y_{t-1} + \epsilon_t \, ,$$

can be rewritten using the lag operator as:

$$(1-\alpha L)y_t = \epsilon_t \, .$$

Also consider a *finite distributed lag* model:

$$y_t = \beta_0 x_t + \beta_1 x_{t-1} + \beta_2 x_{t-2} + \ldots + \beta_n x_{t-n} + \epsilon_t .$$

In the notation using the lag operator, this becomes:

$$y_t = b(L)x_t + \epsilon_t , \quad m = 0 .$$

If lagged values of y_t are added to this distributed lag model, the result is called an *autoregressive distributed lag model*, and is denoted as:

$$y_t = a_1 y_{t-1} + a_2 y_{t-2} + \ldots a_k y_{t-k} + \beta_0 x_t + \beta_1 x_{t-1} + \beta_2 x_{t-2}$$
$$+ \ldots \qquad\qquad + \beta_n x_{t-n} + \epsilon_t ,$$

or, in the more concise notation using the polynomial lag operator:

$$a(L)y_t = b(L)x_t + \epsilon_t ,$$

where:

$$a(L) = \sum_{i=0}^{k} a_i L^i , \quad a_0 = 1 , \quad a_i = - a_i , \quad i = 1, 2, \ldots, k.$$

In order for the variable y_t to meet what are called 'stationarity conditions' (see Chapter 5 below), it is required that the roots of the lag polynomial $a(L)$ 'lie outside the unit circle'. That is, they are larger than one in absolute value (see Granger and Newbold (1986, pp. 6–10)).

For simplicity, it is often assumed that a general *ADL* model contains no leads (that is $m \ge 0$) and that the number of lags for all the variables is identical, so that in the equation above, $k = n$. For such a case the notation *ADL(k)* denotes an autoregressive distributed lag model containing lags for all the variables up to the level of k. For an *ADL* model with unequal number of lags for each variable, the commonly used notation is $ADL(k_1, k_2,..., k_m)$; for example, an ADL model with three variables in which there are five lags imposed on the first two variables and two lags on the third would be written as $ADL(5, 5, 2)$.

The lag polynomial notation may be generalized to include models with more than one explanatory variable, for instance where there are N right–hand side variables x_{1t}, x_{2t}, ..., x_{Nt}. One of these variables may be the intercept if required. The ADL model for this case may be denoted:

$$a(L)y_t = \sum_{i=1}^{N} b_i(L)x_{it} + \epsilon_t.$$

Consider a simple $ADL(1)$ model with one explanatory variable:

$$y_t = \alpha_1 y_{t-1} + \beta_0 x_t + \beta_1 x_{t-1} + \epsilon_t. \qquad (4.1)$$

This is in the form of:

$$a(L)y_t = b(L)x_t + \epsilon_t, \qquad (4.2)$$

where:

$$a(L) = \sum_{i=0}^{1} a_i L^i \ , \ a_0 = 1 \ , \ a_1 = -\alpha_1 \ , \ b(L) = \sum_{i=0}^{1} \beta_i L^i.$$

There are at least ten economically sensible specific models that can be derived from the general model (4.1) by the imposition of restrictions on the parameters α_1, β_0 and β_1. (For a more detailed discussion and generalization of this example see Hendry and Richard (1983) or Hendry, Pagan and Sargan (1984, pp. 1040– 1049).)

Eight out of the ten of these possible restrictions on (4.1) are straightforward:

1. $\alpha_1 = \beta_1 = 0$: static regression,

2. $\beta_0 = \beta_1 = 0$: first–order autoregressive process,

3. $\alpha_1 = \beta_0 = 0$: leading indicator equation,

4. $\alpha_1 = 1$, $\beta_0 = -\beta_1$: equation in first differences,

5. $\alpha_1 = 0$: first–order finite distributed lag equation,

6. $\beta_1 = 0$: partial adjustment equation,

7. $\beta_0 = 0$: 'dead–start' model, with lagged information only,

8. $\beta_1 = -\alpha_1$: proportional response model: the explanatory variables are x_t and $(y_{t-1} - x_{t-1})$.

Case 9 is algebraically more difficult to work out. We would like to derive an equation in first differences with an error–correction mechanism. In order to do so, subtract y_{t-1} from both sides of (4.1), and add and subtract $\beta_0 \cdot x_{t-1}$ to the right–hand side of (4.1). After some simplification this gives:

$$\Delta y_t = (\alpha_1 - 1)y_{t-1} + \beta_0 \Delta x_t + (\beta_0 + \beta_1)x_{t-1} + \epsilon_t .$$

This equation contains an error–correction mechanism of the type $y_{t-1} - x_{t-1}$ (see Chapter 3) if the following restriction is fulfilled:

9. $\alpha_1 - 1 = -(\beta_0 + \beta_1).$

The final restriction on the parameters of (4.1) which will be considered involves the concept of *common factors*. To introduce this concept, let λ_i be a root of a polynomial $a(L) = 0$. That is, it is a solution of the equation:

$$a(L) = \sum_{i=0}^{n} a_i L^i = 0 .$$

In addition, let δ_i be a root of a polynomial $b(L) = 0$, or:

$$b(L) = \sum_{i=0}^{s} b_i L^i = 0 .$$

If some $\lambda_i s$ coincide with $\delta_i s$, we say that the polynomials have *common factors*. In the context of *ADL* modelling one is often interested in a special case, where the *ADL* model:

$$a(L)y_t = b(L)x_t + \epsilon_t ,$$

can be written down with the use of polynomial lag operators containing one common root:

$$a(L) = (1 - \rho L)a^*(L) \quad , \quad b(L) = (1 - \rho L)b^*(L) ,$$

giving a model with first order autocorrelated disturbances:

$$a^*(L)y_t = b^*(L)x_t + u_t ,$$

where:

$$u_t = \rho u_{t-1} + \epsilon_t \ , \text{or} \ u_t = (1 - \rho L)^{-1}\epsilon_t .$$

The relevance of the common factor restriction can be illustrated by a simple static regression equation with first order autocorrelated disturbances:

$$y_t = \beta_0 x_t + u_t ,$$

where:

$$u_t = \rho u_{t-1} + \epsilon_t \ , \qquad |\rho| < 1 ,$$

which can also be rewritten as:

$$y_t = \beta_0 x_t + \rho y_{t-1} - \rho \cdot \beta_0 x_{t-1} + \epsilon_t,$$

or as:

$$(1-\rho L) \cdot y_t = \beta_0 (1-\rho L) \cdot x_t + \epsilon_t,$$

which is an $ADL(1)$ model with a common factor.

This last equation is in fact a version of (4.1) with the nonlinear restriction:

10. $\beta_1 = -\alpha_1 \cdot \beta_0$, since ρ replaces α_1 .

Restriction 10 is usually called a *common factor* or *COMFAC* restriction. The importance of this result will be developed in Section 4.4 of this chapter. However, it is worth noting here that if restriction 10 is valid, then rather than estimate equation (4.1) with a nonlinear restriction, a simpler procedure would be to estimate the simple static regression model allowing for first order autocorrelated errors. If the restriction is rejected, then evidence of autocorrelation in the simple static equation reflects 'misspecified dynamics' in that the variables x_{t-1} and y_{t-1} have been erroneously omitted from this equation.

The examples above illustrate that there is a practically infinite number of specific models which are economically sensible which can be derived from a general autoregressive distributed lag model. The $ADL(1)$ model alone covers at least ten important specific models, including one with serially correlated errors. This finding suggests a systematic way of developing a specific model which avoids the worst features of data mining. We should start from a sufficiently general ADL model and then gradually reduce its size by examining restrictions imposed on parameters.

4.2 Testing Restrictions

An important implication of Section 4.1 is that we must have a tool which can be used for testing whether or not the restrictions of interest which lead to a specific model are valid, or equivalently, whether or not the restrictions contradict the general model. Thus we want a statistical test of the null hypothesis that the restrictions imposed on the general model are true, or more precisely, that these restrictions cannot be rejected at a given level of significance. In some cases there is little problem. For instance, in equation (4.1) the test of any of the restrictions 5 , 6 or 7 that $\alpha_1 = 0$, $\beta_1 = 0$ or $\beta_0 = 0$

can simply be performed with the use of the Student–t test. If the Student–t ratio indicates that the tested coefficient in the estimated general model is significantly different from zero, the restriction is not valid and the model cannot be simplified by dropping the corresponding variable. Also, joint tests for linear restrictions such as restrictions 1 to 4 in (4.1) can be performed with the use of the F test for linear restrictions, described in virtually all textbooks of econometric theory (for example Harvey (1990, p.64), Johnston (1984, pp. 182–189) or Kmenta (1986, pp. 416–422)). For m linear restrictions in a linear regression model with normal disturbances, T observations and k estimated parameters in the general (unrestricted) model, the well-known F test for the validity of these restrictions is:

$$ F = \frac{(SSE_0 - SSE)/m}{SSE/(T - k)} \, , $$

where SSE_0 stands for the residual sum of squares of the restricted model and SSE for the residual sum of squares of the unrestricted model. Under the null hypothesis that the linear restrictions imposed are true, the statistic has an F distribution with $(m , T - k)$ degrees of freedom (see Section 3.3).

However, the above test is not general enough to cover more complex restrictions which are likely to arrive in the process of general to specific modelling. For instance, the *COMFAC* restriction 10, discussed in Section 4.1, is nonlinear and therefore cannot be tested with the use of the *F* statistic above.

Several tests have been suggested for testing both linear and nonlinear restrictions in a general econometric model. The most well known are the Likelihood Ratio, Wald and Lagrange Multiplier (score) tests. An intuitive account of the nature of these tests following Buse (1982) is given below.

Consider a simple null hypothesis relating to a single parameter θ of the form $\theta = \theta_0$. The alternative hypothesis is $\theta \neq \theta_0$. The maximum likelihood estimate of θ is the value which maximizes the likelihood function, given the set of sample data (for instance, see Freund and Walpole (1987, pp. 350–354)). That is, it is the value of θ which maximizes the probability of obtaining the observed data. We may call this value the unrestricted estimate of θ, and denote it as $\hat{\theta}$. Unless the unconstrained estimate is equal to θ_0, the value taken by the likelihood function using θ_0 as the value of the parameter will be lower than that using the unconstrained estimate. If $logL(\hat{\theta})$ and $logL(\theta_0)$ denote the values of the (natural) logarithms of the likelihood functions for $\hat{\theta}$ and θ_0 respectively, then the Likelihood Ratio (*LR*) statistic may be defined as:

$$LR = 2 \cdot (logL(\hat{\theta}) - logL(\theta_0)) .$$

This statistic has an asymptotic χ^2 distribution with one degree of freedom. 'Large' values of *LR* thus indicate substantial differences between the 'most likely' value for θ suggested by the sample data, and the value suggested by the null hypothesis, which is the rationale for rejecting the null hypothesis in such cases. For any specific difference between θ_0 and $\hat{\theta}$, the value of the *LR* statistic will depend on the degree of curvature of the loglikelihood function, and *vice versa*. This curvature may be measured by the absolute value of the change in the slope of the loglikelihood function, or $d^2 logL(\theta)/d\theta^2$.

The Wald (*W*) test weights the (squared) distance between θ_0 and $\hat{\theta}$ by the expected curvature of the loglikelihood function, or:

$$W = \left(\hat{\theta} - \theta_0\right)^2 \cdot I(\hat{\theta}) ,$$

where $I(\hat{\theta}) = E\left(d^2 logL(\theta)/d\theta^2\right)$ evaluated at $\theta = \hat{\theta}$. $I(\theta)$ is called the information matrix. *W* is asymptotically distributed as χ^2 with one degree of freedom, and as with the *LR* test, 'large' values of the test statistic will lead to rejection of the null hypothesis.

The Lagrange multiplier (*LM*) test also involves the curvature of the loglikelihood function, but in this case it is for the constrained rather than the unconstrained model. By definition, the slope of the loglikelihood function is zero at its maximum value. If θ_0 is 'close' to $\hat{\theta}$, then the slope at this point should be about zero. The *LM* test weights the (squared) slope of the loglikelihood function evaluated at $\theta = \theta_0$, denoted by $S(\theta_0)$, by the inverse of the curvature at this point. Since the greater is the curvature of the loglikelihood function at θ_0 the closer θ_0 will be to $\hat{\theta}$, the inverse of this curvature is taken so that values of the test statistic will be small when θ_0 is close to $\hat{\theta}$. Thus the *LM* statistic in this case is defined as:

$$LM = (S(\theta_0))^2 \cdot I(\theta_0)^{-1},$$

where as before, the expected value of the curvature is used, but where it is now evaluated at θ_0 rather than at $\hat{\theta}$. As with the Likelihood Ratio and Wald test statistics for this case, this statistic has an asymptotic χ^2 distribution with one degree of freedom. 'Large' values of LM leading to rejection of the null hypothesis will be obtained when the slope of the loglikelihood function at θ_0 differs markedly from zero.

The differences between the Likelihood Ratio, Wald and Lagrange Multiplier tests are illustrated in Figure 4.1 (adapted from Buse (1982)).

The curve AA′ represents a loglikelihood function for a parameter θ, denoted as $logL(\theta)$. Its unconstrained maximum value $(logL(\hat{\theta}))$ is at $\theta = \hat{\theta}$, while its value at the constrained parameter value θ_0 is $logL(\theta_0)$. Hence, according to the

Likelihood Ratio formula, the distance between $logL(\hat{\theta})$ and $logL(\theta_0)$ is $LR/2$. If, however, the loglikelihood function has a different curvature, say BB′, the value of the loglikelihood function at the constrained parameter value is $logL(\theta_0)'$ and then the value of the Likelihood Ratio test differs from that for AA′, despite the fact that the distance between $\hat{\theta}$ and θ_0 is unchanged. The Wald statistic may not depend so strongly upon the change in the curvature, since the curvature itself (or, strictly speaking, its estimate) is used for weighting the squared differences between the constrained and unconstrained parameter values. For the Lagrange Multiplier test, the unconstrained loglikelihood function is not estimated. What is estimated instead is the constrained loglikelihood function CC′ (that is the function when the restrictions implied by the null hypothesis are imposed). The extent of the difference from zero of the slope of the constrained function

Fig. 4.1: Likelihood Ratio, Wald and Lagrange Multiplier tests

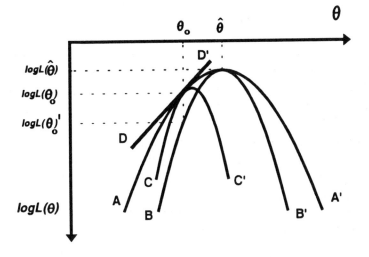

CC′ at θ_0 (weighted by the curvature) forms the basis of the test. This slope is depicted in Figure 4.1 by the line DD′.

All three of these tests have natural generalizations to vectors of parameters rather than the single parameter case that has been considered here. Whilst all three statistics have the same asymptotic distribution, the following relationship between the sample values may be shown to hold for linear models (for example see Maddala (1988, pp. 84–86) or Berndt and Savin (1977)):

$$W \geq LR \geq LM .$$

Thus, in practice, it is possible (say) to reject a null hypothesis by the W test but fail to reject this same hypothesis by the other two tests.

One feature of the tests is the different information they require. The Likelihood Ratio test requires computations involving both restricted and unrestricted parameters. The Wald test only requires computations based on the unrestricted estimates, and the Lagrange Multiplier test only computations based on the restricted estimates. As the estimation of models subject to restrictions may be difficult in practice, the Wald test may be a particularly attractive option in some circumstances.

Let us consider the application of both Lagrange Multiplier and Wald tests to the testing of restrictions in an *ADL* model. (An example of a Likelihood Ratio test is given in Chapter 6 below.) We will firstly describe the Lagrange Multiplier (*LM*) test.

In order to test a set of (possibly nonlinear) restrictions, start from the ordinary least squares estimation of the *restricted model* (STEP 1). If the total number of parameters in the unrestricted model is k and there are m restrictions imposed, the number of parameters estimated in STEP 1 is $k - m$. For the estimated restricted model compute residuals, say ϵ_{0t} (STEP 2). Next, regress ϵ_{0t} on all the variables which appear in the *unrestricted*, that is general, model (STEP 3). At STEP 3 the total number of estimated parameters is k. For this regression, where ϵ_{0t} acts as the dependent variable, compute the coefficient of determination denoted as R_0^2 (STEP 4). From R_0^2, the *LM* statistic is computed as:

$$LM = T \cdot R_0^2 . \qquad (4.3)$$

Given some general assumptions, under the null hypothesis (that is under the hypothesis that the tested restrictions are valid) *LM* has an asymptotic χ^2 distribution with m degrees of freedom. Although the *LM* statistic in (4.3) has been used extensively in econometric inference, it has been shown (see Kiviet (1986)) that it rejects true null hypotheses too often, and that the Lagrange Multiplier statistic in its F distribution form (denoted herewith by *LMF*) has better statistical properties. This is also a straightforward function of the coefficient of determination R_0^2, namely:

$$LMF = \frac{T - k}{m} \cdot \frac{R_0^2}{1 - R_0^2} , \qquad (4.4)$$

where T is the sample size and k is the number of coefficients in the unrestricted model. The LMF statistic under the null hypothesis has an asymptotic F distribution with $(m, T - k)$ degrees of freedom.

The second test outlined here for verifying hypotheses relating to linear and nonlinear restrictions is the Wald test. As was noted earlier, one major advantage of this test compared with the LMF test is that it only requires the estimation of the unrestricted model, which is particularly useful if the restricted model is difficult to estimate.

The general form of the Wald test is relatively simple for the testing of linear restrictions, but considerably more complicated for the testing of multiple nonlinear restrictions (see Harvey (1990, pp. 166–168)). However, for the case of a single nonlinear restriction, the Wald test may be computed as follows:

$$W = \frac{[f(\hat{\beta})]^2}{g(\hat{\beta}) \cdot V(\hat{\beta}) \cdot g(\hat{\beta})'} ,$$

where:

$f(\hat{\beta}) = 0$ is the restriction written in terms of the unrestricted estimates,

$g(\hat{\beta})'$ is the transpose of the $1 \times k$ vector of partial derivatives of the restriction evaluated at the k unrestricted parameter estimates; and

$V(\hat{\beta})$ is the estimated variance–covariance matrix of the unrestricted parameter estimates (for example, see Johnston (1984, p.173 and pp. 180–181)).

As an example, consider the form of the Wald test for restriction 10 in Section 4.1 above.

The unrestricted model was:

$$y_t = \alpha_1 y_{t-1} + \beta_0 x_t + \beta_1 x_{t-1} + \epsilon_t,$$

and the nonlinear restriction to be tested was:

$$\beta_1 + \alpha_1 \beta_0 = 0.$$

If the unrestricted estimates of the parameters are denoted as $\hat{\alpha}$, $\hat{\beta}_0$ and $\hat{\beta}_1$, then in the notation above:

$$f(\hat{\beta}) = \hat{\beta}_1 + \hat{\alpha}_1 \hat{\beta}_0,$$

and

$$g(\hat{\beta}) = \left[\frac{\partial f(\hat{\beta})}{\partial \hat{\alpha}_1}, \frac{\partial f(\hat{\beta})}{\partial \hat{\beta}_0}, \frac{\partial f(\hat{\beta})}{\partial \hat{\beta}_1} \right] = (\hat{\beta}_0 \ \hat{\alpha}_1 \ 1).$$

The Wald statistic for this case is then:

$$W = \frac{(\hat{\beta}_1 + \hat{\alpha}_1 \cdot \hat{\beta}_0)^2}{[\hat{\beta}_0 \ \hat{\alpha}_1 \ 1] \begin{bmatrix} \\ V(\hat{\beta}) \\ \\ \end{bmatrix} \begin{bmatrix} \hat{\beta}_0 \\ \hat{\alpha}_1 \\ 1 \end{bmatrix}}.$$

Under the null hypothesis that the restriction is valid, W is asymptotically distributed as χ^2 with one degree of freedom.

One drawback of the Wald test is that it may be sensitive to the particular way in which the nonlinear restriction is expressed, in that its calculated value may be different for algebraically equivalent ways of expressing the restriction. Thus if the nonlinear restriction in the example above was rewritten as:

$$1 + \frac{\alpha_1 \beta_0}{\beta_1} = 0 \, ,$$

the numerical value of the Wald test statistic in finite samples may differ from that calculated using the original formulation of the nonlinear restriction.

To summarize, general to specific modelling consists of:

1. Formulating and estimating a general unrestricted *ADL* model, and,
2. Successive testing for particular restrictions, perhaps by the use of Lagrange Multiplier or Wald tests.

4.3. Modelling the UK Consumption Function

In this section we return to the example of modelling quarterly UK aggregate consumption for the period 1957–1975. We will determine whether or not a consumption function analogous to that of the *DHSY* model can be derived and empirically supported from a general autoregressive distributed lag model. The transformations required are algebraically more involved than those given in Section 4.1, partly because we are now dealing with a model based on quarterly data.

We start with a general *ADL* model. In the final version of the original *DHSY* model the maximum lag length for $cons_t$ was equal to four, the maximum lag length for inc_t was five , and the maximum lag length for the inflation variable (inf_t) was one (see (3.13)). The fifth lag for inc_t is not

immediately obvious in (3.13) but note that $\Delta\Delta_4(inc_t) = \Delta(inc_t - inc_{t-4}) = (inc_t - inc_{t-4}) - (inc_{t-1} - inc_{t-5})$. It seems reasonable to start from a general *ADL* model with five lags for $cons_t$ and for inc_t and one lag for inflation, that is an *ADL*(5, 5, 1) model. In the notation using the lag operator the general model becomes:

$$a(L)cons_t = b(L)inc_t + c(L)inf_t + \epsilon_t, \qquad (4.5)$$

where:

$$a(L) = 1 - \alpha_1 L - \alpha_2 L^2 - \alpha_3 L^3 - a_4 L^4 - \alpha_5 L^5,$$

$$b(L) = \beta_0 + \beta_1 L + \beta_2 L^2 + \beta_3 L^3 + \beta_4 L^4 + \beta_5 L^5,$$

$$c(L) = \gamma_0 + \gamma_1 L.$$

Altogether, there are 13 parameters to estimate in this general model. To increase the efficiency of the estimators we increase the sample period by including the 20 post sample observations (see Section 3.2), which gives a total number of 71 observations.

The estimates of this 13 parameter general equation are given under MODEL 4.1 in Section 4.6. As before, bear in mind the differences between the text and the computer output notation. The logarithm of *per capita* personal consumption, or $cons_t$, is denoted in the computer output as 'lc',

the logarithm of total *per capita* disposable personal income, inc_t, by 'li' and the inflation variable $(\Delta_4 p_t)$ by 'inf'. Cursory inspection of MODEL 4.1 does not reveal anything exciting. The model seems to fit the data well, with the coefficient of determination virtually equal to one. This is hardly surprising for a model with 13 explanatory variables. Nevertheless there are a lot of seemingly 'insignificant' variables.

The static long run equation is computed from the estimates in MODEL 4.1 by equating each variable at all of its lags, that is:

$$cons^* = cons_t = cons_{t-1} = ... = cons_{t-5} \, ,$$

$$inc^* = inc_t = inc_{t-1} = ... = inc_{t-5} \, ,$$

$$inf^* = inf_t = inf_{t-1} \, ,$$

and solving the equation for $cons^*$. This gives:

$$cons^* = \beta^* inc^* + \gamma^* inf^* \, ,$$

where:

$$\beta^* = \frac{\displaystyle\sum_{j=0}^{5} \beta_j}{1 - \displaystyle\sum_{j=1}^{5} \alpha_j} \, , \qquad \gamma^* = \frac{\displaystyle\sum_{j=0}^{1} \gamma_j}{1 - \displaystyle\sum_{j=1}^{5} \alpha_j} \, .$$

The computed long run coefficients β^* and γ^* are given in the long run equation below MODEL 4.1. We will not discuss here how the asymptotic standard errors of the estimated β^* and γ^* coefficients reported in brackets below the estimates have been computed (for the full formulae see Hendry (1989, pp. 51–53)). Note that the estimated standard error for β^*, equal to 0.0108, is relatively low in comparison with the corresponding parameter (1.005), and the result is consistent with a long run unitary income elasticity of consumption.

However, the joint tests on the significance of each set of variables shows that none of the explanatory variables in (4.5), namely $cons_t$ lagged from one to five, inc_t lagged from zero to five and inf_t lagged from zero to one, can be entirely eliminated. The F statistics reported below the static long run solution for MODEL 4.1 for the particular sets of explanatory variables treated as omitted variables are significant so that none of these variables can be entirely excluded from the model on purely statistical grounds. The 5% critical value of the F distribution with $(2, 60)$ degrees of freedom is 3.15, while the lowest computed F value is 11.445. The degrees of freedom in the numerator (five for $cons_t$, six for inc_t, and two for inf_t) are the number of restrictions imposed on the general model. The degrees of freedom in the denominator (63) is the difference between the sample size of 71 plus the five observations retained for forming the lagged variables (see Chapter 3.2) less the 13 estimated parameters. These F statistics are the Lagrange Multiplier LMF statistics described in Section 4.2. For instance, the value 14.142 for inc_t has been obtained in an equivalent way to the following. First, MODEL 4.1 was re–estimated with all six of the inc_t variables excluded. This is equivalent to estimating the ADL model with restrictions, $\beta_0 = \beta_1 = \beta_2 = \beta_3 = \beta_4 = \beta_5 = 0$. Next, the residuals of this restricted model were regressed on the entire set of 13 explanatory variables, including all the inc_t variables. For this regression, the coefficient of determination was computed. This coefficient of determination, say R_0^2, was used in turn to compute the Lagrange Multiplier statistic according to the formula (4.4):

$$LMF = \frac{76 - 13}{6} \cdot \frac{R_0^2}{1 - R_0^2} = 14.142 .$$

Analogously, the Lagrange Multiplier tests for the joint significance of each lag (that is jointly $cons_{t-1}$, inc_{t-1}, inf_{t-1}, and then $cons_{t-2}$ and inc_{t-2}, etc.) have been calculated. The insignificant values for lags two and three indicates that the two and three period lags on the variables do not contribute significantly to the model. In other words, an hypothesis that the coefficients of $cons_{t-2}$ and inc_{t-2}, or that $cons_{t-3}$ and inc_{t-3} are jointly zeros, cannot be rejected.

The *first stage of model reduction* may now be performed by eliminating all the explanatory variables lagged by two and three periods. This reduces the total number of the parameters to be estimated to nine.

The results of estimating this reduced model are shown as MODEL 4.2 in Section 4.6. The PROGRESS to DATE results compare the residual sum of squares and the estimated standard error of the residuals of both models. The differences are evidently not great. This intuitive finding is confirmed by the Lagrange Multiplier test for testing the four restrictions which, if valid, transform the general equation (4.5) into the more specific form:

$$cons_t = \alpha_1 cons_{t-1} + \alpha_4 cons_{t-4} + \alpha_5 cons_{t-5} + \beta_0 inc_t +$$
$$\beta_1 inc_{t-1} + \beta_4 inc_{t-4} + \beta_5 inc_{t-5} + \gamma_0 inf_t +$$
$$\gamma_1 inf_{t-1} + \epsilon_t, \tag{4.6}$$

by imposing the restrictions: $\alpha_2 = \alpha_3 = \beta_2 = \beta_3 = 0$ on the general equation. The *LMF* statistic for testing the reduction from equation (4.5) to equation (4.6) is equal to 0.69, which is clearly not significant. Therefore the four explanatory variables lagged by two and three periods can be safely eliminated from the model. Note that in this and succeeding model reduction procedures, the five observations used to form lagged variables are not used by *PC–GIVE* to calculate the degrees of freedom in the denominator of the *LMF* statistics, but only the 71 sample observations.

The next step in the process of sequential reduction is to attempt to move to the original *DHSY* function. In fact, a slightly simplified form of the *DHSY* model is derived which omits the variable DO_t (compare with equation (3.13)), that is:

$$\Delta_4 cons_t = \theta_1 \Delta_4 inc_t + \theta_2 (cons_{t-4} - inc_{t-4}) + \theta_3 \Delta\Delta_4 inc_t +$$

$$\theta_4 inf_t + \theta_5 \Delta inf_t + error_t , \qquad (4.7)$$

(The notation of the parameters of the *DHSY* model has been changed in comparison with that used in Chapter 3, in that the coefficients are now denoted by θs rather than by βs.) It is difficult immediately to spot the required restrictions on (4.6) which will give rise to (4.7). They become more evident if equation (4.6) is transformed by adding and subtracting four period lags of the variables $cons_t$ and inc_t multiplied by coefficients of the non–lagged variables, and $\gamma_1 inf_t$ to the right–hand side of equation (4.6). That is, add and subtract $cons_{t-4}$, $\beta_0 inc_{t-4}$, and $\gamma_1 inf_t$ to the right–hand side of (4.6). After a little manipulation, the following may be derived:

$$\Delta_4 cons_t = \alpha_1 cons_{t-1} + (\alpha_4 - 1) cons_{t-4} + \alpha_5 cons_{t-5} +$$

$$\beta_0 \Delta_4 inc_t + (\beta_0 + \beta_4) inc_{t-4} + \beta_1 inc_{t-1} +$$

$$\beta_5 inc_{t-5} + (\gamma_0 + \gamma_1) inf_t - \gamma_1 \Delta inf_t + \epsilon_t . \qquad (4.8)$$

If the following four restrictions are imposed on (4.8):

1. $\alpha_1 = 0$,
2. $\alpha_4 - 1 = -(\beta_0 + \beta_4)$,
3. $\alpha_5 = 0$,
4. $\beta_1 = -\beta_5$,

then model (4.8) becomes:

$$\Delta_4 cons_t = \beta_0 \Delta_4 inc_t + (\gamma_0 + \gamma_1) inf_t + (\alpha_4 - 1)(cons_{t-4} - inc_{t-4})$$

$$+ \beta_1 \Delta_4 inc_{t-1} - \gamma_1 \Delta inf_t + \epsilon_t . \qquad (4.9)$$

At first sight, the model in (4.9) does not look like the *DHSY* model, but in fact equation (4.9) *is* numerically equivalent to equation (4.7). That is, its parameters are deterministic linear functions of those of the *DHSY* model. To see this add and subtract $\beta_1 \Delta_4 inc_t$ to and from the right–hand side of (4.9), and rearrange terms to give:

$$\Delta_4 cons_t = (\beta_0 + \beta_1)\Delta_4 inc_t - \beta_1(\Delta_4 inc_t - \Delta_4 inc_{t-1}) +$$

$$(\alpha_4 - 1)\cdot(cons_{t-4} - inc_{t-4}) + (\gamma_0 + \gamma_1)inf_t -$$

$$\gamma_1 \Delta inf_t + \epsilon_t. \tag{4.10}$$

Now, it is easy to see that (4.10) is identical to the *DHSY* model (4.7) where:

$$\theta_1 = \beta_0 + \beta_1, \qquad \theta_2 = \alpha_4 - 1, \qquad \theta_3 = -\beta_1,$$
$$\theta_4 = (\gamma_0 + \gamma_1), \qquad \theta_5 = -\gamma_1, \qquad error_t = \epsilon_t.$$

To confirm the equivalence of models (4.7) and (4.9), one could estimate them both and compare the results (see MODEL 4.3 and MODEL 4.4 in Section 4.6). The notation for the variables in the computer output is identical to that used in Chapter 3 (that is 'lc_li 4' stands for $(cons_{t-4} - inc_{t-4})$, 'dd4li' for $\Delta\Delta_4 inc_t$, etc.) The estimates of equations (4.7) and (4.9) are identical, with the exception of the 'composite' coefficient on $\Delta_4 inc_t$. The original *DHSY* coefficient of $\Delta_4 inc_t$, rounded up to 0.495 in MODEL 4.3 is the sum of the coefficients of $\Delta_4 inc_t$ and $\Delta_4 inc_{t-1}$ in MODEL 4.4, that is 0.284 and 0.211.

Model reduction has proceeded by a sequence of steps. Firstly, equation (4.5) (the general *ADL* model with 13 parameters to estimate) was reduced to equation (4.6) (the general *ADL* model with four zero–type restrictions on the coefficients of the variables lagged by two and three periods), resulting in a model with nine parameters to estimate. Secondly, equation (4.6) was in its turn reduced to the *DHSY* model in the form of equation (4.9), with five parameters. The PROGRESS to DATE printout under MODEL 4.4 in Section 4.6 shows an increase in the residual sum of squares while moving from equation (4.6) to equation (4.9) (*RSS* rises from 0.0025 to 0.0029). The significance of this rise may be tested by the Lagrange Multiplier test for the validity of the restrictions imposed on the general model. If equation (4.9) is tested as the restricted form of equation (4.5), that is with all the $4 + 4 = 8$ restrictions imposed, the *LMF* statistic is 1.38 and is not significant (the degrees of freedom for this F distribution are $(8, 58)$. Consequently, we cannot reject the hypothesis that the *DHSY* model is a specific form of the general autoregressive distributed lag model. Similarly, if we test equation (4.9) as a restricted form of equation (4.6) (the more specific *ADL* model, with lags of order two and three removed), with four restrictions imposed, the *LMF* statistic is 2.11. The 5% critical value for an $F(4, 62)$ distribution is (by interpolation) 2.52. Hence, at the 5% level of significance we cannot reject the hypothesis that the *DHSY* model is a restricted form of (4.6), that is of an *ADL* model which contains lags of order one, four and five. In the terminology that will be developed in Chapter 8, we may say that equation (4.9) is *nested* within equations (4.5) and (4.6).

Of course, being acceptable as a specific form of a general *ADL* model is not in itself sufficient for an estimated equation to be taken as a satisfactory description of the process being investigated. Further requirements on the equation have been suggested by Hendry and Richard (1982, 1983) as criteria for model acceptance. Three of these, namely consistency with an economic theory, parameter constancy, and randomness of model residuals, we have encountered already. Others, such as properties of *weakly exogenous regressors* and *encompassing* will be discussed in Chapters 7 and 8 below.

4.4 *COMFAC* Analysis

The presence of autocorrelated errors as evidenced by (say) a significant Durbin–Watson test statistic may be the result of some misspecification of the model, for example that some important variables have been omitted from the regression (see Maddala (1988, pp. 208–209)). The common factor (*COMFAC*) approach introduced in Section 4.1 showed, however, that the existence of autocorrelation in a static model did not necessarily imply that something was wrong with the model. It might merely be an indication of the fact that the valid model is in fact an autoregressive distributed lag model with some common factor restrictions present. In this case, such autocorrelation can be regarded as a 'simplific-ation, not a nuisance' (Hendry and Mizon (1978)) in that it allows the use of a simpler model which follows from the imposition of restrictions on the general model.

Consider the estimation of a static consumption function with the same variables as those in the *DHSY* model. The static equation is:

$$cons_t = \varphi_1 inc_t + \varphi_2 inf_t + u_t, \qquad (4.11)$$

and its estimates are given as MODEL 4.5 in Section 4.6. Our primary interest is now in the autocorrelation diagnostics of this model. The Durbin–Watson statistic of 1.525 is on the verge of being significant at the 5% level of significance. (The appropriate tables in this case are those of Farebrother (1980) as there is no intercept in the regression.) The estima-ted first order autocorrelation coefficient is equal to 0.444. However, it is also worth testing for autocorrelation of a higher order, especially as the model is estimated using seasonally unadjusted quarterly data with no seasonal dum-mies. Indeed, in this case, there appears to be quite large error autocorrelation coefficients at lags four and five as well as at the first lag. For testing the joint presence of autocorre-lation of orders 1, 2, 3, 4 and 5, the familiar Lagrange Multi-plier approach has been applied once again. This consists

simply of computing the ordinary least squares residuals of
(4.11), denoted by $\hat{u}_t$, and testing whether in the equation:

$$cons_t = \varphi_1 inc_t + \varphi_2 inf_t + \rho_1 \hat{u}_{t-1} + \rho_2 \hat{u}_{t-2} + \rho_3 \hat{u}_{t-3} + \rho_4 \hat{u}_{t-4} + \rho_5 \hat{u}_{t-5},$$

the hypothesis that $\rho_1 = \rho_2 = \rho_3 = \rho_4 = \rho_5 = 0$ can be maintained.

Technically, this test is as described in Section 4.2.
Equation (4.11) is estimated by ordinary least squares, and
the residuals are computed. These residuals are regressed on
inc_t, inf_t and their own values lagged up to five times, and
the coefficient of determination for this regression is computed. The LM and the LMF statistics may now be calculated
according to the formulae given in Section 4.2 (see Hendry
(1989, p.55), or Harvey (1990, p.278)). Hence, in this case,
the LM statistic has a $\chi^2(5)$ distribution and the LMF statistic has an $F(5, 65)$ distribution. For the model considered
here, both statistics are significant ($LM = 41.951$ and $LMF =
18.15$), so that we may reject the hypothesis that all five
autocorrelation coefficients are jointly equal to zero. Inspection of the values of the autocorrelation coefficients of MODEL 4.5 suggests that the fourth order autocorrelation coefficient, equal to 0.8083, may contribute a lot towards this rejection of the null hypothesis.

Having established the presence of autocorrelation in the
errors of equation (4.11), it is reasonable to enquire whether
this is a result of the fact that the valid model is an autoregressive distributed lag model with common factors. If we
start from the general $ADL(5,5,1)$ model introduced in the
previous section, with five lags for consumption and income,
and one for the inflation variable, then there can be at most
one common factor in the model. From the discussion of case
10 in Section 4.1, we may recall that common factors reflect
common roots in the lag polynomials of each variable. Thus

there cannot be more common factors than the order of the lag distribution with the smallest number of lags. If we work with a model with a single lag on the inflation variable, then even if a common factor is found, model simplification on this account can only be to move to a model which omits the longest lag on each variable and which exhibits first order autocorrelated errors.

However, given that up to fifth order autocorrelation in the residuals of the static model have been detected, it will be more interesting to start from an $ADL(5)$ model, with five lags on each variable. This model can have up to five common factors present, and will allow us to test whether a static equation with fifth order autocorrelated errors (the simplest form potentially equivalent to the general $ADL(5)$ model) is an acceptable simplification of the general model.

That is, consider the $ADL(5)$ model:

$$cons_t = \sum_{i=1}^{5} \alpha_i cons_{t-i} + \sum_{i=0}^{5} \beta_i inc_{t-i} + \sum_{i=0}^{5} \gamma_i inf_{t-i} + error. \quad (4.12)$$

We would like to determine what simplifications of equation (4.12) might be possible due to the existence of common factors in the lag polynomials of this equation, and whether, in the limit, the empirical evidence is consistent with the data having been generated from the static consumption function (equation (4.11) with fifth order autocorrelated errors:

$$u_t = \sum_{j=1}^{5} \rho_j u_{t-j} + \epsilon_t. \quad (4.13)$$

To help resolve these issues, a series of common factor tests are performed. First, a test for one common factor is carried out. If this is not rejected, then a further test for a second common factor is performed, and so on. Only if all five common factor tests are not rejected will we not be able to reject the simplified model (equation (4.11) with (4.13)).

These common factor tests are undertaken using COMFAC WALD (W) χ^2 tests. The relevant statistics to study are those of the *incremental* values of the Wald statistics which are independent of each other, rather than the cumulative values. For tests at the 5% level of significance each incremental value is compared in turn with the tabulated $\chi^2(2)$ value of 5.991. Thus, the incremental value for one common factor is compared with 5.991. If the calculated incremental value is larger than this tabulated figure, the hypothesis of one common factor may be rejected. Only if the calculated value is smaller than the tabulated value can one proceed to test for a second common factor, by comparing the incremental value for this second factor with the same tabulated value.

Empirical results illustrating this test are given in Section 4.6 under MODEL 4.6. Although we do not present the full results here, we may note in passing that the more restricted $ADL(5, 5, 1)$ model used in the previous section, with a single lagged inflation variable, cannot be rejected as a specific form of the $ADL(5)$ model in the form of equation (4.12). The Lagrange Multiplier F test for the joint significance of the four lagged inflation variables $(inf_{t-2}$ to $inf_{t-5})$ is only 1.16, and is not significant. MODEL 4.6 also

presents the COMFAC WALD (W) χ^2 test statistics needed to test for common factors. By comparing each incremental χ^2 value with the tabulated $\chi^2(2)$ value of 5.991, we cannot reject the null hypothesis that three common factors are present, but can reject four (or more) at the 5% significance level. Hence, the empirical evidence does not support a static consumption function with fifth order autocorrelated errors. Despite this, some model simplification (for example, the use of a model with two period lags on each variable and a third order autoregressive process for the errors) might be suggested. Whilst Harvey (1990, p.287) points to some difficulties in using the results of *COMFAC* analysis to determine model specification precisely, it may still be a useful part of a general to specific modelling sequence.

4.5 General to Specific Modelling and Data Mining

The message of this chapter is that in econometric model building, in order to derive credible models, it is preferable to start with a general model and attempt to reduce it by a sequence of tests of economically sensible restrictions. In the example in Section 4.3, the sequence of restrictions imposed (or model reductions) was directed by knowledge of the specific form (the *DHSY* formulation of the aggregate consumption function) which was ultimately to be tested. However, there need not be a unique model reduction sequence that leads from a general model to a specific form. For example, we moved to the *DHSY* specification in two steps, whilst a similar analysis carried out by Hendry, Muellbauer and Murphy (1990) involved a sequence of nine steps. In the special case where the sequence of tests is properly nested (contained within each other) it is possible to compute the true significance level α^* (see Section 2.2) for the jth test in the sequence by the following expression:

$$\alpha^* = 1 - (1 - \alpha_1) \cdot (1 - \alpha_2) \cdot \ldots \cdot (1 - \alpha_j),$$

where α_i, $i = 1, 2, \ldots, j$, is the significance level used in the ith test (see Maddala (1988, p.425)). For instance, for a sequence of three nested reductions, at a nominal significance level of 5%, the true significance level of the last test is $1 - (0.95)^3 = 0.143$.

In practice, the restrictions to be tested may not be nested one within the other so as to allow such a sequence of tests to be performed. For example, the Lagrange Multiplier tests for the joint significance of each lag in Section 4.3 are not nested within each other. There seems to be no theoretical reason for believing that in the general *ADL* model, all variables lagged one period, or two periods, etc. should be zero rather than any other particular combination of lags on these variables. Thus, we must admit to some arbitrariness in the initial selection of zero restrictions to be tested. The tests of the joint significance for either lag two or lag three may be reasonable given the insignificance of these terms in the estimated unrestricted equation (MODEL 4.1 in Section 4.6) but to decide on the sequence of tests to be performed in this way is of course subject to the strictures on preliminary tests of significance discussed in Section 2.3.

The charge of data mining that can be directed against the general to specific methodology seems to be potentially more serious where the investigator does not have a clear idea as to the specific form that the investigation should lead to. Thus, for example, in Section 4.1 there were ten economically plausible models presented which could be derived from a simple $ADL(1)$ model. If the investigator were interested in only one of these, then the situation would be as existed in Section 4.3, where the specific form of the general model was known. However, if the investigator has no firm view as to the specific form of the final model to be considered, the interesting question remains as to whether general to specific modelling can be viewed as a method of model simplification, that is as a method of discovery, rather than of confirmation. There is a clear dilemma here. With a number of economic theories acceptable to the investigator, it seems inevitable that a data mining problem exists. General to specific modelling (model reduction through the testing of restrictions) may well lead to multiple admissible models not nested within each other. (Chapter 8 will consider the testing of non—nested models.) There is no systematic way of ordering the sequence of tests in general (though Pagan (1987) suggests that $COMFAC$ analysis provides a systematic way of choosing the dynamics of a system), but the particular sequence adopted could be crucial in the selection of the specific form finally accepted.

On the positive side, however, general to specific modelling does seem to represent a major advance over 'bottom up' or 'simple to general' approaches, where models are successively complicated or altered in response to indications of model misspecification. Thus, for example, there is little theoretical justification for the common practice of adding new variables to a model because of evidence of serial correlation in the errors of a fitted equation. Not only are conventional test statistics normally invalid in models with omitted variables, but there is no reason why two investigators starting from the same simple model will converge on the same final equation. If a test suggests an extension to a model, and subsequently another test on this extended model indicates some misspecification, then clearly the original decision to change the model in the way indicated was wrong. Accordingly, the entire approach is questionable. The major problem of 'simple to general' approaches to econometric modelling is that if one starts with a misspecified model, then the attempt to improve upon this model by extending it on the basis of statistical tests is likely to be based on erroneous statistical procedures. As was noted in Chapters 1 and 2, it was unstructured data mining and 'bottom up' modelling that led to the existence of a plethora of alternative models which so undermined the credibility of econometrics to many people.

The strength of general to specific modelling is that model construction proceeds from a very general model in a more structured, ordered (and statistically valid) fashion, and in this way avoids the worst excesses of data mining.

4.6   Stylized Computer Output (*PC–GIVE*)

Generalized *ADL* model for *cons*$_t$

MODEL 4.1: Modelling lc (equation (4.5) in text)

The Sample is 1958 (2) to 1975 (4) less 0 Forecasts

VARI	COEF	STD ERR	t–VALUE
lc 1	−.0013	.11611	−.0116
lc 2	.00383	.02892	.13230
lc 3	−.0330	.02844	−1.160
lc 4	.95111	.03164	30.061
lc 5	.00374	.11892	.03149

li	.28969	.04395	6.5919
li 1	.19232	.06049	3.1794
li 2	−.0390	.05135	−.7596
li 3	.04350	.05160	.84301
li 4	−.1905	.05594	−3.406
li 5	−.2198	.06225	−3.532
inf	−.3106	.08983	−3.457
inf 1	.18238	.09773	1.8661

$R^2 = .9999$ $\sigma = .00647$ $F(13, 58) =$ very large DW = 2.247
RSS $= .002428$ for 13 Variables and 71 Observations

Solved   STATIC LONG RUN Equation

$$lc \quad = \quad 1.005\ li \quad - \quad 1.695\ inf$$
$$S.E. \qquad\quad (.01080) \qquad\quad (.61921)$$

Tests on the Significance of each set of variables

Variable	F[NUM,DENOM] =	Value
lc	F[5, 63]	229.33
li	F[6, 63]	14.142
inf	F[2, 63]	11.445

Tests on the Significance of each LAG

LAG	F[NUM,DENOM] =	Value
5	F[2, 63]	11.0
4	F[2, 63]	648
3	F[2, 63]	.701
2	F[2, 63]	.710
1	F[3, 63]	5.10

First stage of testing restrictions: elimination of lags 2 and 3

MODEL 4.2: Modelling lc (equation (4.6) in text)

The Sample is 1958 (2) to 1975 (4) less 0 Forecasts

VARI	COEF	STD ERR	t–VALUE
lc 1	−.0017	.11294	−.0155
lc 4	.94576	.02985	31.680
lc 5	.00983	.11396	.08626
li	.28998	.04341	6.6799
li 1	.17691	.05730	3.0872
li 4	−.1944	.04894	−3.973
li 5	−.2254	.06036	−3.735
inf	−.3144	.08694	−3.616
inf 1	.20873	.09516	2.1934

$\sigma = .00640$ F(9, 62) = very large DW = 2.296
RSS = .00254 for 9 Variables and 71 Observations

PROGRESS TO DATE:

MODEL	PARAMETERS	RSS	σ
1	13	.002428	.00647
2	9	.002543	.00640

TESTS OF MODEL REDUCTION

From Model 1 to Model 2
Model 1: F(4, 58) =   .69

Second stage of testing restrictions: seasonal differences and error correction

The *DHSY* model re–estimated without DO_t

MODEL 4.3: Modelling d4lc by OLS (equation (4.7) in text)

The Sample is 1958 (2) to 1975 (4) less 0 Forecasts

VARI	COEF	STD ERR	t–VALUE
d4li	.49489	.03130	15.8097
dd4li	−.2107	.04177	−5.0455
lc_li 4	−.0871	.01305	−6.6754
inf	−.1126	.02433	−4.6278
dinf	−.2357	.09325	−2.5278

$\sigma = .00661$ F(5, 66) = 229.42   DW = 2.218
RSS = .002889 for 5 Variables and 71 Observations

The *DHSY* model in an equivalent form

MODEL 4.4: Modelling d4lc by OLS (equation (4.9) in text)
The Sample is 1958 (2) to 1975 (4) less 0 Forecasts

VARI	COEF	STD ERR	t–VALUE
d4li	.28415	.03723	7.63265
d4li 1	.21073	.04177	5.04554
lc_li 4	−.0870	.01305	−6.6754
inf	−.1126	.02433	−4.6278
dinf	−.2357	.09325	2.52786

$\sigma = .00661$ F(5, 66) = 229.42 DW = 2.218
RSS = .002889 for 5 Variables and 71 Observations

PROGRESS TO DATE:

MODEL	PARAMETERS	RSS	σ
1	13	.002428	.00647
2	9	.002543	.00640
3	5	.002889	.00661

TESTS OF MODEL REDUCTION

From Model 1 to Model 2
Model 1: F(6, 55) =   .69
  Reductions from models 1 through 2 to model 3
Model 1: F(8, 58) =   1.38
Model 2: F(4, 62) =   2.11

Estimation of a static consumption function

MODEL 4.5: Modelling lc by OLS (equation (4.11) in text)

The Sample is 1958 (1) to 1975 (4) less 0 Forecasts

VARI	COEF	STD ERR	t–VALUE
linc	.98472	.00073	1356.45
inf	−.5685	.08572	−6.6329

$\sigma = .0345$ $F(2, 70) = 2346794$ $DW = 1.525$
$RSS = .08365$ for 2 Variables and 72 Observations

Testing for Serial Correlation from Lags 1 to 5

$CHI^2(5) = 41.951$ and F–Form $(5, 68) = 18.15$

Error Autocorrelation Coefficients:

.4444   .0464   −.0847   .8083   −.4315

ADL(5) model estimated for further COMFAC analysis

MODEL 4.6: Modelling lc by OLS (equation (4.12) in text)

The Sample is 1959 (2) to 1975 (4) less 0 Forecasts

VARI	COEF	STD ERR	t–VALUE
lc 1	−.0830	.12334	−.6729
lc 2	.00493	.03137	.15714
lc 3	−.0219	.03111	−.7052
lc 4	.93807	.03394	27.63
lc 5	.07001	.12427	.56339
li	.29236	.04562	6.4093
li 1	.22682	.06442	3.5210
li 2	−.0408	.06488	−.7235
li 3	.01556	.05692	.27337
li 4	−.1801	.05737	−3.139
li 5	−.2217	.06280	−3.530
inf	−.3420	.11760	−2.908
inf 1	.23999	.17858	1.3438
inf 2	−.0788	.14328	−.5503
inf 3	−.090	.13205	−.687
inf 4	.05186	.13671	.37934
inf 5	.12473	.10413	1.1978

$\sigma = .0064$ $F(17, 50) = 7408252$ DW $= 2.286$
RSS $= .002080$ for 17 Variables and 67 Observations

Solved STATIC LONG RUN equation

lc	$=$	1.001 li	$-$	1.035 inf
S.E.		(.00946)		(.36227)

Tests on the Significance of each variable

LAG	F[NUM,DENOM] $=$	Value
lc	F[5,59]	172.4
li	F[6,59]	14.10
inf	F[6,59]	4.905

Tests on the significance of each LAG

LAG	F[NUM,DENOM] $=$	Value
5	F[3, 59]	6.426
4	F[3, 59]	373.0
3	F[3, 59]	.4534
2	F[3, 59]	.4614
1	F[3, 59]	4.926

COMFAC WALD Test Statistic CHI^2

Order	CHI df	Value	Incremental CHI	
			df	Value
1	2	.105	2	.105
2	4	.324	2	.219
3	6	1.13	2	.814
4	8	18.1	2	16.9
5	10	24.7	2	6.58

4.7 Suggestions for Further Reading

Full details of general to specific modelling are in fact more complex and rigorous than described above and go beyond the scope of this book (for a quite sophisticated description see Hendry (1983, 1987); much simpler presentations of this approach are those given in Pagan (1987), Cuthbertson (1985), Gilbert (1986) and Cuthbertson, Hall and Taylor (1992)). A development to general to specific Bayesian methodology can be found in Lubrano and Marimotou (1988). Traditional 'bottom up' and general to specific modelling are compared in Maddala (1988, pp. 423–425) and Gilbert (1989, pp. 122–125).

General to specific modelling has been criticized by Darnell (1986, 1988) and Darnell and Evans (1990), mainly on the grounds of a lack of a proper interpretation of the dynamic long run solution. It has, however, been defended by Phillips (1988a) who evaluated it positively as a tool for achieving an optimal inference procedure.

For Lagrange Multiplier, Likelihood Ratio and Wald tests, more advanced references are those of Judge *et al.* (1985, pp. 182–187), Amemiya (1985, pp. 141–146), Engle (1984) and Spanos (1986, pp. 328–336). An examination of the practical importance of the sensitivity of the Wald test to the form in which nonlinear restrictions are expressed has been given by Gregory and Veall (1986), and Lafontaine and White (1986).

Spanos (1988) examines the general to specific methodology within the broader context of constructing a coherent methodological framework for econometrics. Empirical applications using the general to specific approach are still scarce. Muscatelli (1989) has used it for modelling money demand in the UK. Applications of *ADL* model to East European parallel markets are given in Charemza (1990c, 1991), and to modelling financial markets in India in Ghatak and Charemza (1989) and Italy in Muscatelli and Papi (1988). An example of dynamic econometric modelling considered in the light of the general to specific approach has been given by Spanos (1986, pp. 553–570).

Chapter 5

Cointegration Analysis

5.1 Introductory Concepts

Cointegration analysis in time series econometrics was introduced in the mid 1980s, and has been regarded by many econometricians as the most important recent development in empirical modelling. The basic computational ideas of applied cointegration analysis are simple to understand and to use, as they require only the application of the method of ordinary least squares. The theory behind the computations is not so straightforward. In this chapter we concentrate entirely on those ideas which can be understood without the need for complex mathematics and which can be used without resorting to sophisticated computer software. Nevertheless, it is necessary to start with a description of some elementary concepts of stochastic processes and time series analysis. Those already familiar with the basic concepts of stochastic processes may ignore the first two sections of this chapter and move straight to Section 5.3.

We start with a definition of a *stochastic process*. By a stochastic process we will mean a family of real valued random variables, indexed by t, where t represents time. Since a random variable is usually denoted by a capital letter, say X, a stochastic process will be denoted as the set $\{X_t\}$. Simply put, each element X_1, X_2,..., X_t of the stochastic process $\{X_t\}$ is a random variable. In order to conform with econometric practice, and if there is no room for misunderstanding, we will refer to the stochastic process $\{X_t\}$ as X_t.

If all the random variables X_t have means (expected values), we may describe the *mean of a stochastic process*

Fig. 5.1: Stochastic process with nonstationary mean

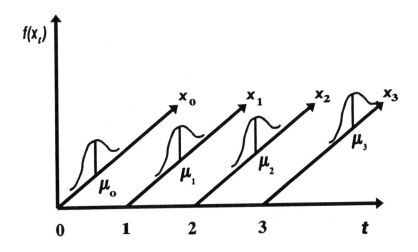

$\{X_t\}$ as a series of means (expected values) for particular X_ts or as a function of t. By analogy with the notation used for describing a single random variable, where μ conventionally denotes a mean, we may denote the mean of a stochastic process by μ_t. Analogously, the variance of a stochastic process is denoted by σ_t^2, and the covariance between two of the variables, say X_t and X_{t+j}, which belong to the stochastic process by $\sigma_{t,t+j}$.

The concept of a mean being a function of time is illustrated in Figure 5.1, where some random variables of a stochastic process $\{X_t\}$, for $t = 0, 1, 2,...$, etc. are shown. The figure illustrates a case in which the means μ_0, μ_1, etc. are an increasing function of time.

A stochastic process is said to be *stationary* (or, more precisely, is *stationary in a strict or strong sense*), if the joint and conditional probability distributions of the process are unchanged if displaced in time. In practice, it is more usual to deal with *weak sense* stationarity, restricting attention to the means, variances and covariances of the process (see Spanos (1986, pp.137–140)). Then, a stochastic process $\{X_t\}$ is said to be stationary if:

$$E(X_t) = \text{constant} = \mu \; ; \quad Var\,(X_t) = \text{constant} = \sigma^2 \; ;$$

and:

$$Cov\,(X_t X_{t+j}) = \sigma_j \, .$$

Thus the means and the variances of the process are constant over time, while the value of the covariance between two periods depends only on the gap between the periods, and not the actual time at which this covariance is considered. If one or more of the conditions above are not fulfilled, the process is *nonstationary*. Hence, the process shown in Figure 5.1 would appear to be nonstationary because its means seem to be an increasing function of time. The stochastic process depicted by Figure 5.2 *may* be stationary, although we cannot say for certain whether or not it really is. It appears that its means are constant (identical for different *ts*) and the variances of the random variables also look to be the same. We cannot say anything about the covariance, since it cannot be shown on a diagram such as this.

An important form of a nonstationary variable is illustrated below by a simple and not (we hope) very realistic example. Suppose we are between two bars and we are trying to decide which one to use by tossing a coin. If it is a head, we move two steps to the right; if it is a tail we move two steps to the left. After moving, we repeat the tossing of the coin, etc. (for simplicity assume that the number of steps to each of the bars is infinite, which may be realistic if we had visited a couple of bars already). Let us describe our journey as a

Fig. 5.2: Stochastic process with stationary mean

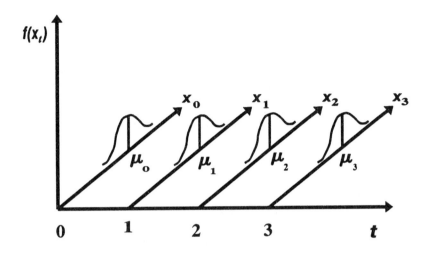

series of random variables Z_t. Each of the random variables Z_t takes the value -2 if we move towards the bar to the left and $+2$ if we decide to move towards the bar to the right. That is:

$$Z_t = \begin{cases} -2 & \text{with probability } 0.5 \\ \\ +2 & \text{with probability } 0.5 \end{cases}$$

Each of the random variables Z_t has its mean equal to zero and its variance equal to four and is independent from every other variable in the series, that is from Z_{t+j} for any $j \neq 0$. The stochastic process describing the 'bar–or–bar' dilemma (that is the position reached relative to the starting position after the ith toss of the coin) is then given as:

$$X_1 = Z_1 \ , \ X_2 = X_1 + Z_2 \ , \ X_3 = X_2 + Z_3, \ ..., \text{etc.} \ ,$$

or more generally as:

$$X_t = X_{t-1} + Z_t \ . \tag{5.1}$$

The fact that all the variables Z_t are identical and independent does not mean that the process described by (5.1) is stationary. Although in the above example $E(X_t) = 0$ (since the expected value of Z_t is zero), the variance of X_t can be expressed as:

$$Var(X_1) = Var(Z_1) = 4 \ ,$$
$$Var(X_2) = Var(X_1) + Var(Z_2) = 8 \ ,$$

or, in general:

$$Var(X_t) = 4 \cdot t \ .$$

As we can see, the variance of this process is a linear function of time and the stochastic process X_t is nonstationary.

The 'bar–or–bar' example is a special case of an important nonstationary stochastic process called *a random walk*. A random walk is usually described in the form of equation (5.1), where Z_t represents a series of identical and independent random variables. They may not necessarily be discrete variables; for instance, Z_t may represent a series of identically and normally distributed random variables. In a similar fashion to our example, random walk stochastic processes are nonstationary. In the example above, the process was nonstationary as the variance of X_t was not constant. It is easy to check that if the mean of Z_t is not zero (as would be the case in our example where the coin tossed is biased), the mean of

X_t is also a function of t.

Another, quite similar, example of a nonstationary stochastic process is:

$$X_t = \mu + X_{t-1} + Z_t , \quad \mu \neq 0 , \tag{5.2}$$

where Z_t is defined as before as a series of identically distributed independent random variables and μ is a constant. The difference between (5.1) and (5.2) is that in (5.1), $\mu = 0$. Referring to the 'bar–or–bar' example, if μ was equal to 1, the bar visitor takes one step towards the right before each toss of the coin. Consequently, there is a tendency for him (her) to float towards the right. Not surprisingly, the stochastic process given by (5.2) is called a *random walk with drift*.

In the literature, the concept of a *time series* is often used alongside the concept of a stochastic process. There is some ambiguity here. According to some authors a stochastic process and a time series are the same provided only that t can be interpreted as time, whilst according to some others a time series is a single realization of a stochastic process. In the case of an economic investigation, this distinction does not really matter, since what we usually observe is a sequence of data ordered in time. If we understand the time series to be a single realization of a stochastic process, then such a single realization can be as depicted in Figure 5.3.

Let us assume, for simplicity, that a stochastic process and a time series are the same. Unfortunately, conventional economic time series analysis uses a slightly different notation from that of the calculus of probability. To be consistent with econometric textbooks, and also with the other chapters of this book, let us use the symbol ϵ_t to denote a series of identically distributed continuous random variables with zero means (that is ϵ_t replaces Z_t) and y_t (instead of X_t) to denote a time series. If in addition the errors ϵ_t are independently distributed, then the stochastic process $\{\epsilon_t\}$ is called

Fig. 5.3: Single realization of a stochastic process

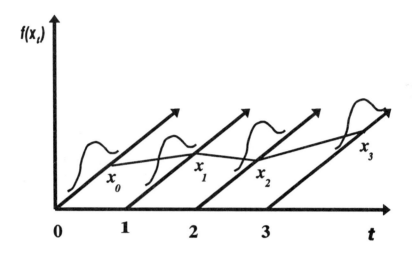

a 'white noise' process. In this case, instead of (5.1) we will use:

$$y_t = y_{t-1} + \epsilon_t, \tag{5.3}$$

as a description of a random walk process, and instead of (5.2) use:

$$y_t = \mu + y_{t-1} + \epsilon_t, \tag{5.4}$$

to represent a random walk with drift.

In economics, the form of nonstationarity in a time series may well be evident from an examination of the series. If the form of nonstationarity is a propensity of the series to move in one direction, we will call this tendency a *trend*.

A series may drift slowly upwards or downwards purely as a result of the effects of stochastic or random shocks. This is true for the random walk process. We have seen that the variance of this process increases over time, but so too does the correlation between neighbouring values (see Cryer (1986, pp. 11–13)). These results imply that there may be long periods in which the process takes values well away from its mean value. In Figure 5.3 there is a clear (stochastic) tendency for such movement and consequently this series is called a time series with a *stochastic trend*. A formal definition of a stochastic trend may be found in Harvey (1990, p.31).

Another example of a developing tendency in a nonstationary stochastic process is where the mean of the process is itself a specific function of time. If such a function is linear then the process can be described as:

$$y_t = \mu_t + \epsilon_t \, ,$$

where:

$$\mu_t = \alpha + \beta \cdot t \, ,$$

or:

$$y_t = \alpha + \beta \cdot t + \epsilon_t \, . \tag{5.5}$$

In this case it is said that the process has a *deterministic trend*. A mixed stochastic–deterministic trend process is also possible. That is, the process can be described as:

$$y_t = \alpha + \beta \cdot t + y_{t-1} + \epsilon_t \, .$$

In these expressions, it has been assumed that the expected values of ϵ_t are zero and that the stochastic process $\{\epsilon_t\}$ is white noise, but these conditions may be relaxed to allow for autocorrelation in the series of ϵ_t. If the ϵ_ts are autocorrelated, the processes (5.3) and (5.4) can no longer be called random walks. The variable y_t will still be nonstationary.

5.2   Nonstationary Series and Integrated Processes

Nonstationarity of time series has always been regarded as a problem in econometric analysis.   It has been shown in a number of theoretical works (for example Phillips (1986)) that, in general, the statistical properties of regression analysis using nonstationary time series are dubious. Without going into this theory, we will indicate that if series are nonstationary one is likely to finish up with a model showing promising diagnostic test statistics even in the case where there is no sense in the regression analysis.

This point is illustrated below by a rather silly regression of a linear on a quadratic trend.   Let a variable y_t be defined as: $y_1 = 1$, $y_2 = 2$,..., $y_n = n$, and a variable x_t as: $x_1 = 1$, $x_2 = 4$,..., $x_n = n^2$. For $n = 30$, the results of regressing y_t on x_t are as follows:

$$y_t = 5.92 + 0.030\, x_t,$$
$$\quad (9.9) \quad (21.2)$$

where Student–t ratios are given in brackets below the estimates, the coefficient of determination $R^2 = 0.94$, and the Durbin–Watson statistic $DW = 0.06$.

If an investigator 'forgets' to report the Durbin–Watson statistic, the regression equation looks quite interesting, although in fact it represents a totally spurious relationship. Indeed, the only sign that something may be wrong in this regression is the very low Durbin–Watson statistic.   As is evident from Figure 5.4, the observed and fitted values have no common pattern in their development over time.   This somewhat extreme case shows the danger in interpreting regression results for two deterministically trended variables which diverge in time.

Fig. 5.4: Regression of a linear on a quadratic trend

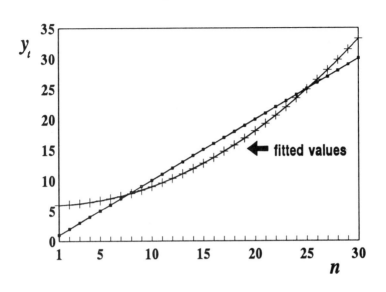

The second example shows the problem of spurious relationships in the case where the variables are subject to stochastic rather than deterministic trends. This example is a particular but representative case of those given in Newbold and Davies (1978) and repeated in Granger and Newbold (1986). Suppose that two variables, y_t and x_t, are independently generated by random walk processes:

$$y_t = y_{t-1} + \epsilon_{1t},$$
$$x_t = x_{t-1} + \epsilon_{2t},$$

where ϵ_{1t}, ϵ_{2t} are independent standard normal random variables. That is, they are independent normally distributed random variables having zero means and variances equal to unity. Since y_t and x_t are independently generated, we would not expect to find a significant relationship between them. When, however, 1,000 samples of y_t and x_t were generated from the above model for $t = 1, 2,..., 50$, with initial values $y_0 = x_0 = 100$ and 1,000 ordinary least squares regressions of y_t on x_t were computed, it was found that about 67% (that is about 670 out of 1,000) of these regressions had 'significant' Student–t ratios for the regression parameter at a significance level of 5%.   These regressions also had very low Durbin–Watson statistics: on average about 0.33.

The above two examples show why economists do not like performing regressions on time series which are subject to stochastic or deterministic trends.   These regressions often give apparently good results, and therefore may make it impossible to determine whether or not an economic relationship suggested by a theory has in fact any support from the data.

If one argues, for instance, that aggregate consumption in the UK is predominantly related to a random walk process with drift, it is possible to get some support from the following regression. $CONS_t$ is the original data for aggregate consumption for the period of 1957 (second quarter) to 1975 (fourth quarter) that was used for estimating versions of the Absolute and Permanent Income Hypotheses in Chapter 3. The variable x_t is a random walk with drift generated from the model:

$$x_t = 1 + x_{t-1} + v_t ,$$

where the series v_t consists of pseudo–random numbers generated from the standard normal distribution.   Regress $CONS_t$ on x_t , an intercept, and the seasonal dummy variables, $Q1_t$, $Q2_t$ and $Q3_t$ defined in Chapter 3 above.   The result looks remarkably good:

$$CONS_t = 5578 + 42.68x_t - 741Q1_t - 386Q2_t - 311Q3_t ,$$
$$(112.7) \quad (47.0) \quad (-14.6) \quad (-7.7) \quad (-6.2)$$

$$R^2 = 0.972 , \quad DW = 0.67 ,$$

where Student–t values are given in brackets, R^2 is the conventionally calculated coefficient of determination and DW is the Durbin–Watson statistic. Apart from the Durbin–Watson statistic, the equation looks very promising, but obviously the way the computer generates its random numbers does not have a lot in common with UK aggregate consumption. It is worth noting that *no* data mining was undertaken for the above 'modelling'; the reported results are the very first that came out of the computer, for the first set of 72 random numbers generated.

The discussion above implies that regression analysis makes sense only for data which are not subject to a trend. Since almost all economic data series contain trends, it follows that these series have to be *detrended* before any sensible regression analysis can be performed. It was shown in Chapter 3 that a convenient way of getting rid of a trend in a series is by using first differences (that is, the difference between successive observations) rather than levels of the variables. For a time series with a stochastic trend of the type (5.3):

$$y_t = y_{t-1} + \epsilon_t ,$$

we define the detrended variable:

$$\Delta y_t = y_t - y_{t-1} = \epsilon_t ,$$

and Δy_t is evidently stationary. Similarly, for a random walk with drift (5.4) we have:

$$\Delta y_t = y_t - y_{t-1} = \mu + \epsilon_t .$$

and, again, Δy_t is stationary.

It is not necessary for a series to be a random walk for its differencing to achieve stationarity. The variables ϵ_t can be correlated with each other, that is they may not constitute a white noise process. For instance, if the process is of the type:

$$y_t = y_{t-1} + \epsilon_t,$$

with $\qquad \epsilon_t = \rho \cdot \epsilon_{t-1} + \xi_t,$

where ξ_t is a white noise variable, first differencing of y_t gives a stationary series, provided that $|\rho| < 1$.

Sometimes it is necessary to difference a series more than once in order to achieve stationarity. In this context it is convenient to use the concept of an *integrated series*. Following Engle and Granger (1987) we may define such a series as follows:

Definition: A nonstationary series which can be transformed to a stationary series by differencing d times is said to be *integrated of order d.*

A series x_t integrated of order d is conventionally denoted as:

$$x_t \sim I(d).$$

Thus, for example, if $x_t \sim I(2)$, the first differences of the first differences of x_t achieve stationarity, that is:

$$\Delta\Delta x_t = \Delta\left(x_t - x_{t-1}\right) = \left(x_t - x_{t-1}\right) - \left(x_{t-1} - x_{t-2}\right)$$

$$= x_t - 2x_{t-1} + x_{t-2}.$$

This operation will be termed second (order) differencing, and the resulting variables called second differences. It is important to note that this operation is not the same as taking the difference between the observations on the variable x_t at time periods t and $t-2$. In general, $\Delta\Delta x_t = \Delta^2 x_t \neq x_t - x_{t-2}$.

If x_t is stationary, then no differencing is necessary; that is $x_t \sim I(0)$. If we have two series, x_{1t} and x_{2t} and $x_{1t} \sim I(0)$ while $x_{2t} \sim I(1)$, then $(x_{1t} + x_{2t}) \sim I(1)$. Also, if $x_t \sim I(d)$, then $(\alpha + \beta \cdot x_t) \sim I(d)$, where α and β are constants.

The definition, and indeed the entire problem of enquiry into stationarity, becomes more complex in the case where the series x_t is subject to seasonality. For a series measured s times per annum (so $s = 4$ for quarterly data and $s = 12$ for monthly data), if the series has a seasonal pattern then the differencing which removes seasonality should be s rather than one. That is, an operator $x_t - x_{t-s}$ should be applied rather than $x_t - x_{t-1}$. The difference $x_t - x_{t-s}$ is termed a seasonal difference, and the operation in which these variables are obtained is called *seasonal differencing*, or *s*–differencing. (A numerical example of this operation was given in Chapter 3.) Very occasionally, *s*–differencing may have to be performed more than once on the data to remove the seasonal pattern. Often (and contrary to the impression given in many textbooks) *s*–differencing also removes a trend, but where the trend is nonlinear, first differencing of the *s*–differences may be necessary in order to make the series stationary. Hence, the definition of a *seasonally integrated* series is the following. (This is a somewhat simplified version of a definition given by Engle, Granger and Hallman (1989).)

Definition: A nonstationary series is said to be *seasonally integrated* of order (d, D), denoted $SI_s(d, D)$, if it can be transformed to a stationary series by applying *s*–differences D times and then differencing the resulting series d times using first differences.

Normally, the value of s is known *a priori*, being equal to 4 in a series of quarterly data and equal to 12 in a series of monthly data. Therefore the subscript s can be safely omitted in order to keep the notation simple.

To reiterate, many series (for example those with additive seasonality) can be transformed to stationary series by applying only seasonal differencing. That is, they are $SI_4(0, 1)$ for quarterly data, or $SI_{12}(0, 1)$ for monthly data even if the nonseasonal component of the series is $I(1)$. However, in some situations, further nonseasonal (normally first) differencing is necessary. Such a procedure is required if there is multiplicative seasonality and (or) the nonseasonal component of the series is integrated of order greater than one, which could be the case for a nonlinear trend.

5.3   Testing for the Order of Integration

Before any sensible regression analysis can be performed, it is essential to identify the order of integration of each variable (provided, of course, that the variable can be transformed into a stationary variable through differencing). Two simple tests are described below.

Suppose that we wish to test the hypothesis that a nonseasonal variable y_t (for example a variable measured annually or one with no seasonal pattern) is integrated of order one, that is that y_t is generated by:

$$y_t = y_{t-1} + \epsilon_t,$$

where ϵ_t represents a series of identically distributed stationary variables with zero means.

At first sight, a straightforward procedure would seem to be to test for $\rho = 1$ in the autoregressive equation:

$$y_t = \rho \cdot y_{t-1} + \epsilon_t. \tag{5.6}$$

If the error term in equation (5.6) is a white noise process, then this equation represents a random walk process when $\rho = 1$. We have already seen that such a process generating y_t is nonstationary. However, if $|\rho| < 1$, then the process generating y_t in (5.6) is integrated of order zero and is stationary (see Granger and Newbold (1986, pp. 8–10)). It is tempting to estimate equation (5.6) by ordinary least squares, and to test the hypothesis that $\rho = 1$ by a Student–t test. However, this is not the test used. The ordinary least squares estimate of ρ may be substantially biased in an autoregressive equation and little is known about the distribution of the Student–t statistic where the variable y_t is nonstationary.

An appropriate and simple method of testing the order of integration of y_t in (5.6) has been proposed by Dickey and Fuller (1979), hereafter called the *DF* test. Strictly speaking, the *DF* test is a test of the hypothesis that in (5.6) $\rho = 1$, the so–called *unit root test.* This test is based on the estimation of an equivalent regression equation to (5.6), namely:

$$\Delta y_t = \delta \cdot y_{t-1} + \epsilon_t. \tag{5.7}$$

Equation (5.7) can be re–written as:

$$y_t = (1 + \delta) \cdot y_{t-1} + \epsilon_t,$$

which is the same as (5.6) with $\rho = (1 + \delta)$. Hence, if in (5.7) δ is negative, then in (5.6) ρ becomes smaller than one. The Dickey–Fuller test consists of testing the negativity of δ in the ordinary least squares regression of (5.7). Rejection of the null hypothesis: $\delta = 0$ in favour of the alternative: $\delta < 0$ implies that $\rho < 1$ and that y_t is integrated of order zero.

In order to test the null hypothesis it is necessary to know the distribution of the statistic used for the test and the associated critical region for its evaluation. Since in (5.7) we want to evaluate a hypothesis which concerns only a single parameter, the natural choice would seem to be that of a

Student–t ratio, namely the ratio of the ordinary least squares estimate of δ to its ordinary least squares standard error.

Unfortunately, for equation (5.7), this ratio or statistic does not have the familiar Student–t distribution. If $y_t \sim I(1)$, as implied by the null hypothesis, equation (5.7) represents a regression of an $I(0)$ variable on a $I(1)$ variable. Not surprisingly, in such a case the t–ratio does not have a limiting normal distribution. Its distribution is negatively skewed with most of its mass below zero. Hence, the critical values in the left hand tail should be smaller than those of the conventional Student–t distribution.

Tables of critical values (percentiles) for the distribution of the Student–t statistic in the Dickey–Fuller regression equation (5.7) are given in the Appendix. They are constructed differently to other tables available (for instance Fuller (1976), Guilkey and Schmidt (1989) and MacKinnon (1991)). Since the distribution of the Student–t statistic in this case is not known precisely, it has to be simulated and therefore the critical values are subject to some error (for a more detailed description of the simulation technique used and the generation of initial values see Blangiewicz and Charemza (1990) and the notes to the Appendix). The tables in the Appendix reflect this error. For testing integration using the Dickey–Fuller test, the two columns headed *lower* and *upper* for $m = 0$ are used. If the computed Student–t statistic is smaller than the lower critical value for a particular number of observations (n), the null (unit root) hypothesis has to be rejected and the alternative of stationarity of y_t accepted. (When reading the tables remember that the minus sign is omitted from each entry; hence 2.86 stands for –2.86, etc.) If the calculated Student–t statistic is greater than the upper critical value, the null hypothesis cannot be rejected. There is an inconclusive range between the lower and upper limits. Since the true critical value is unknown, if the calculated statistic falls within this range, then one is unsure whether or not to reject the null hypothesis.

It is important to remember that the critical values given in the Tables in the Appendix, just like the Fuller (1976), Guilkey and Schmidt (1989) and MacKinnon (1991) tables, are *simulated* and not derived analytically. They are model dependent in that they may vary depending on the structure of the model used for simulation. If one has to have more accurate critical values, then so—called *customized testing* is advisable (see Blangiewicz and Charemza (1990)).

But what if the null hypothesis cannot be rejected? In such a case the variable y_t might be integrated of order higher than zero, or might not be integrated at all. Consequently, the next step would be to test whether the order of integration is one. If $y_t \sim I(1)$, then $\Delta y_t \sim I(0)$. Hence we can repeat the test using Δy_t instead of y_t. The Dickey—Fuller equation is now:

$$\Delta \Delta y_t = \delta \cdot \Delta y_{t-1} + \epsilon_t \, ,$$

and again our interest is in testing the negativity of δ. If the null hypothesis is rejected and the alternative $\delta < 0$ can be accepted, the series Δy_t is stationary and $y_t \sim I(1)$. If the null hypothesis cannot be rejected, we may subsequently test whether $y_t \sim I(2)$. That is, we run the Dickey—Fuller regression using $\Delta \Delta \Delta y_t$ as the left—hand side variable and $\Delta \Delta y_{t-1}$ as the right—hand side variable. We can continue the process until we establish an order of integration for y_t, or until we realize that y_t cannot be made stationary by differencing. It is unusual in practice for economic series to be integrated of an order greater than two. Obviously it might be the case that the series is not integrated at all, so that no differencing of any order will transform it into a stationary series. It is also possible that a series is integrated of some order, but the tests applied fail to give a clear indication of this order. In both cases there is a danger of *overdifferencing*, that is of applying the difference operator too many times. Overdifferencing normally results in a very high positive (instead of negative) value of the *DF* test accompanied by a very high coefficient of determination for the fitted regression. Consider the following typical but fictitious example. Suppose that the *DF* statistic computed for a series x_t is 1.23, which obviously is not 'significantly negative', so we apply the test for first differences. For the differenced series Δx_t the *DF* statistic becomes −1.00, which is still not significantly negative so we move to second differences. However, for the series $\Delta\Delta x_t$, the *DF* statistic becomes 8.2 (positive!) and the coefficient of determination for the regression of $\Delta\Delta\Delta x_t$ on $\Delta\Delta x_t$ is 0.991.

This is a clear indication of overdifferencing, and either the series x_t is $I(1)$ but the test has failed to discover this, or the series is not an integrated time series and differencing cannot transform it into a stationary series.

The Dickey–Fuller test can also be used for testing the order of integration for a variable generated as a stochastic process with drift, that is by tests on the equation:

$$\Delta y_t = \mu + \delta \cdot y_{t-1} + \epsilon_t, \qquad (5.8)$$

where μ is a constant representing drift (see (5.4)). The technique is analogous to that described before, but the distribution of the Student–t statistic for δ is different and consequently different tables of critical values should be used (see Table 3 in the Appendix, for $m = 0$). In practice, it is unclear when one should use this test, and when one should use the *DF* test without a constant. Experience suggests that tests with the constant sometimes give unexpected results that are hard to interpret. Also, for $m = 0$ the critical values of the test are dubious; see technical note in the Appendix.

Statistical inference about a stochastic trend is often combined with a deterministic trend. A straightforward modification of the Dickey–Fuller equation which accounts for both drift and a linear deterministic trend is the following:

$$\Delta y_t = \mu + \alpha \cdot t + \delta \cdot y_{t-1} + \epsilon_t. \qquad (5.9)$$

In the above equation it is possible to test simultaneously for the absence of a stochastic trend ($\delta < 0$) and the existence of a deterministic trend ($\alpha \neq 0$). Since in this case the null hypothesis involves more than one parameter, an appropriate test is the Lagrange Multiplier test, again with non–conventional critical values (see Dickey and Fuller (1981) or Guilkey and Schmidt (1989)).

A weakness of the original Dickey–Fuller test is that it does not take account of possible autocorrelation in the error process ϵ_t. If ϵ_t is autocorrelated (that is, it is not white noise) then the ordinary least squares estimates of equation (5.7), and of its variants described above, are not efficient. A simple solution, advocated by Dickey and Fuller (1981), is to use lagged left–hand side variables as additional explanatory variables to approximate the autocorrelation. This test, called the Augmented Dickey–Fuller test, and denoted conventionally as *ADF*, is widely regarded as being the most efficient test from among the simple tests for integration and is at present the most widely used in practice.

The *ADF* equivalent of (5.7) is the following:

$$\Delta y_t = \delta \cdot y_{t-1} + \sum_{i=1}^{k} \delta_i \cdot \Delta y_{t-i} + \epsilon_t . \tag{5.10}$$

The practical rule for establishing the value of k (the number of lags for Δy_{t-i}) is that it should be relatively small in order to save degrees of freedom, but large enough to allow for the existence of autocorrelation in ϵ_t. For instance, if for $k = 2$ the Durbin–Watson autocorrelation statistic is low, indicating first order autocorrelation, it would be sensible to increase k with the hope that such autocorrelation will disappear.

The testing procedure is the same as before, with an examination of the Student–t ratio for δ. The critical values of the test are the same as for the Dickey–Fuller test (that is using Table 2 in the Appendix with $m = 0$ if there is no intercept in the *ADF* equation, or Table 3 if an intercept is present). It is straightforward to augment equation (5.9) analogously, by adding lagged left–hand side variables to the set of regressors. Again, this should not affect the critical values of the test. The comments made earlier relating to overdifferencing apply equally to the *ADF* test.

If only a quick guide is needed as to whether a variable is integrated of order zero, a useful tool is a simple test developed on the basis of the Durbin–Watson statistic. Instead of running the regressions needed for the *DF* and *ADF* tests, we may compute for the variable y_t, a Durbin–Watson type statistic (the *integration Durbin–Watson statistic, IDW*):

$$IDW = \frac{\Sigma(y_t - y_{t-1})^2}{\Sigma(y_t - \bar{y}_t)^2} \, , \tag{5.11}$$

where $\bar{y}_t$ stands for the arithmetic mean of y_t. If $\rho = 1$ in (5.6), the numerator in (5.11) is equal to $\Sigma \epsilon_t^2$. In other words, y_{t-1} represents the 'fitted' value for a regression of y_t on y_{t-1} under the restriction that the coefficient on y_{t-1} is equal to one. Intuitively, in such a case the value of *IDW* should be close to zero.

The *IDW* test should provide a rough guide to the stationarity of a variable. If it is low (say lower than 0.5), one might suspect that the variable in question is not stationary and that further, more thorough testing is required. If the value of *IDW* is close to two, the stationarity of the examined variable might be relatively safely assumed, without the need for further investigation.

Testing for seasonal integration is more complicated. From the various tests proposed, the simplest is probably that suggested by Dickey, Hasza and Fuller (1984) and modified by Osborn *et al.* (1988), denoted *DHF* hereafter. It resembles a generalization of the *ADF* test. For a series measured s times *per annum*, this test is based on the Student−t statistic for the *OLS* estimate of the parameter δ in the regression equation:

$$\Delta_s y_t = \delta \cdot z_{t-s} + \sum_{i=1}^{k} \delta_i \cdot \Delta_s y_{t-i} + \epsilon_t \quad , \qquad (5.12)$$

where the variable z_{t-s} is constructed in the following way. First, regress $\Delta_s y_t$ (where $\Delta_s y_t = y_t - y_{t-s}$) on its own values, lagged up to k periods. That is, estimate the equation:

$$\Delta_s y_t = \sum_{i=1}^{k} \lambda_i \cdot \Delta_s y_{t-i} + \xi_t . \qquad (5.13)$$

Next, use the *OLS* estimates of $\lambda_1, \lambda_2,..., \lambda_k$, (denoted as $\hat{\lambda}_1$, $\hat{\lambda}_2 ,..., \hat{\lambda}_k$) to construct the variable z_t from y_t, $y_{t-1},..., y_{t-k}$ as:

$$z_t = y_t - \sum_{i=1}^{k} \hat{\lambda}_i \cdot y_{t-i} .$$

Finally, substitute the lagged value of z_t, namely z_{t-s}, into (5.12), estimate the equation and compute the Student−t statistic for δ. (Rather than $\Delta_s z_t$ which was originally suggested by Dickey, Hasza and Fuller (1984), we have followed the practice adopted by Osborn *et al.* (1988, p.365)) and used $\Delta_s y_t$ as the dependent variable in equation (5.12)).

Computation of the *DHF* test with the use of econometric packages such as *PC–GIVE* is feasible as the example in Section 5.7 illustrates. The critical values for the test are given in Dickey, Hasza and Fuller (1984), Table 7. For a quarterly seasonal series, that is for $s = 4$, the critical values in Table 3 in the Appendix for $m = 4$ give a rough approximation to the *DHF* critical values, and thus provide an *ad hoc* evaluation of the *DHF* statistic. If the estimate of δ in (5.12) is significantly negative, the null hypothesis of the existence of a seasonally integrated process may be rejected in favour of the alternative hypothesis that either there is no stochastic seasonality, or that stochastic seasonality which can be removed by using *s*-differences does not exist.

If the null hypothesis is not rejected, it is usual to consider the order of nonseasonal differencing required to achieve stationarity, rather than consider higher orders of seasonal differencing. That is, economic data series are generally expected to be $SI_s(0, 0)$, or $SI_s(0, 1)$ or $SI_s(d, 1)$ so that, at most, using *s*-differences once is expected to remove seasonal nonstationarity. Hence, if the null $(\delta = 0)$ in (5.12) above is not rejected (that is, the null hypothesis that the variable is $SI_s(0,1)$ cannot be rejected), the next step is to consider whether the variable is $SI_s(1, 1)$ rather than $SI_s(0, 1)$ with the former representing the new null hypothesis, and the latter the new alternative hypothesis. Hence, the following equation is constructed and estimated in the same way as the *ADF* test above:

$$\Delta\Delta_s y_t = \delta \cdot \Delta_s y_{t-1} + \sum_i \delta_i \cdot \Delta\Delta_s y_{t-i} + \epsilon_t,$$

and the significant negativity or otherwise of δ is examined. If the null hypothesis that the variable is $SI_s(1, 1)$ is not rejected, then this forms the next alternative hypothesis for the null that the variable is $SI_s(2, 1)$, tested by a test on the negativity of δ in the equation:

$$\Delta\Delta\Delta_s y_t = \delta \cdot \Delta\Delta_s y_{t-1} + \sum_i \delta_i \cdot \Delta\Delta\Delta_s y_{t-i} + \epsilon_t,$$

and so on. Note that the constructed variable z_t is needed only for the *DHF* test for the order of seasonal integration. It is not used in the later tests for the order of nonseasonal integration.

For a 'rough and ready' simplification of the Dickey-Hasza–Fuller test, a straightforward generalization of the *DF* or *ADF* tests can be used. The constructed variable z_{t-s} can be replaced in (5.12) by y_{t-s}. If, in addition, all the δ_is are assumed to be equal to zero, the test becomes the *Dickey-Fuller seasonal integration test* (*DFSI*), based on the significant negativity or otherwise of the parameter δ in the regression:

$$\Delta_s y_t = \delta \cdot y_{t-s} + \epsilon_t . \tag{5.14}$$

Otherwise it becomes the *Augmented Dickey–Fuller seasonal integration test* (*ADFSI*), based on the regression:

$$\Delta_s y_t = \delta \cdot y_{t-s} + \sum_{i=1}^{k} \delta_i \cdot \Delta_s y_{t-i} + \epsilon_t . \tag{5.15}$$

The critical values for the *DFSI* and *ADFSI* tests are the same as for the *DHF* test, so that for quarterly data they can be roughly approximated by those given in Table 3 in the Appendix for $m = 4$. However, it must be remembered that neither of these two tests is strictly appropriate and should be used as a rough approximation only. Moreover, the critical values given in the Appendix are inexact. (The values given in the Appendix have been computed for the purpose of cointegration analysis and their similarity to the critical values for the seasonal integration test is presumably accidental.) The sequence of tests for seasonal and nonseasonal integration using the *DFSI* and *ADFSI* approaches is the same as that for the *DHF* test above.

In Section 5.7, an example of testing for seasonal integration as well as for the order of non–seasonal integration is given, using the *DHF* and *ADF* approaches for the principal variables in the *DHSY* model.

Testing for seasonal integration using the *DHF* test is equivalent to testing for what may be termed *stochastic seasonality*. The simplest form of stochastic seasonality is where seasonal differences are stationary, or where a process can be expressed as:

$$y_t = y_{t-s} + \epsilon_t \, ,$$

or:

$$\Delta_s y_t = \epsilon_t \, ,$$

where ϵ_t is a series of identically distributed independent random variables.

Such a process may exhibit a seasonal pattern which changes over time. This is in contrast with deterministic seasonality of the form (for quarterly data):

$$y_t = \alpha_1 Q1_t + \alpha_2 Q2_t + \alpha_3 Q3_t + \alpha_4 Q4_t + \epsilon_t \, ,$$

where the Qi_t , ($i = 1, 2, 3, 4$) variables are seasonal dummy variables. The principal difference between the two forms of seasonality is that shocks in the deterministic seasonal model die out in the long run, while in the stochastic seasonal model they have a *permanent* effect. Thus in the stochastic seasonal model, a positive shock at time t will not only increase the value of y_t, but also the value of y_{t+s}, y_{t+2s} , etc. Deterministic seasonality therefore may be a rather poor approximation to stochastic seasonality.

Clearly it would be useful to be able to discriminate between these two models of seasonality. A test is available which not only allows for such discrimination, but which also gives a richer insight into the nature of the seasonal pattern for a variable. This test has been proposed by Hylleberg, Engle, Granger and Yoo (1990), hereafter termed the *HEGY* test. To discuss this test more fully, it will be useful to recall from Chapter 4 the concept of the lag operator L, where

$Ly_t = y_{t-1}$ and $L^j y_t = y_{t-j}$. In this notation, a seasonal difference may be written as $(1-L^s)y_t$. The *HEGY* tests for quarterly data use the representation:

$$\Delta_4 y_t = \sum_{i=1}^{4} a_i Q i_t + \sum_{i=1}^{4} b_i Y_{i,t-1} + \sum_{i=1}^{k} c_i \Delta_4 y_{t-i} + \epsilon_t ,$$

where k is the number of lagged terms included, the Qi_t are seasonal dummy variables, and the $Y_{i,t}$ variables are constructed from the series on y_t as:

$$Y_{1,t} = (1+L)(1+L^2) \cdot y_t \qquad = y_t + y_{t-1} + y_{t-2} + y_{t-3} ;$$

$$Y_{2,t} = -(1-L)(1+L^2) \cdot y_t \qquad = -y_t + y_{t-1} - y_{t-2} + y_{t-3} ;$$

$$Y_{3,t} = -(1-L)(1+L) \cdot y_t \qquad = -y_t + y_{t-2} ;$$

$$Y_{4,t} = -(L)(1-L)(1+L) \cdot y_t \qquad = Y_{3,t-1} = -y_{t-1} + y_{t-3} .$$

The *HEGY* model may be estimated by ordinary least squares. If the null hypothesis of stochastic seasonality rather than deterministic seasonality is true, then all the a_is will be equal to each other and all the b_is will be equal to zero. If the a_is are different, and at least one of the b_is is nonzero, then there is a combination of both deterministic and stochastic seasonality. Each negative b_i has a different interpretation. For example, if only b_1 is negative, then there is no non–seasonal stochastic stationary component (that is no component corresponding to an $I(0)$ process). If only b_2 is negative, then there is no semi–annual cycle. Both b_3 and b_4 are related to the annual cycle, and may be tested jointly.

Critical values and examples of these tests are provided in the Hylleberg *et al.* (1990) paper.

In order to justify the *HEGY* tests, those mathematically inclined may wish to check that the expression $(1-L^4)$ may be factorized as:

$$1-L^4 = (1-L)(1+L)(1+L^2) = (1-L)(1+L)(1-i\cdot L)(1+i\cdot L),$$

where i is an imaginary part of a complex number such that $i^2 = -1$.

Technically, this factorization shows that a quarterly stochastic seasonal unit root process has four roots of modulus one. One root $(1-L)$ described as being at 'zero frequency' removes the trend. The three other roots $(1 + L)$, and $(1 \pm i\cdot L)$ which remove the seasonal structure imply stochastic cycles of semi–annual and annual periodicity. For a more detailed explanation of the concepts of seasonal frequencies and seasonal fluctuations see Granger and Newbold (1986, Chapter 2). An elegant introduction to complex numbers and complex number dynamics can be found in Dhrymes (1970a, Mathematical Appendix).

A simple model which can be useful in practical investigations is where it is assumed that the process may have been generated by a combination of stochastic and deterministic seasonality and trend of the type:

$$y_t = \alpha_0 + y_{t-1} + \sum_{i=1}^{3} \alpha_i Qi_t + \epsilon_t,$$

where the Qi_t are seasonal dummy variables. In such a model, the order of integration can be tested by a conventional *DF* or *ADF* test. However, the distribution of the Student–*t* statistic is different and the critical values should be taken from Table 4 in the Appendix (again for $m = 0$) rather than from Tables 2 or 3.

5.4 The Concept of Cointegration

The main message from Section 5.2 was that trended data can be regarded as potentially a major problem for empirical econometrics. Trends, either stochastic or deterministic, may give rise to spurious regressions, uninterpretable Student–t values and other statistics, goodness of fit measures which are (R^2) 'too high' and, in general, make regression results extremely difficult to evaluate.

The grim fact is that, in economics, most time series (data ordered by time) are subject to some type of trend. Section 5.3 suggested one remedy, namely to difference a series successively until stationarity is achieved. Nevertheless, this does not seem to be an ideal solution. It was shown earlier (Chapter 3) that applying first differences to the variables in the *DHSY* consumption function (or, strictly speaking, to logarithms of the variables), led to the loss of long–run properties, since the model in differences did not have a long run solution. The desire to evaluate models which combine both short run and long run properties and which at the same time maintain stationarity in all of the variables, has prompted a reconsideration of the problem of regression using variables measured in their levels.

Let us consider the variables x_t and y_t in Figures 5.5 and 5.6. In both cases these variables are clearly nonstationary as they are both subject to a positive trend. However, the variables in Figure 5.5 are drifting apart. They diverge in time or, in other words, the difference between x_t and y_t does not seem to be stationary. The variables depicted in Figure 5.5 may or may not be integrated of the same order (possibly x_t is $I(1)$ and y_t is $I(2)$). On the other hand, the variables in Figure 5.6 seem to be floating in time together. They are presumably integrated of the same order and the fact that the differences between x_t and y_t do not have a clear tendency to rise or to decline suggests that these differences (or, more generally, a linear combination of x_t and y_t) might be stationary.

Figure 5.6 illustrates the general concept of *cointegration.* If there is a long run relationship between two (or more) nonstationary variables, the idea is that deviations from this long run path are stationary. If this is the case, the variables in question are said to be *cointegrated.* Note that according to these figures, time series can be cointegrated only if they are integrated of the same order.

The formal definition of *cointegration of two variables,* developed by Engle and Granger (1987) is as follows:

Definition: Time series x_t and y_t are said to be *cointegrated of order d, b* where $d \geq b \geq 0$, written as:

$$x_t, y_t \sim CI(d, b),$$

if:

1. both series are integrated of order d,
2. there exists a linear combination of these variables, say $\alpha_1 \cdot x_t + \alpha_2 \cdot y_t$, which is integrated of order $d - b$.

The vector $[\alpha_1, \alpha_2]$ is called a *cointegrating vector.*

A straightforward generalization of the above definition for the case of n variables is the following. If x_t denotes an $n \times 1$ vector of series $x_{1t}, x_{2t}, ..., x_{nt}$ and:

a) each of them is $I(d)$,
b) there exists an $n \times 1$ vector α such that $x_t' \cdot \alpha = \sim I(d - b)$, then:

$$x_t' \cdot \alpha \sim CI(d, b).$$

(It is shown later that there are special cases where condition a) above can be relaxed.)

For empirical econometrics, the most interesting case is where the series transformed with the use of the cointegrating vector become stationary, that is where $d = b$, and the cointegrating coefficients (the coefficients which constitute the cointegrating vector) can be identified with parameters in the

Fig. 5.5: Two series drifting apart

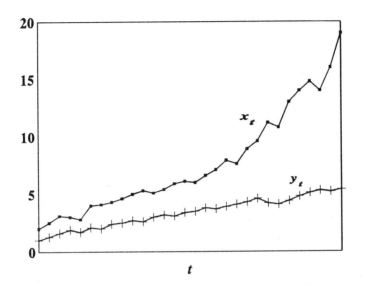

Fig. 5.6: Two series drifting together

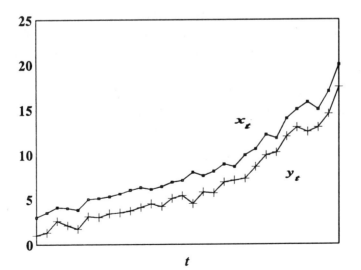

long run relationship between the variables. In this chapter we will concentrate on such situations, that is where $x_t' \cdot \alpha \sim CI(d, d)$.

Let us suppose that x_t, y_t are both $I(1)$ and that the long run relationship between them is given by:

$$y_t^* = \beta \cdot x_t .$$

An important situation occurs if the variables x_t, y_t are $CI(1, 1)$, and have the cointegrating vector $[\beta, -1]$, so that the deviations of y_t from its long run path y_t^* are $I(0)$. If this is the case, a model in first differences incorporating an error correction mechanism can be sensibly developed (see Chapter 3). Specifically for the equation:

$$\Delta y_t = \beta_1 \Delta x_t + \beta_2 (y_{t-1} - \beta \cdot x_{t-1}) + \epsilon_t , \qquad (5.16)$$

both the dependent variable Δy_t and the regressors Δx_t and $(y_{t-1} - \beta x_{t-1})$ are $I(0)$. Thus there is no danger of estimating a spurious regression because of the presence of stochastic or deterministic trends in the data. The model incorporates both a long run solution and has an error correction mechanism (ECM) when β_2 is negative.

As explained in Chapter 3 above, the starting point for deriving model (5.16) is a static equation with a single explanatory variable. Let the stochastic variable u_t represent deviations of y_t from its long run path y_t^*, that is:

$$ECM = y_t - y_t^* = y_t - \beta \cdot x_t = u_t ,$$

or:

$$y_t = \beta \cdot x_t + u_t . \qquad (5.17)$$

Hence, u_t in (5.17) can be viewed in the same light as the term $(y_{t-1} - \beta \cdot x_{t-1})$ which appears in (5.16) to reflect the error correction aspect of that equation.

Let us consider various possibilities of integration and cointegration in (5.17).

1. if $y_t \sim I(1)$ and $x_t \sim I(0)$, then $u_t \sim I(1)$ and the variables x_t, y_t are not cointegrated;
2. if $y_t \sim I(1)$ and $x_t \sim I(1)$, then it *may* be that $u_t \sim I(0)$ and the variables x_t, y_t are cointegrated, *only if* $[\beta , -1]$ constitutes a cointegrating vector;
3. if $y_t \sim I(0)$ and $x_t \sim I(0)$, then $u_t \sim I(0)$ and the enquiry about cointegration does not really make sense;
4. if $y_t \sim I(0)$ and $x_t \sim I(1)$, then $u_t \sim I(1)$ and the variables x_t, y_t are not cointegrated.

Consequently, in a long run relationship between two variables both must be integrated of the same order if the error term is to be $I(0)$. Stationarity of the error term is especially important if one is going to examine models incorporating error correction mechanisms such as equation (5.16).

If the number of variables involved in the long run relation increases, the problem becomes much more complicated than that implied by the definition above. Consider, for example, a three variable case:

$$y_t = \beta_1 x_{1t} + \beta_2 x_{2t} + u_t . \tag{5.18}$$

Now *it is* possible for the variables to be integrated of different orders and for the error term u_t to be stationary (later in the text we will assume, rather imprecisely, that stationarity is a synonym for $I(0)$). Suppose that $y_t \sim I(0)$, $x_{1t} \sim I(1)$ and $x_{2t} \sim I(1)$. By analogy with the previous analysis we might expect that in such a case $u_t \sim I(1)$. It may happen, however, that $[\beta_1, \beta_2]$ constitutes a cointegrating vector for x_{1t}, x_{2t}, so that $(\beta_1 x_{1t} + \beta_2 x_{2t}) \sim I(0)$, since x_{1t}, x_{2t} are integrated of the same order. If this is the case, u_t may be stationary, since $y_t \sim I(0)$ and $(\beta_1 x_{1t} + \beta_2 x_{2t}) \sim I(0)$.

In economics a more common situation would be for $y_t \sim I(1)$, $x_{1t} \sim I(2)$ and $x_{2t} \sim I(2)$. Despite the different orders of integration, the error term could still be stationary provided $(\beta_1 x_{1t} + \beta_2 x_{2t}) \sim I(1)$. That is, if x_{1t}, $x_{2t} \sim CI(2, 1)$ with the cointegrating vector $[\beta_1, \beta_2]$. This leads to a major complication of the entire concept of cointegration in a long run relationship and in the stationarity of the error term, but there is a practical hint that can simplify testing procedures. If variables in a long run relationship are of a different order of integration and the order of integration of the dependent variable is lower than the highest order of integration of the explanatory variables, there must be at least two explanatory variables integrated of this highest order if the necessary condition for stationarity of the error term is to be met.

Where seasonal data are used, the entire concept of cointegration becomes more difficult. The previous section outlined four tests that could be used to investigate the seasonal integration properties of a series. The *HEGY* representation stresses the possibility that series may be transformed into stationary series by seasonal and/or other differencing. For cointegration analysis, this means additional complications. Let us say that the null hypothesis is that the variables x_t and y_t are not cointegrated, so that $u_t = y_t - \beta \cdot x_t$ is not stationary. In the case of seasonality this could mean that either $u_t \sim SI_s(0, 1)$, or $u_t \sim SI_s(1, 0)$ or $u_t \sim SI_s(1, 1)$ to mention only the most straightforward possibilities. As for integration analysis, each case requires further analysis based on different lengths of differences.

5.5   Testing for Cointegration

Consider firstly the problem of testing for nonseasonal cointegration. Technically, the test for cointegration of the type $CI(d, b)$, for $b = d$, is analogous to testing for integration. A Dickey–Fuller, Augmented Dickey–Fuller or Durbin–Watson statistic can be used in order to determine whether the linear combination of two (or more) variables is $I(0)$. Cases of the type $CI(d, b)$, for $b < d$, are not of primary interest, since for $b < d$ the cointegrating vector is not stationary and does not have a straightforward economic interpretation. Nevertheless, special care is required since the distribution of the Student–t values, and consequently the critical values of the cointegration test, both depend heavily on the number of *unknown* cointegrating coefficients. A two–step algorithm for testing for cointegration in a long run relationship is given below. This algorithm is derived for a 'classical' Engle–Granger type enquiry into cointegration described more fully in Section 5.6.

Step 1:
Test for the order of integration of the variables involved in the postulated long run relationship (for example, equation (5.17)). If only two variables appear in the long run relation, both have to be of the same order of integration. If the number of variables is greater than two (that is if there is more than one explanatory variable), the order of integration of the dependent variable cannot be higher than the order of integration of any of the explanatory variables. Moreover, there must be either none or at least two explanatory variables integrated to an identical order higher than the order of integration of the dependent variable.

Step 2:
Decide whether the cointegrating vector is known, or has to be estimated. Sometimes the cointegrating vector may be known *a priori*. For instance, suppose one assumes that in a consumption function, where $cons_t$ denotes the logarithm of consumption and inc_t stands for the logarithm of income,

the long run income elasticity of consumption is equal to unity. One form of the long run consumption function consistent with this is simply:

$$cons^*_t = inc_t \,,$$

where long run consumption ($cons^*_t$) is equal to income. If this is believed to be the appropriate form of the long run function the cointegrating vector would be [1 , −1]. In the general case, however, the long run relationship is of the form of equations (5.17) or (5.18) and the cointegrating vector is given by [1 , − β] or [1 , − β_1 , −β_2] respectively. Coefficients in these vectors have to be estimated, usually by ordinary least squares. Hence, we have two cases at step 2:

Step 2a:
The cointegrating vector is known *a priori*. In this case the procedure is the same as that described earlier for testing the order of integration. In equations (5.7), (5.10) or (5.11) we have to replace y_t by the appropriate linear combination of the variables which we expect to be stationary. As an example, consider the consumption model mentioned above. The hypothesis to be tested is whether $cons_t$, $inc_t \sim CI(1 , 1)$ with the known *a priori* cointegrating vector [1 , −1]. Let us assume that the integration test (step 1) reveals that $cons_t \sim I(1)$ and $inc_t \sim I(1)$. The Dickey–Fuller cointegration test, by analogy with (5.7), consists in testing the significance of the Student–*t* ratio for δ in the ordinary least squares regression:

$$\Delta u_t = \delta \cdot u_{t-1} + \epsilon_t \,. \tag{5.19}$$

where $u_t = cons_t - inc_t$. The critical values of the test are the same as used for testing integration. That is, they may be read from the Table 2 given in the Appendix for $m = 0$. Analogously, the Augmented Dickey–Fuller test uses the

Student–t ratio for δ from the equation:

$$\Delta u_t = \delta \cdot u_{t-1} + \sum_{i=1}^{k} \delta_i \cdot \Delta u_{t-i} + \epsilon_t \, , \qquad (5.20)$$

Step 2b:
The cointegrating vector is not known *a priori*. That is, we are dealing with a long run relationship of the type:

$$y_t = \beta_1 x_{1t} + \beta_2 x_{2t} + ... + \beta_m x_{mt} + v_t \, , \qquad (5.21)$$

and the cointegrating vector $[1 \, , \, -\beta_1 \, , \, -\beta_2 \, ,..., \, -\beta_m]$ is not known and has to be estimated. Computationally, little changes; we use the Dickey–Fuller or Augmented Dickey–Fuller equations like (5.19) and (5.20), with the estimated residuals from (5.21) instead of u_t, so that:

$$\Delta \hat{v}_t = \delta \cdot \hat{v}_{t-1} + \xi_t \, , \qquad (5.22)$$

(Dickey–Fuller), or:

$$\Delta \hat{v}_t = \delta \cdot \hat{v}_{t-1} + \sum_{i=1}^{k} \delta_i \cdot \Delta \hat{v}_{t-i} + \xi_t \, , \qquad (5.23)$$

(Augmented Dickey–Fuller), where the $\hat{v}_t$ are the ordinary least squares residuals in (5.21) and can be interpreted as the deviations of y_t from its long run path.

As was the case for the integration test, the Student–t ration that results from the regression of an $I(0)$ variable on an $I(1)$ variable (as is (5.22) or (5.23)) does not have the conventional Student–t distribution if the null hypothesis is true. The important difference between Step 2a and Step 2b is the fact that in Step 2b, coefficients in the cointegrating vector are estimated and *the distribution of the Student–t ratio depends on the number of coefficients estimated.* In the integration test and in the cointegration test with the cointegrating vector known, the number of coefficients estimated is zero, and consequently one can read the critical values of the test from Table 2 in the Appendix for $m = 0$. If there is a positive number of estimated coefficients in the cointegrating vector, we have to use the appropriate critical values. For instance, if a long run relationship is given by (5.18), where there are two explanatory variables, and the number of observations is equal to 30, the approximate critical values for the cointegration test are for the 5% level of significance: −3.31 (lower bound) and −3.15 (upper bound). One would reject the null hypothesis of no cointegration if the Student−t value for δ in equation (5.22) or (5.23) is below −3.31, would not reject the null if the value was above −3.15, and be unsure whether to reject or not if the value lies between −3.31 and −3.15 in the inconclusive region. Now, m is taken as two as there are two estimated coefficients in the cointegrating vector.

In the same way as was discussed for the case of testing for the order of integration, a Durbin−Watson analogue can be applied as a 'rough and ready' method for testing for cointegration. The *cointegration Durbin−Watson test* (*CIDW*) consists in computing a Durbin−Watson statistic for the estimated deviations from a long run path which, under the cointegration hypothesis, are stationary:

$$CIDW = \frac{\Sigma(\hat{v}_t - \hat{v}_{t-1})^2}{\Sigma(\hat{v}_t - \bar{v}_t)^2} , \qquad (5.24)$$

where $\bar{v}_t$ is the arithmetic mean for the residuals $\hat{v}_t$. The distribution of *CIDW* has not been fully investigated yet and its critical values are not known. By analogy with *IDW*, we might expect that the smaller is *CIDW*, the greater is the chance that the hypothesis that the series are cointegrated should be rejected. It is known that the power of *CIDW* depends positively on the goodness of fit of the *OLS* estimate of the long run relationship (5.21). Hence, Banerjee *et al.* (1986) proposed a simple 'rule of thumb' for a quick evaluation of the cointegration hypothesis: if $CIDW$ computed for $\hat{v}_t$ of an equation like (5.21) is smaller than the coefficient of determination (R^2) for this equation, the cointegration hypothesis is likely to be false; otherwise, when $CIDW > R^2$, cointegration may occur. We may then state that if the conventional Durbin–Watson statistic, computed for the residuals of a static model representing a long run relationship, is close to 2, there is no danger of the lack of cointegration of the variables.

As has been mentioned earlier, the testing for cointegration and the estimation of cointegrating vectors when one is dealing with seasonal data is more problematic than that for annual data, and this area is still in the process of development. Some progress has been made, however. Testing for cointegration and the estimation of a long run cointegrating model using seasonal data may be performed in a number of ways. Engle, Granger and Hallman (1989) have pointed out that the use of seasonal data to estimate the long run model may give rise to inconsistent estimates of the long run parameters. Annual data could be used to estimate these long run parameters thereby avoiding the need to model the seasonality, and the standard tests for cointegration applied. Alternatively, seasonal data may be used provided the series which may be cointegrated are 'filtered' or 'seasonally adjusted' first. Once the data is seasonally adjusted, one of the tests outlined in Step 2b above (for example, the ADF test of equation (5.23)) may be applied to the seasonally adjusted data. There are several suggested approaches to this seasonal adjustment. For instance, if there are two series x_t and y_t which have been shown to be seasonally integrated of the same order, then applying the operator $(1-L^s)/(1-L)$ to each series will yield seasonally adjusted series which can be tested for non–seasonal cointegration. Alternatively, the $HEGY$ tests outlined above may identify the seasonal roots that should be extracted from the raw data before cointegration tests are applied. A straightforward (but probably generally sub–optimal) procedure is to assume that stochastic seasonality can be approximated by deterministic seasonal dummy variables, and include these in the long run relationship, or long run cointegrating vector. In such a case, Table 4 in the Appendix can be used for quarterly data, where m is the number of estimated coefficients in the long run cointegrating vector excluding those for the intercept and seasonal dummies. An example of this approach is given in Section 5.7 below.

The testing of seasonal cointegration and the estimation of seasonal cointegrating vectors is probably best approached by an extension of the Johansen method which is discussed in Chapter 6 below. Currently, there is little published work in this field, although an example of the technique has been provided by Kunst (1990). No doubt further examples will become available when this extension is incorporated in standard econometric software packages.

5.6   Modelling Cointegrated Series through Error Correction Models

This section describes how cointegrated nonstationary variables can be used to formulate and estimate a model with an error correction mechanism. The fact that variables are cointegrated implies that there is some adjustment process which prevents the errors in the long run relationship becoming larger and larger. Engle and Granger (1987) have shown that any cointegrated series have an error correction representation. The 'Granger representation theorem' which establishes this result is outlined in Chapter 6. The converse is also true, in that cointegration is a necessary condition for error correction models to hold (see Engle and Granger (1991, pp. 7–8)). A detailed analysis of cointegration and error correction mechanisms is given by Hylleberg and Mizon (1989). Phillips and Loretan (1991) have considered a variety of ways of representing cointegrated systems with particular emphasis on error correction model representations. Such models currently represent the most common approach to situations where it is wished to incorporate both the economic theory relating to the long run relationship between variables, and short run disequilibrium behaviour. Two of the simplest and most widely used procedures will be described, which require only the use of ordinary least squares estimation (for references to more complicated methods see the suggested further reading at the end of this chapter, and also at the end of Chapter 6).

The first approach was originally suggested by Engle and Granger (1987). It is particularly convenient for the case in which the variables appearing in the long run relation are all $I(1)$, or where the dependent variable is $I(1)$, and the explanatory variables are $CI(d + 1, d)$. For simplicity we will only consider the case with a single explanatory variable in the long run relation. (The extension to the multivariate case is direct.) Thus, reconsider equation (5.17),

$$y_t = \beta \cdot x_t + u_t, \tag{5.25}$$

where both y_t and x_t are $I(1)$. Suppose that the coefficient β is unknown, but for its *OLS* estimate $\hat{\beta}$, the Dickey–Fuller and/or Augmented Dickey–Fuller tests indicate stationarity of the *OLS* residuals $\hat{u}_t$. In other words, cointegration of y_t and x_t of order $(1, 1)$ with the cointegrating vector $[1, -\hat{\beta}]$ can be positively accepted. Logically, the next move would be to switch to a short run model with an error correction mechanism:

$$\Delta y_t = \alpha_1 \Delta x_t + \alpha_2 (y_{t-1} - \beta \cdot x_{t-1}) + \epsilon_t, \tag{5.26}$$

where ϵ_t is an error term and α_2 is negative. It is tempting to estimate (5.26) by unrestricted ordinary least squares, since the parameters in the unrestricted version of (5.26) are exactly identified. That is, they may be recovered from the regression:

$$\Delta y_t = \alpha_1 \Delta x_t + \alpha_2 y_{t-1} - \alpha_2 \beta \cdot x_{t-1} + \epsilon_t . \qquad (5.27)$$

However, direct estimation of (5.27) probably would not be the best way forward. Firstly, in addition to $\hat{\beta}$ obtained from the regression of equation (5.25), we would now have another estimate of β, say $\tilde{\beta}$, and we do not know whether $\tilde{\beta}$ is a cointegrating coefficient for y_t and x_t. Secondly, and more important is the fact that in (5.27) the variables have, by assumption, different orders of integration. Both Δy_t and Δx_t are $I(0)$ while y_{t-1} and x_{t-1} are $I(1)$. Unless an additional restriction: $(\alpha_2 y_t - \alpha_2 \beta \cdot x_t) \sim I(0)$ is met, these different orders of integration imply a 'hidden' assumption for ϵ_t, namely that $\epsilon_t \sim I(1)$. In other words, the error term is nonstationary.

The Engle–Granger remedy consists of a two–step procedure. *First* estimate (5.25) by ordinary least squares and test for stationarity of the residuals. *Second*, if this is not rejected, estimate (5.26) replacing β by its previously computed *OLS* estimate $\hat{\beta}$. Now the condition of the identical order of integration for the variables in (5.26) is met: Δy_t, Δx_t and $(y_{t-1} - \hat{\beta} \cdot x_{t-1})$ are all $I(0)$ and consequently, provided the model is properly specified, ϵ_t is also $I(0)$.

One doubt about the Engle–Granger procedure concerns its first step. The variables y_t and x_t are nonstationary. Hence, what is the sense of estimating (5.25) by ordinary least squares? Further investigation has shown that the properties of the *OLS* estimators are not all bad. Indeed, under some general assumptions they are consistent. Unfortunately, the *OLS* estimate of the standard error of $\hat{\beta}$ is not consistent in this case and most researchers do not even bother to report it. (For a method better than *OLS* for computing standard errors for a regression with nonstationary variables, see West (1988).)

When using the Engle–Granger method, we must be aware of the fact that *we do not prove that the relation* (5.25) *is really a long run one.* This is an assumption and cannot be statistically verified. We have to have a strong belief in a long run equilibrium relationship between the variables that is supported by relevant economic theory. It may be that the theory suggests a convenient assumption about a long run relationship. In Section 5.5 we considered an example where we assumed the theory suggested that long run consumption and income were equal. Consequently in (5.25) $\beta = 1$, if y_t stands for the logarithm of consumption and x_t for the logarithm of income. In this case the Engle–Granger method simplifies to a direct estimation of

$$\Delta y_t = \alpha_1 \Delta x_t + \alpha_2 (y_{t-1} - x_{t-1}) + \epsilon_t \, ,$$

provided that y_t , $x_t \sim CI(1 , 1)$ with the cointegrating vector $[1 , -1]$.

There may be other views about how the long run relationship (5.25) should be estimated (see Phillips and Loretan (1991)). For example, this could be approached through the use of an autoregressive distributed lag model (*ADL* models were introduced in Chapter 4). The unrestricted *ADL*(n) model for the variables y_t and x_t is formulated as:

$$y_t = \sum_{i=1}^{n} \alpha_i y_{t-i} + \sum_{i=0}^{n} \beta_i x_{t-i} + \epsilon_t \, , \tag{5.28}$$

where α_i, β_i are coefficients and ϵ_t is an error term. Equation (5.28) can be estimated instead of (5.25) by *OLS* and then the long run coefficient β^* (when $y_t = y_{t-i}$ and $x_t = x_{t-i}$ for all i) is derived from the estimated *OLS* coefficients as:

$$\beta^* = \frac{\sum_{i=0}^{n} \hat{\beta}_i}{1 - \sum_{i=1}^{n} \hat{\alpha}_i} . \tag{5.29}$$

After testing for cointegration of y_t, x_t with the cointegrating vector $[1, -\beta^*]$, the model (5.26) can now be estimated by *OLS*, substituting β^* in place of β.

The general idea of the Engle–Granger and *ADL* methods is the same. Both methods start from the estimation of the long run relationship (5.25), either directly in the case of Engle–Granger or by using (5.28) in the *ADL* method, and then insert the deviations from the long run path, lagged appropriately, as the error correction mechanism in the short run equation. The difference consists in the method of estimation of the long run relationship.

5.7   An Example of Cointegration Analysis

In this section we examine the orders of integration and possible cointegration of the variables which appear in the *DHSY* aggregate consumption model, using the same sample data as in that study (Davidson *et al.* (1978)). The tests presented below were not available at the time this paper was published.

Following the steps suggested in the previous sections, we start with testing for the order of integration of the variables involved, namely: $cons_t$ (logarithm of consumption), inc_t (logarithm of income) and inf_t (inflation measured as the seasonal difference of the logarithm of the price deflator, or $\Delta_4 p_t$). In the computer output below, these are denoted as 'lc', 'li' and 'inf' respectively.

First, we determine the order of seasonal integration of each variable using the Dickey–Hasza–Fuller (*DHF*) and the *ADFSI* and *DFSI* tests. This is followed by testing whether first differences used once and twice after seasonal differencing make the variables stationary. In other words, for each variable we test the hypothesis that the variable is $SI_4(0 \ , \ 1)$, then $SI_4(1 \ , \ 1)$ and then $SI_4(2 \ , \ 1)$ as the alternatives.

Next, we test whether a postulated equality in the long run relationship between consumption and income gives a stationary error. Both *DF* and *ADF* tests are used here. In order to develop a model with an error correction mechanism, we estimate an autoregressive distributed lag (*ADL*) model for consumption, income and inflation and use the long run solution of this model for constructing possible cointegrating coefficients. The errors from this long run model are in turn tested for stationarity, that is for the cointegration of $cons_t$, inc_t and inf_t, with the cointegrating vector estimated from the *ADL* long run solution. Only the long run and not seasonal cointegrating vectors are considered.

We start by testing for seasonal integration using the Dickey–Hasza–Fuller test. MODELS 5.1 and 5.2 in the computer output given in Section 5.8 of this chapter show the two–stage *DHF* procedure for consumption. MODEL 5.1 gives the estimates of coefficients $\lambda_1,...,\ \lambda_4$ from a regression of the type (5.13) and the method of computing the variable z_t with the use of these coefficients is shown. MODEL 5.2 presents the Student–*t* value (2.24) for the Dickey–Hasza-Fuller test for consumption, that is the boldfaced and underlined figure. Analogously, MODEL 5.3 and MODEL 5.4 show the seasonal *ADF* and *DF* statistics respectively (boldfaced and underlined), computed according to (5.15) and (5.14) respectively. Results for income and inflation were obtained in a similar way (the details of these computations are

unreported here). The computations for the inflation variable
are based on four fewer observations than those for either
consumption or income, due to the way this variable is
constructed from the price deflator series. The set of results
is given below (recall: *DHF* stands for the Dickey–Hasza–
Fuller, *DFSI* for the seasonal Dickey–Fuller and *ADFSI* for
the seasonal Augmented Dickey–Fuller test statistic).
Figures in brackets are values of the Durbin–Watson statistic
used for testing for autocorrelation in the residuals formed in
the construction of each seasonal integration test:

	$cons_t$	inc_t	inf_t
DHF	2.24 (1.94)	2.46 (1.84)	11.23 (0.06)
DFSI	12.0 (0.55)	8.57 (0.72)	−7.04 (0.51)
ADFSI	2.57 (1.92)	2.56 (1.82)	11.23 (0.06)

These results clearly indicate that there are no grounds
for accepting that any of the original series measured as the
levels of logarithms of consumption or income, or the inflation variable, are $SI_4(0, 0)$. The Dickey–Hasza–Fuller
critical values for a sample size of 60 (which is the closest
reported to the sample size of the original *DHSY* study) are
−4.85 (1%), −4.14 (5%) and −3.79 (10%). Comparing the
computed statistics given above with these critical values is
really an academic exercise. Obviously the positive numbers
in the table above cannot be 'significantly negative'. The
very low values of the Durbin–Watson statistics associated
with the *DFSI* test statistics mean that in these cases (including the seemingly significant value of −7.04 for the inflation
variable) the *DFSI* tests are unreliable.

If the hypothesis that the series in levels are $SI_4(0, 0)$
cannot be accepted, the next step is to test the hypothesis
that the series are $SI_4(0, 1)$, that is that seasonal differencing
will make them stationary. MODEL 5.5 shows the way the
ADF statistic for consumption (−1.2385) has been obtained.
The computer output notation *dd4lc* stands for $\Delta\Delta_4 cons_t$,
that is for the first difference of the seasonal difference of the

logarithm of consumption, and *d4lc* for the seasonal difference of the logarithm of consumption. For the three variables the statistics are:

	$\Delta_4 cons_t$	$\Delta_4 inc_t$	$\Delta_4 inf_t$
ADF	−1.24 (1.97)	−1.37 (1.94)	3.72 (1.38)

For inf_t, we may conclude that the series in seasonal differences is still nonstationary without even looking at the critical values, since the value of 3.72 cannot be 'significantly negative'. For $cons_t$ and inc_t however, it is better to look.

According to Table 2 in the Appendix, the upper limits of the critical values for a sample size of 75 and $m = 0$ are: −2.40 (1%) , −1.86 (5%) and −1.53 (10%). Hence, the computed *ADF* statistics are not significant even at the 10% level of significance. At conventional levels of significance, we cannot accept the hypothesis that the series are $SI_4(0 , 1)$. We proceed to the next step, namely to test whether they are $SI_4(1 , 1)$. In other words, to test whether the variables are stationary after taking seasonal differences and then first differences. (Actually, the order in which these differences are taken is immaterial.) MODEL 5.6 shows the result for consumption. The *ADF* statistic is equal to −4.475 and *ddd4lc* stands for $\Delta\Delta_4 cons_t$, that is the first difference of the first difference of the seasonal difference of the logarithm of consumption. For all the variables the results are:

	$\Delta\Delta_4 cons_t$	$\Delta\Delta_4 inc_t$	$\Delta\Delta_4 inf_t$
ADF	−4.48 (1.98)	−4.81 (1.99)	−4.64 (2.06)

All these statistics are significant at a significance level of 1% (the lower limit of the critical value for a sample size of 75 is −2.72). Therefore, our search for the appropriate order of integration of the variables which appear in the *DHSY* model is over. According to our findings, all variables are $SI_4(1 , 1)$,

that is they are stationary after computing seasonal differences and then first differences of the seasonal differences.
This result does not support the original formulation of the
DHSY consumption function. In the *DHSY* consumption
function the dependent variable is $\Delta_4 cons_t$ and this,
according to our findings, may not be stationary. Similarly,
one of the explanatory variables, $\Delta_4 inc_t$ may not be
stationary.

Before we proceed to the cointegration analysis, it is
interesting to see whether or not the integration Durbin-
Watson test, *IDW* (see equation (5.11)) would give us similar
results. As was stated in Section 5.3, the lower is the value of
the Durbin–Watson statistic computed for a tested variable,
the more it is likely that the variable is nonstationary. Given
below are the values of the *IDW* statistic computed for all
three variables for their seasonal differences and first
differences of the seasonal differences.

	$cons_t$	inc_t	inf_t
Δ_4	0.56	0.73	0.30
$\Delta\Delta_4$	2.20	2.26	1.67

For all the variables the message is clearly the same as that
from the *ADF* testing. That is, low values of the *IDW*
statistic for seasonal differences and higher for the first
differences of the seasonal differences indicate nonstationarity
of the former and stationarity of the latter.

Despite being unable to confirm that the appropriate
differencing for the variables in the *DHSY* model was as
presented by *DHSY*, provided the variables $cons_t$, inc_t and
inf_t are integrated of the same order (which they seem to be)
there is a chance that their linear combination is stationary.

Let us first consider the *DHSY* model that excluded
inflation (equation (3.7)) which is equivalent to assuming
values for the long run cointegrating vector (Step 2a in

Section 5.5). The error correction term in this function is of the form:

$$cons_t - inc_t \ .$$

If the entire *DHSY* function is to be stationary (assuming, for the sake of argument, that the other terms in the *DHSY* function have been differenced appropriately), the term above must also be stationary. That is, the variables $cons_t$ and inc_t should be cointegrated of order (1 , 1) with the cointegrating vector [1 , −1].

MODEL 5.7 shows the output for the *ADF* cointegration test for consumption and income, or equivalently, the integration test for the variable defined as $cons_t - inc_t$. In the computer output, this variable is denoted as *lc_li*, with a first difference *dlc_li*. The computed Student–*t* value, which is the value for the *ADF* cointegration test is equal to 1.89480. Formally, we should compare it with the critical values given in Table 2 in the Appendix for $m = 0$, since no estimated coefficients were needed in order to define the cointegrating vector. As before, the value of the test is so visibly positive that we can spare ourselves the effort of looking into the tables to find out whether 1.89480 is 'significantly negative'. It is definitely not. MODEL 5.8 gives the results for the corresponding *DF* test. The Student–*t* value is negative but small, so that the conclusion is the same as for the *ADF* test.

The conclusion is that the error correction mechanism of the *DHSY* model is not stationary. In other words, the variables $cons_t$ and inc_t are not cointegrated (1 , 1) with the cointegrating vector [1 , −1]. This is confirmed by a relatively low value of the cointegration Durbin–Watson test statistic (*CIDW*) of 0.79 which may be computed for $cons_t - inc_t$. This, as far as testing nonstationarity is concerned, is not very low, but it looks rather suspicious.

Let us now consider the testing of long run cointegration in the *DHSY* model where the coefficients in the potential long run cointegrating vector are unknown (Step 2b in Section 5.5). In order to extend the analysis, the long run model will be taken to be multivariate rather than bivariate (see equation (5.18) above), so that the inflation variable is also considered. An unrestricted $ADL(5, 5, 1)$ model for $cons_t$, inc_t and inf_t (that is five lags for both consumption and income, and a single lag for inflation) has been estimated and the results given in Section 5.8 as MODEL 5.9. Note that this model also includes seasonal dummy variables to approximate stochastic seasonality for the reasons outlined in Section 5.5 above. The estimated coefficients are then used to compute the long run parameters, in a similar fashion to (5.29). They are directly computed by *PC–GIVE* and printed together with their asymptotic standard errors. Since they are equal to 0.943 for inc_t and -1.294 for inf_t, the error correction mechanism, representing deviations of $cons_t$ from its long run path, is computed as:

$$ECM = cons_t - 0.943 \cdot inc_t + 1.294 \cdot inf_t - intercept \ and$$

$$seasonal\ dummy\ variables\ .$$

MODEL 5.10 gives the value of the *ADF* statistic for this error term (denoted by *ECM* and its first differences by *decm*). This statistic is equal to -0.89278, which is not significantly negative as may be confirmed by inspection of the critical values in Table 4 in the Appendix for $m = 2$. This is the appropriate value for m as the tested cointegrating vector is now [1 , -0.943 , 1.294, plus an intercept and seasonal coefficients], that is it contains two estimated coefficients apart from the coefficients representing the deterministic seasonality. Our conclusion is that the consumption, income and inflation series in the *DHSY* model are not (nonseasonally) cointegrated, if the cointegrating vector is that of the long run solution to an *ADL* model. However, Hendry, Muellbauer and Murphy (1990) found a cointegrating vector for the variables which appeared in the *DHSY* model using techniques which will be described in Chapter 6.

5.8 Stylized Computer Output (*PC–GIVE*)

Computing coefficients λ_i for the Dickey–Hasza–Fuller test

MODEL 5.1 Modelling d4lc by OLS

The Sample is 1959 (1) to 1975 (4) less 0 Forecasts

VARI	COEF	STD ERR	H.C.S.E.	t–VALUE
d4lc 1	<u>.84338</u>	.12490	.12088	6.7524
d4lc 2	<u>.09487</u>	.16470	.14891	.57602
d4lc 3	<u>.02541</u>	.16243	.14983	.15643
d4lc 4	<u>−.0489</u>	.12774	.14191	−.3830

$\sigma = .01163$ $F(4, 64) = 80.43$ $DW = 1.968$
$RSS = .008662$ for 4 Variables and 68 Observations

Creating variable z_t for the Dickey–Hasza–Fuller test

z1	= lc 1 *	.8434
z2	= lc 2 *	.0949
z3	= lc 3 *	.0254
z4	= lc 4 *	−.0489
z12	= z1	+ z2
z123	= z3	+ z12
z1234	= z4	+ z123
z	= lc	− z1234

Computing the Dickey–Hasza–Fuller test for consumption

MODEL 5.2 Modelling d4lc   by OLS

The Sample is 1959 (4) to 1975 (4) less 0 Forecasts

VARI	COEF	STD ERR	H.C.S.E.	t–VALUE
d4lc 1	.77069	.12785	.14207	6.0281
d4lc 2	.06386	.16041	.15229	.39807
d4lc 3	−.0295	.15910	.14169	−.1855
d4lc 4	−.1493	.13367	.16896	−1.117
z 4	.00964	.00430	.00549	**<u>2.2426</u>**

$\sigma = .01116$ $F(5, 60) = 66.60$ $DW = 1.938$
RSS = .0074808 for 5 Variables and 65 Observations

Augmented Dickey–Fuller test for seasonal integration (*ADFSI* test) consumption

MODEL 5.3 Modelling d4lc by OLS

The Sample is 1959 (1) to 1975 (4) less 0 Forecasts

VARI	COEF	STD ERR	H.C.S.E.	t–VALUE
d4lc 1	.75257	.12485	.13536	6.0276
d4lc 2	.06157	.15845	.15001	.38858
d4lc 3	−.0145	.15651	.13747	−.0931
d4lc 4	−.1755	.13200	.16780	−1.329
lc 4	.00095	.00037	.00047	**2.5722**

$\sigma = .01115$ $F(5, 63) = 71.31$ $DW = 1.922$
RSS = .007839 for 5 Variables and 68 Observations

Dickey–Fuller test for seasonal integration (*DFSI* test), consumption

MODEL 5.4 Modelling d4lc by OLS

The Sample is 1959 (1) to 1975 (4) less 0 Forecasts

VARI	COEF	STD ERR	H.C.S.E.	t–VALUE
lc 4	.00260	.00022	.00022	**11.9797**

$\sigma = .01574$ $F(1, 67) = 143.51$ $DW = .550$
RSS = .016616 for 1 Variable and 68 Observations

Augmented Dickey–Fuller test for $SI_4(0, 1)$, consumption

MODEL 5.5 Modelling dd4lc by OLS

The Sample is 1959 (2) to 1975 (4) less 0 Forecasts

VARI	COEF	STD ERR	H.C.S.E.	t–VALUE
dd4lc 1	−.14200	.12136	.12115	−1.1700
dd4lc 2	−.05943	.12540	.11909	−.47393
dd4lc 3	−.06731	.12800	.13919	−.52587
dd4lc 4	−.29815	.12414	.10880	−2.4017
d4lc 1	−.06575	.05309	.05542	**−1.2385**

$\sigma = .01129$ F(5, 62) = 1.92 DW = 1.968
RSS = .007903 for 5 Variables and 67 Observations

Augmented Dickey–Fuller test for $SI_4(1 , 1)$, consumption

MODEL 5.6 Modelling ddd4lc by OLS

The Sample is 1959 (3) to 1975 (4) less 0 Forecasts

VARI	COEF	STD ERR	H.C.S.E.	t–VALUE
ddd4lc 1	−1.119	.12564	.12867	−8.911
ddd4lc 2	−1.142	.18537	.16934	−6.160
ddd4lc 3	−1.186	.23630	.25364	−5.019
ddd4lc 4	.00333	.12981	.15011	.02567
dd4lc 1	−1.488	.33258	.34997	**−4.475**

$\sigma = .01130$ F(5, 61) = 19.16 DW = 1.981
RSS = .007798 for 5 Variables and 66 Observations

Augmented Dickey–Fuller test for cointegration of
$cons_t$ and inc_t, with the cointegrating vector [1 , −1]

MODEL 5.7 Modelling dlc_li by OLS

The Sample is 1958 (2) to 1975 (4) less 0 Forecasts

VARI	COEF	STD ERR	H.C.S.E.	t–VALUE
dlc_li 1	−.7147	.13164	.16275	−5.4294
dlc_li 2	−.6287	.13764	.17917	−4.5680
dlc_li 3	−.6573	.13508	.18301	−4.8659

| dlc_li 4 | .26882 | .12912 | .16539 | 2.08198 |
| lc_li 1 | .02670 | .01409 | .01904 | **1.89480** |

$\sigma = .01812$ F(5, 66) = 60.81 DW = 1.961
RSS = .021673 for 5 Variables and 71 Observations

Dickey–Fuller test for cointegration of
$cons_t$ and inc_t, with the cointegrating vector $[1, -1]$

MODEL 5.8 Modelling dlc_li by OLS

The Sample is 1958 (2) to 1975 (4) less 0 Forecasts

VARI	COEF	STD ERR	H.C.S.E.	t–VALUE
lc_li 1	−.02302	.02786	.02851	**−.82622**

$\sigma = .04146$ F(1, 70) = .68 DW = 2.891
RSS = .12035 for 1 Variable and 71 Observations

Unrestricted *ADF* model

MODEL 5.9 Modelling lcons by OLS

The Sample is 1958 (1) to 1975 (4) less 0 Forecasts

VARI	COEF	STD ERR	t–VALUE
lc 1	.03053	13112	.2328
lc 2	.01394	.1054	.1322
lc 3	.07911	.10182	.7769
lc 4	.70831	.10461	6.771
lc 5	.07467	.12669	.5893
li	.29710	.04499	6.604
li 1	.16266	.06215	2.616
li 2	−.0466	.05543	−.842
li 3	.04847	.05361	.9041
li 4	−.1640	.05714	−2.87
li 5	−.2093	.06304	−3.32
inf	−.2934	.09007	−3.25
inf 1	.17256	.09829	1.755

INCPT	.06620	.18601	.3559
Q1	−.0364	.01573	−2.31
Q2	−.0147	.01169	−1.26
Q3	−.0211	0.0154	−1.37

$R^2 = 0.9999$ $\sigma = .0075$ $F(16, 54) = 1686.84$ DW = 2.211
RSS = .00217 for 17 Variables and 71 Observations

Long run relation used for deriving the error correction mechanism

Solved STATIC LONG RUN Equation

lc	=	.943 li	−	1.294 inf +		.708
S.E.		(.18)		(1.29)		(1.3)

	−.390 Q1	−	.158 Q2 −		.226Q3
	(.47)		(.22)		(.29)

WALD Test $Chi^2(6) = $ 192339.613

Augmented Dickey–Fuller test for cointegration of $cons_t$, inc_t, and inf_t with the estimated cointegrating vector

MODEL 5.10 Modelling decm by OLS

The Sample is 1958 (2) to 1975 (4) less 0 Forecasts

VARI	COEF	STD ERR	H.C.S.E.	t–VALUE
decm 1	−.2389	.09859	.10086	−2.4239
decm 2	−.2419	.09499	.08471	−2.5468
decm 3	−.2684	.09437	.07917	−2.8444
decm 4	.71314	.09576	.08127	7.44741
ECM 1	−.03	.03518	.03316	<u>−.89278</u>

$\sigma = .0298$ $F(5, 62) = 710.56$ DW = 1.930
RSS = .05532 for 5 Variables and 67 Observations

5.9   Suggestions for Further Reading

Problems of spurious regression and correlation have been recognized since the early days of statistics. A new perspective to these problems has been given by Granger and Newbold (1974, 1986). Desai (1981, Chapter 3) discusses spurious correlation within the general framework of testing economic theories. A thorough approach to this problem is highly complicated and formal (see Phillips (1986), or Stock and Watson (1988)). Methodological aspects of the lack of stationarity of variables in an econometric model are discussed by Charemza (1990b) and Nelson and Kang (1981). A useful and wide–ranging account of stochastic processes is that provided by Spanos (1986, Chapter 8).

For integration analysis (unit root testing) the seminal papers are those of Dickey and Fuller (1979, 1981) and, for the Durbin–Watson integration statistic, that by Sargan and Bhargava (1983). A more general model is discussed by Said and Dickey (1984). The first critical values for the *DF* and *ADF* tests were given by Fuller (1976), where a detailed statistical introduction to the problem of unit root analysis can be found. Dickey and Pantula (1987) suggested a step–by–step algorithm which might be useful for determining the proper order of differencing of an integrated series. The widely known example of the empirical testing of stochastic and deterministic trends is that provided by Nelson and Plosser (1982) and a more sophisticated one has been provided by Perron (1989).

The foundations for cointegration analysis were given by Engle and Granger (1987), although their ideas had been known about since 1984, due to conference and discussion papers. Since 1986, the number of publications in this field has been growing rapidly. There were special issues of the journals *Oxford Bulletin of Economics and Statistics* (1986) and *Journal of Economic Dynamics and Control* (1988) devoted exclusively to the problems of cointegration. From the numerous publications now available one might note the following. Applications of cointegration analysis which are relatively easy to read and follow can be found in the special issue of the *Oxford Bulletin of Economics and Statistics* (1986) mentioned above. Other applications are by Miller (1988) and Taylor (1988). The link between cointegration and error correction mechanisms is discussed in Mills (1990, pp. 273–274), and in Cuthbertson, Hall and Taylor (1992, pp. 133–134)). An interesting extension to the Engle–Granger two–step procedure is given by Engle and Yoo (1987) and an alternative by Wickens and Breusch (1988). Some theory and analysis of seasonal integration and cointegration can be found in Osborn *et al.* (1988), Engle, Granger and Hallman (1989), Kunst (1989, 1990) and Hylleberg *et al.* (1990). Problems of seasonality and unit roots are also discussed in Franses (1990), Ghysels (1990) and Ghysels and Perron (1990); note, however, that at the time of writing, all these papers were unpublished. Selected papers on cointegration are published in the volume edited by Engle and Granger (1991). Developments of statistical inference into cointegration are available in Park and Phillips (1988, 1989), Phillips (1988b) and Phillips and Ouliaris (1990). There is also a developed cointegration analysis within the vector autoregressive approach. This will be analysed in Chapter 6.

Chapter 6

Vector Autoregression: Forecasting, Causality and Cointegration

6.1   A Reconsideration of Structural Modelling

The previous chapters of this book have been directed towards the modelling of a single economic phenomenon which could be described by a single equation, with a single dependent variable. In this chapter (and also in Chapter 7) we will outline some problems and approaches of econometric modelling in situations where one is dealing with relationships described by a system of more than one equation. Before considering some relatively new approaches to multiple equation econometric modelling, it will be useful briefly to reconsider the traditional structural (Cowles Commission) method of constructing such models.

Structural multi–equation modelling is described in, for example, Goldberger (1964), Dhrymes (1978) or Johnston (1984) and only the central ideas will be outlined here. We will illustrate the main features of traditional structural multi–equation modelling by the use of two equation models, used widely in the literature. The first of these models is a simple Keynesian model, in which the Absolute Income Hypothesis (see Chapter 3) is complemented by an identity which defines the formation of income in a closed economy:

$$C_t = \alpha + \beta Y_t + \epsilon_t, \qquad (6.1a)$$
$$Y_t = C_t + I_t, \qquad (6.1b)$$

where C_t stands for the level of aggregate consumption, Y_t is aggregate income, I_t is the level of investment, ϵ_t is an error term and α and β are coefficients. Completing the Absolute

172

Income Hypothesis by the equilibrium condition (6.1b) that saving is equal to investment has an important consequence for the entire process of model estimation and use. Let us first make an *ad hoc* intuitive analysis of the effect of a sudden unexpected change in C_t through a change in ϵ_t. From (6.1a) it is clear that, for instance, a rise in ϵ_t causes a rise in C_t. At the same time a rise in C_t must also change Y_t through (6.1b). Hence, in the system of equations (6.1a — 6.1b), it is not possible to change C_t without causing Y_t to change. Similarly, it is not possible to change Y_t without affecting C_t. It is, however, possible to affect C_t and Y_t by a change in I_t but not the other way round; one may change C_t and Y_t and leave I_t intact. Consequently, the variables C_t and Y_t in the system of equations (6.1a — 6.1b) are described as the *endogenous* variables (values determined within the system) whilst I_t is called an *exogenous* variable (its value is determined outside of the system). The endogenous variables are also described as being *jointly dependent* variables. It is usual to make a distinction between exogenous and lagged endogenous variables, despite the fact that the values of both can be considered as having been determined already for any time period of interest. Exogenous and lagged endogenous variables together make up what are described as the *predetermined* variables in a system. The distinction between the types of variable appearing in a multiple equation system is in sharp contrast with single equation structural modelling, where little attention is paid to the problem of endo–exogenous division of variables. Usually, what is on the left–hand side of a single equation structural model is simply treated as endogenous and what is on the right–hand side is treated as exogenous.

The observed simultaneity of C_t and Y_t has an important consequence for the entire process of econometric modelling. It is easy to show that in (6.1a) the right–hand side variable

Y_t is correlated with the error term ϵ_t. This can be demonstrated by solving the system of equations (6.1a − 6.1b) for the endogenous variables:

$$C_t = \beta^* \alpha + \beta^* \beta I_t + \beta^* \epsilon_t , \tag{6.2a}$$
$$Y_t = \beta^* \alpha + \beta^* I_t + \beta^* \epsilon_t , \tag{6.2b}$$

where $\beta^* = \dfrac{1}{1 - \beta}$. Clearly, Y_t is directly related to the error term, ϵ_t.

A structural model solved for the endogenous variables as functions of the predetermined variables only, like (6.2a − 6.2b), is usually called the *reduced form* of the model. However, to clarify what is to come, we will call a system of equations like (6.2a − 6.2b) a *restricted reduced form* and abbreviate, if necessary, as *RRF*. Coefficients of an *RRF* are often denoted as π_{11} , π_{12} , π_{21} , etc., so that in this notation, the restricted reduced form of (6.2a − 6.2b) would be written as:

$$C_t = \pi_{11} + \pi_{12} I_t + v_{1t} , \tag{6.2c}$$
$$Y_t = \pi_{21} + \pi_{22} I_t + v_{2t} . \tag{6.2d}$$

If (6.2a − 6.2b) and (6.2c − 6.2d) are compared, it can be seen that the form in which the coefficients enter into the former imply certain restrictions on the parameters in the latter, more general, notation. In this case, the restrictions are that $\pi_{11} = \pi_{21}$, and $(\pi_{22} - \pi_{12}) = 1$. The second restriction follows from noting that the coefficient on variable I_t in (6.2a) is β times the coefficient on I_t in (6.2b), and that β^* is a function of β.

It will be useful for what follows to note that knowledge of the true (not estimated) values of the restricted reduced form coefficients in (6.2c − 6.2d) would allow the coefficients in the original system (6.1a − 6.1b) to be retrieved.

Specifically, $\beta = \dfrac{\pi_{12}}{\pi_{22}}$ and $\alpha = \dfrac{\pi_{21}}{\pi_{22}}$. The possibility of retrieving the coefficients of the original model from knowledge of the values of the restricted reduced form coefficients is termed *the identification problem*. We will return to this problem shortly.

The *unrestricted reduced form* (*URF*) is the set of linear equations expressing the jointly dependent variables as functions of the predetermined variables only, with no restrictions on the values of the coefficients in these equations. For the case of equations (6.1a − 6.1b) this gives:

$$C_t = \pi_{11}^* + \pi_{12}^* I_t + \epsilon_{1t} , \qquad (6.3a)$$

$$Y_t = \pi_{21}^* + \pi_{22}^* I_t + \epsilon_{2t} , \qquad (6.3b)$$

where no restrictions are imposed on the parameters π_{11}^*, π_{12}^*, π_{21}^* and π_{22}^*.

The original system (6.1a − 6.1b) is called the *structural form* of the model. As was noted above, in this structural form the covariance between Y_t and ϵ_t is not zero. It follows from equation (6.2b) that $E(Y_t \epsilon_t) = \beta^* \sigma^2$, where σ^2 is the variance of ϵ_t. Consequently, equation (6.1a) cannot be consistently estimated by the ordinary least squares method, because the assumption that there is no correlation between the explanatory variable and the error term is violated. This fact, called *simultaneity bias* or *Haavelmo bias* (after the Cowles Commission member who first noted this problem) has been a persistent worry to structural modellers who, especially in the 1950s and 1960s, developed a great number of estimation methods to deal with this problem. One or more of these methods are thoroughly described in most textbooks of econometrics.

There is another problem of econometric inference in simultaneous equations structural models that was touched upon briefly above. This is the problem of the *identification* of structural parameters, that is the parameters which are present in the structural form of a model. Logically, this problem is prior to that of the estimation of the structural equations, in that estimation would not be sensible if the equation were not identified.

For example, consider a simple supply–demand system of two equations in which it is assumed that market clearing (equilibrium) is achieved in each period:

$$Q_t = \alpha_0 + \alpha_1 P_t + u_{1t}, \tag{6.4a}$$

$$Q_t = \beta_0 + \beta_1 P_t + u_{2t}. \tag{6.4b}$$

Here, equation (6.4a) represents a demand equation and (6.4b) a supply equation, Q_t is the quantity supplied and demanded of a good, and P_t is the price of the good. It is clear that the variables Q_t and P_t are jointly dependent, as were C_t and Y_t in (6.1a − 6.1b); one cannot change one of them independently of the other. Therefore, there is simultaneous equation bias in the system, since Q_t and P_t are correlated with both u_{1t} and u_{2t}. The model (6.4a − 6.4b) might be perfectly admissible from the point of view of economic theory, especially if we expect α_1 to be negative and β_1 to be positive. Nevertheless, intuition suggests that when it comes to estimation of the parameters α_0, α_1, β_0 and β_1 using two series of data for Q_t and P_t, something is wrong. How can we estimate four parameters from two series of data? Even, if we ignore the constant terms by, for instance, working with variables measured in deviations from their means, we are still left with two structural coefficients (α_1 and β_1) to be determined from the running of only one regression with a single explanatory (right–hand side) variable. If we run a regression of Q_t on P_t, how will we know whether the result is a demand equation, a supply equation or a mixture of both? In this case, the equations (6.4a − 6.4b), and hence the model, are said to be *not identified* or *underidentified*. Another way of seeing this is to note that it is not possible to recover the structural parameters α_0, α_1, β_0 and β_1 from knowledge of the *RRF* of the model, since the *RRF* contains only two coefficients and we have four structural parameters to determine. Even if we knew the true values of the restricted reduced form coefficients, there would be no way to determine or unscramble the values of the structural parameters from these known coefficients. This is in contrast to our result earlier for model (6.1a − 6.1b) which was identified, since knowing the four coefficients in the *RRF* (6.2a − 6.2b) it was possible to solve for the structural parameters α and β. Equations (6.4a − 6.4b) become identified if (on the grounds of economic theory) additional variables are added to the system, say an interest rate r_t to the demand equation and lagged price P_{t-1} to the supply equation. The model would then be given by:

$$Q_t = \alpha_0 + \alpha_1 P_t + \alpha_2 r_t + u_{1t}, \qquad (6.5a)$$
$$Q_t = \beta_0 + \beta_1 P_t + \beta_2 P_{t-1} + u_{2t}. \qquad (6.5b)$$

Note that in (6.5a − 6.5b) the division between endogenous and exogenous variables no longer corresponds with that of jointly dependent and predetermined variables. The jointly dependent (simultaneous) variables are still Q_t and P_t, but the predetermined variables are divided into the *lagged dependent* variables (in this case, just the one, P_{t-1}) and the *exogenous* variables (again, just one in this case, r_t). The structural parameters in (6.5a − 6.5b) are identified, since it is possible to solve for the structural parameters from knowledge of the values of the restricted reduced form coefficients of the model. Stewart and Wallis (1981, pp. 78–86) provide details of such a solution.

Structural models may be presented using matrix notation (see, for example, Goldberger (1964, Chapter 7) or Judge *et al.* (1985, Chapter 14)) as:

$$y_t' \Gamma + x_t' B = u_t', \qquad (6.6)$$

where y_t' is a $(1 \times M)$ row vector of the observations at time t on the M jointly dependent variables, Γ is an $(M \times M)$ matrix of structural coefficients of the current jointly dependent (or endogenous) variables, x_t' is a $(1 \times H)$ row vector of the observations at time t on the H predetermined variables, B is an $H \times M$ matrix of coefficients on the predetermined variables, and u_t' is a $(1 \times M)$ row vector of disturbance terms. If lagged dependent variables are to be distinguished from the exogenous variables, the model may be written as:

$$y_t' \Gamma + x_t^{*\prime} B_0 + \sum_{i=1}^{k} y_{t-i}' B_i = u_t', \qquad (6.7)$$

where k is the maximum lag length entertained for any of the endogenous variables. In this notation, $x_t^{*\prime}$ stands for the vector of observations on the exogenous rather than the predetermined variables at time t. For the sake of simplicity, we have assumed that there are no lagged exogenous variables in the model. If there were, either they could be simply included in the set of exogenous variables, or if a separate treatment of them was required, another set of terms on the lines of those introduced for the lagged endogenous variables could be introduced into (6.7).

For model (6.1a − 6.1b), the matrices Γ and B are:

$$\Gamma = \begin{bmatrix} 1 & -1 \\ -\beta & 1 \end{bmatrix}, \qquad B = \begin{bmatrix} \alpha & 0 \\ 0 & 1 \end{bmatrix}.$$

For model (6.4a – 6.4b) these matrices are:

$$\Gamma = \begin{bmatrix} 1 & 1 \\ -\alpha_1 & -\beta_1 \end{bmatrix} \quad , \qquad B = [\ -\alpha_0 \ \ -\beta_0] \ ,$$

and for model (6.5a – 6.5b):

$$\Gamma = \begin{bmatrix} 1 & 1 \\ -\alpha_1 & -\beta_1 \end{bmatrix} \quad , \qquad B = \begin{bmatrix} -\alpha_0 & -\beta_0 \\ -\alpha_2 & 0 \\ 0 & -\beta_2 \end{bmatrix} \ .$$

In model (6.5a – 6.5b) there is a lagged dependent variable. We may therefore split the set of predetermined variables into lagged endogenous (P_{t-1}) and exogenous (the intercept term and r_t) variables. The matrices of the parameters of (6.5a – 6.5b) in the form of equation (6.7) become:

$$\Gamma = \begin{bmatrix} 1 & 1 \\ -\alpha_1 & -\beta_1 \end{bmatrix} \ , \ B_0 = \begin{bmatrix} -\alpha_0 & -\beta_0 \\ -\alpha_2 & 0 \end{bmatrix} \ , \ B_1 = [\ 0 \ \ -\beta_2] \ .$$

For equations (6.6), the restricted reduced form can be obtained by solving the matrix equation with respect to the variables in x_t:

$$y'_t = -x'_t \Pi + V_t \ , \tag{6.8}$$

where $\Pi = B\Gamma^{-1}$, and $V_t = u'_t \Gamma^{-1}$. Analogously, for a model in the notation of equation (6.7), the *RRF* is defined as:

$$y'_t = -x^{*'}_t \Pi_0 - \sum_{i=1}^{k} y'_{t-i} \Pi_i + V_t,$$

where $\Pi_i = B_i \Gamma^{-1}$, $i = 0, 1, \ldots, k$. The form of equations (6.6) and (6.8) indicates the restrictive nature of the identification problem in structural modelling. If a model is to be identified, it must be possible to recover the matrices of structural parameters Γ and B from the equation $\Pi = B\Gamma^{-1}$. Clearly, in general this is not possible. Intuitively, identification is more likely if the matrix Π contains a lot of zero elements or, more precisely, if the matrices Γ and B have zero elements in particular rows and columns. In structural econometrics, the existence of a zero element in the matrix Γ or B means that a *zero restriction* has been imposed for a particular variable. For instance, for model (6.5a − 6.5b), in matrix B we have zeros as elements {3, 1} and {2, 2}. This means that we know *a priori* that the variable P_{t-1} does not appear in the demand equation and the variable r_t does not appear in the supply equation. It is easy to check that without these restrictions model (6.5a − 6.5b) is not identified. Also, in order to identify parameters of endogenous and exogenous variables, it is necessary to establish prior to any econometric investigation which variable belongs to the set of the endogenous and which to the set of exogenous variables. In other words, the *endo–exogenous division* of the variables in a model has to be imposed. The technical 'order and rank' conditions which provide necessary and sufficient conditions for the identification of an equation in a simultaneous equation system are given in most econometric theory textbooks, and will not be pursued here.

6.2 Principles of Vector Autoregressive Modelling

Structural econometrics, and especially multi–equation modelling, attracted a lot of attention during the 1950s and 1960s. Theoretical advancements were mainly concerned with the development of estimation methods which took account of the 'simultaneous equation bias' that resulted from the correlation of error terms with some of the explanatory variables in an equation. Applications of multi–equation modelling were focused on the building of large and complicated models of economies, in some cases containing several thousand endogenous variables, which were used for forecasting and policy analysis. As was noted in Chapter 1, these models did not perform very well, and this sparked off widespread criticism of structural econometric modelling. As far as single equation models are concerned, the main cause of concern seems to be the practice of data mining (see Chapter 2). For multi–equation modelling, criticism has been mainly directed towards the assumption of zero restrictions and the endo–exogenous division of the variables.

The questioning of the role of zero restrictions imposed in order to achieve identification of a model started over thirty years ago (see Liu (1960)). The danger is that models may be formulated and estimated with some variables added to equations without much economic justification and other variables deleted (that is, zero restrictions imposed), in order to achieve identification. For instance, model (6.4a − 6.4b) may be perfectly supported by economic theory. Nevertheless this theory will never have any econometric confirmation because it is not identified. An investigator might be tempted to add extra, different variables to each equation, merely to satisfy the identification of each equation, even if the economic justification for such variables was weak.

The theoretical restrictions imposed on structural simultaneous equation models were viewed as 'incredible' in a seminal paper by Sims (1980), where the basis for the new methodology of vector autoregressive modelling was first formulated. The principal differences of the Sims modelling methodology from those formulated in the Cowles Commission structural approach are the following:

1. There is no *a priori* endo–exogenous division of variables;
2. No zero restrictions are imposed;
3. There is no strict (and prior to modelling) economic theory within which the model is grounded.

The above principles are quite revolutionary and have far reaching consequences. No zero restrictions and no specified exogenous variables means that the identification problem becomes ill defined. Principle 3 is in fact a consequence of the other two: if there is no variable excluded from any equation of a model and nothing is exogenous, it means that everything causes everything else and there is no room for assuming anything more than very general economic principles as a starting point. This is why the Sims methodology is often called by its critics *atheoretical macroeconometrics*. The standard defence of Sims' position is from an examination of the economist's example of a consumer maximizing his/her lifetime utility function. There is literally no variable which may not enter the consumer's demand and labour supply functions and there is no *a priori* reason to exclude any of them. It has to be stressed, however, that these 'atheoretical' postulates are regarded as testable hypotheses. It is shown later that further inference in a Sims type model may lead to a model form which is consistent with even highly detailed economic theories.

The starting point of modelling in the Sims methodology is the formulation of a *general (unrestricted) vector autoregressive (VAR) model*. As its name implies, this consists in regressing each current (non–lagged) variable in the model on all the variables in the model lagged a certain number of times. In order to stress the difference from structural modelling, suppose that we wish to develop a *VAR* alternative to the structural dynamic model described in matrix form by (6.7), that is a model containing vectors of current and lagged endogenous variables y_t, y_{t-1}, ..., y_{t-k} and current exogenous variables x_t^*. For *VAR* modelling, this division is not relevant and it is also not relevant that there are no lagged exogenous variables. The unrestricted *VAR* alternative to model (6.7) can be described as:

$$Z_t = \sum_{i=1}^{k} A_i Z_{t-i} + \mathcal{E}_t, \qquad (6.9)$$

where
$$Z_t = \begin{bmatrix} y_t \\ x_t^* \end{bmatrix}$$

is a column vector of observations on the current values of all the variables in the model. $\mathcal{E}_t$ is a column vector of random errors, usually assumed to be contemporaneously correlated but not autocorrelated so that it has a non–diagonal covariance matrix. The matrices A_i do not contain any zero elements. There is some resemblance of (6.9) with the reduced form of a structural econometric model. In fact (6.9) constitutes an unrestricted reduced form of a structural model (in the sense defined in the previous section) for the case where there are no exogenous variables, that is where in (6.7) all elements in the B_0 matrix are zeros.

Since the *VAR* model involves only lagged variables on its right–hand side, and since these variables by definition are not correlated with the error term (assuming no autocorrelation), it can be consistently estimated, equation by equation, by ordinary least squares. However, since the multivariate error term $\mathcal{E}_t$ was assumed above to have a non–diagonal covariance matrix, it would be natural to consider applying multivariate regression (or seemingly unrelated regressions) rather than ordinary least squares, in order to take account explicitly of the non–zero covariances of the error terms. In fact, as no restrictions are placed on the coefficients in (6.9), the multivariate least squares estimators are no more efficient than those of ordinary least squares (Harvey (1989, p.72)).

Often, particular equations in a general *VAR* model are completed by an additional set of deterministic components, such as intercept terms, deterministic trends and seasonal dummy variables. Also, the existence of stochastic trends (see Chapter 5) may be accommodated by allowing variables integrated of a given order to enter the *VAR* model after appropriate differencing. Harvey, (1989, pp. 469–470), however, points out some difficulties with this if different series have different orders of integration. In addition, it is possible to allow for time varying elements in A_i by formulating the *VAR* model recursively and to impose some *a priori* knowledge concerning the variability of elements in A_i by assuming Bayesian priors. These types of inference are, however, beyond the scope of this book (for more information see the suggestions for further reading in Section 6.7).

One straightforward application of an unrestricted *VAR* model is for forecasting. A *VAR* forecaster does not worry about the economic theory underlying his or her *VAR* model and, more importantly, does not need to make any assumptions about the values of exogenous variables in the forecasting period. This is in contrast with standard econometric forecasting where forecasts have to be conditioned upon knowledge of exogenous variables.

For instance, suppose a single equation model, say:

$$y_t = \alpha x_t + \xi_t \, ,$$

is estimated for the period $t = 1, 2,..., T$ and is to be used by an econometrician for *ex ante* forecasting for the period $t = T+1,..., T^*$. Provided that the structural coefficient α is unchanged in the forecast period and that the model is an appropriate formulation of the way in which y_t is generated, an unbiased forecast of y_t, say y_t^f, for a period t between $T+1$ and T^* is:

$$y_t^f = \alpha x_t \, ,$$

that is, it is conditional on the information concerning x_t, the value of the exogenous variable in the forecast period. Quite evidently, the future data for x_t are not known, and it would be necessary to make some predictions concerning x_t and condition the forecast on these predictions rather than on the true but unknown values of x_t. Hence, the forecast of y_t will be heavily dependent on the predictions of x_t. In a *VAR* model, however, the problem of conditioning a forecast on an exogenous variable does not exist, since there are no exogenous variables.

If the contemporaneous correlation between the errors of the equations is ignored, a forecast in a *VAR* model can be made in a quite mechanical way. For the first forecast period, the forecasts in (6.9) are made conditional on the last observed values of the variables, as:

$$Z^f_{T+1} = \sum_{i=1}^{k} A_i Z_{T-i+1},$$

and for the later periods recursively or sequentially, conditionally on the forecasts computed for periods for which true values are unknown. That is, in general:

$$Z^f_{T+j} = \sum_{i=1}^{k} A_i Z^f_{T+j-i},$$

where:

$$Z^f_{T+j-i} = \begin{cases} Z^f_{T+j-i} & \text{for } j > i \\ Z_{T+j-i} & \text{for } j \leq i \end{cases}.$$

In practice, it is not possible to avoid imposing some prior restrictions on a *VAR* system. There is always some limit on the number of variables which can be included in a *VAR* model as well as on the maximum number of lags. If we have, for instance, a system of six variables and we wish to impose five lags on each variable, the total number of regressors in each equation would be 30. This could make the entire modelling process impossible if we have only a small data sample. It may happen, then, that some variables have to be excluded prior to modelling. Especially important here is the choice of the appropriate length of the lags to be used. Whilst some quite sophisticated procedures for making this choice have been proposed (for example, see Hsiao (1979, 1981)), it seems of particular importance to establish the maximum lag length in relation to the possible existence of autocorrelation in the disturbances. Since a *VAR* model contains lagged dependent variables as regressors, autocorrelation of error terms can be very serious in that it may lead to inconsistent estimates of parameters if ordinary least squares or multivariate least squares methods are used for estimation. However, as was indicated in Chapter 5 where the role of augmentation for the Dickey–Fuller test was discussed, lagged dependent variables may provide a good approximation to an autoregressive process in the error terms. Hence an intuitive guide to establishing the best lag length in a *VAR* model is to choose such a k in (6.9) which results in estimated model residuals without significant autocorrelation.

An essential, but sometimes overlooked feature of a *VAR* model is that the multivariate error term in (6.9), ε_t , contains nonzero covariances. This feature allows the formulation of 'structural' alternatives to Cowles Commission type models, consistent with a particular economic theory and applicable for economic policy analysis.

In an attempt to make the interpretation of policy analysis in a *VAR* model more straightforward, it has become common practice to transform the model into one having 'orthogonal innovations'; that is to transform the model so that the error terms are no longer contemporaneously correlated. This may be illustrated by an example of a simple *VAR* model containing two variables x_t and y_t and two lags, so:

$$\begin{bmatrix} x_t \\ y_t \end{bmatrix} = \begin{bmatrix} a_1 & b_1 \\ c_1 & d_1 \end{bmatrix} \begin{bmatrix} x_{t-1} \\ y_{t-1} \end{bmatrix} + \begin{bmatrix} a_2 & b_2 \\ c_2 & d_2 \end{bmatrix} \begin{bmatrix} x_{t-2} \\ y_{t-2} \end{bmatrix} + \begin{bmatrix} \epsilon_{1t} \\ \epsilon_{2t} \end{bmatrix} \quad (6.10)$$

where the error terms are contemporaneously correlated, that is $E(\epsilon_{1t}) = E(\epsilon_{2t}) = 0$; $E(\epsilon_{1t}^2) = \sigma_{11}$; $E(\epsilon_{2t}^2) = \sigma_{22}$; $E(\epsilon_{1t} \cdot \epsilon_{2t}) = \sigma_{12}$. In order to obtain a model in which the error terms are contemporaneously uncorrelated we may multiply the first row of (6.10) by $\delta = \sigma_{12}/\sigma_{11}$ and subtract the result from the second row. The result is:

$$\begin{bmatrix} x_t \\ y_t - \delta x_t \end{bmatrix} = \begin{bmatrix} a_1 & b_1 \\ c_1^* & d_1^* \end{bmatrix} \begin{bmatrix} x_{t-1} \\ y_{t-1} \end{bmatrix} + \begin{bmatrix} a_2 & b_2 \\ c_2^* & d_2^* \end{bmatrix} \begin{bmatrix} x_{t-2} \\ y_{t-2} \end{bmatrix} + \begin{bmatrix} \epsilon_{1t} \\ \epsilon_{2t}^* \end{bmatrix},$$
$$(6.11)$$

where:
$$c_i^* = (c_i - \delta a_i) ; \quad d_i^* = (d_i - \delta b_i) ; \quad \epsilon_{2t}^* = (\epsilon_{2t} - \delta \epsilon_{1t}) , \, i = 1, 2 .$$

In (6.11) the error terms ϵ_{1t} and ϵ_{2t}^* are uncorrelated, since:

$$E(\epsilon_{1t} \cdot \epsilon_{2t}^*) = E(\epsilon_{1t} (\epsilon_{2t} - \delta \epsilon_{1t}))$$
$$= E((\epsilon_{1t} \cdot \epsilon_{2t}) - (\sigma_{12}/\sigma_{11}) E(\epsilon_{1t}^2))$$
$$= \sigma_{12} - \sigma_{12} = 0 .$$

As in general the σ_{ij} are unknown, sample values obtained from the residuals of the *VAR* equation estimates will be needed for further analysis. The idea behind making the error terms in (6.11) orthogonal to each other is to enable the equations which form (6.11) to be used separately for policy analysis. In this context, policy analysis refers to the impact of a known random shock on the system. One problem with such analysis is that the results may be sensitive to the ordering of the *VAR* equations, and another is that it is difficult to give a sensible meaning to an orthogonal innovation (see Darnell and Evans (1990, pp. 120–123) or Cooley and LeRoy (1985, pp. 301–303)). In practice, it may be possible to decide on the ordering of the equations following the application of a series of *causality tests* of the type developed in the next section.

In matrix notation, 'orthogonal innovations' may be obtained from (6.9) by multiplying it by the triangular matrix ϕ with units on the main diagonal such that:

$$D = \phi \cdot \Sigma \cdot \phi' \, ,$$

where D is a diagonal matrix and Σ is the covariance matrix of the multivariate error term $\mathcal{E}_t$. Hence, the *VAR* model becomes:

$$\phi \cdot Z_t = \phi \cdot \sum_{i=1}^{k} A_i Z_{t-i} + \mathcal{N}_t \, , \qquad (6.12)$$

where $\mathcal{N}_t = \phi \cdot \mathcal{E}_t$. It can be shown that the random variables which constitute $\mathcal{N}_t$ are orthogonal to each other, so that $E(\mathcal{N}_t \mathcal{N}'_t) = I$ where I is an identity matrix (see Johnston (1984, pp. 143–147)).

For large *VAR* systems, the procedure described above can be difficult since construction of the matrix ϕ can be awkward and may require special ordering algorithms.

6.3   Causality Inference

The general (unrestricted) *VAR* model containing a large number of estimated coefficients can usually be reduced in size by eliminating those coefficients for which the hypothesis that they are jointly equal to zero cannot be rejected (see

Chapter 4 for a description of the Likelihood Ratio, Lagrange Multiplier and Wald tests for such hypotheses). In some situations, testing for zero coefficients can lead to economically relevant results. Often, testing zero restrictions in a *VAR* model is made within the context of *causality analysis*.

The notion of causality (and also of causal relations and causal ordering) is essentially a philosophical rather than an empirical matter. Philosophers do not agree on their understanding and definition of *a cause* and *outcome*. Theories vary from an extreme 'everything causes everything' (Democrit) to denying the existence of any causation whatsoever (Hume, Berkeley). Usually in modern philosophy the meaning of 'causation' is close to 'force' or 'produce'. In empirical econometrics the need for defining 'causality' is clear. One simply wants to know whether an increase of prices results in wages increasing when otherwise they would not have altered, or whether the relation works in the opposite direction, so that it is an increase of wages that results in an increase of prices. Consequently, there is a need to establish an operational and testable definition of causality. In econometrics, causality has a meaning more on the lines of 'to predict' rather than 'to produce'. Nevertheless, philosophical definitions have important influences on statistical counterparts. In particular, there are three important features of contemporary notions of causality. The first two may be summarized as:

1. 'instantaneous causation' does not exist, since there is always a time difference between independent actions,
2. for similar reasons, there is no such thing as 'simultaneous causation'.

In practice, however, it is necessary to speak about 'instantaneous' and 'simultaneous' causation simply because we are unable to maintain continuous observation and we can only analyse data related to a particular time interval or moment. The notion that 'x causes y and simultaneously y causes x' is nothing but a simplification; due to discontinuity of observations, we are unable to define the cause and outcome. The third notion can be stated as:

3. The future cannot 'cause' the present. This is perhaps the most straightforward of the features of the contemporary concept of causality and, as is shown below, plays an important role in testing for the presence of a causal relation.

In econometrics the most widely used *operational definition* of causality is that the *Wiener–Granger* or *Granger definition of causality* (see Granger (1969)). It can be formulated in a simplified way as follows:

Definition:
x is a *Granger cause* of y (denoted as $x \rightarrow y$), if present y can be predicted with better accuracy by using *past* values of x rather than by not doing so, other information being identical.

This definition can be extended to *instantaneous causation*, denoted as $x => y$. Instantaneous causation exists if present y can be predicted better by using *present and past* values of x, *ceteris paribus*. The concepts of Granger causality and Granger instantaneous causality between two variables may be defined in a more formal way. Let us introduce the following notation:

U_t – the set of all past and present information existing at time t;

X_t –the set of all past and present information on a variable x existing at time t, that is $X_t = \{x_1, x_2, ..., x_t\}$. Evidently, X_t is a subset of U_t, or (since we may have more information than just for a single variable):

$$X_t \in U_t ;$$

y_t – the current value of a variable y $(y_t \subset U_t)$;

$\tilde{y}_t$ – an unbiased prediction of y_t.

With the use of the above notation, the definitions can be formulated as:

Granger causality:

if $MSE(\tilde{y}_t|\ U_{t-1}) < MSE(\tilde{y}_t|\ U_{t-1} \backslash X_{t-1})$ then $x \rightarrow y$,

Granger instantaneous causality:

if $MSE(\tilde{y}_t|\ U_t \backslash y_t) < MSE(\tilde{y}_t|\ U_t \backslash X_t, y_t)$ then $x \Rightarrow y$,

where *MSE* stands for the mean square error of prediction and " | " and " \ " are the conventional logical operators; that is " $A\ |\ B$ " means 'A conditional on B' and " $A \backslash B$ " means 'all elements of A which are not B' (if $B \subset A$).

In the above definitions, there is the rather vague notion of *all information*. Since the set of *all information* is not well defined, it is up to a researcher to decide which information to use, and which to ignore. Hence, for practical purposes, the notion of 'all information' has to be replaced by 'all relevant information', and which information is 'relevant' is always arbitrary.

To make progress, let us assume that 'all relevant information' is that which is included in an econometric model. The model may also include 'irrelevant information' and hence we may suppose that a general unrestricted *VAR* may be suitable for our purpose. In light of the above definitions, the problem of testing whether $x \rightarrow y$ reduces to a question of whether x can be eliminated from that part of a *VAR* model which describes y. In the literature on this subject, various tests for causality which use this principle have been proposed. We describe two of the most widely used tests below. These tests are complements rather than substitutes for each other.

The first of these tests, which is called a *Granger* test, is a straightforward and simple modification suggested by Sargent (1976) of the test originally suggested by Granger (1969). Consider an equation describing y_t in an unrestricted bivariate *VAR* model, that is one describing relations between two variables, x and y. This equation may be written as:

$$y_t = A_0 D_t + \sum_{j=1}^{k} \alpha_j y_{t-j} + \sum_{j=1}^{k} \beta_j x_{t-j} + \epsilon_t , \qquad (6.13)$$

where $A_0 D_t$ denotes the deterministic (non–stochastic) part of the equation (intercept, deterministic trend, seasonals, etc.). If $\beta_1 = \beta_2 = ... = \beta_k = 0$ then, in light of the above definition, x does not Granger cause y. A straightforward test for testing the restriction $\beta_1 = \beta_2 = ... = \beta_k = 0$ would be an F test or the Lagrange Multiplier *LM* test. For equation (6.13), the hypothesis $\beta_1 = \beta_2 = ... = \beta_k = 0$ can be tested by the *LM* test in the following way:

1. Regress y_t on all the deterministic components of (6.13) and on $y_{t-1}, ... , y_{t-k}$;
2. Compute the residuals of the above regression, denoted by u_t^*;
3. Regress u_t^* on the entire set of explanatory variables which appear in (6.13), that is the variables used in step 1 and additionally $x_{t-1}, ..., x_{t-k}$;
4. Calculate the coefficient of determination for the above regression, say R_0^2;
5. Test the hypothesis by one of the following Lagrange multiplier statistics:

$$LM = T \cdot R_0^2 ,$$

which under the null has a $\chi^2(k)$ distribution, or:

$$LMF = \frac{T - h}{k} \cdot \frac{R_0^2}{1 - R_0^2} \,,$$

which under the null hypothesis has an $F(k, (T - h))$ distribution (T is the sample size and h is the number of variables in (6.13) including those for the variables in D_t). As has been mentioned in Chapter 4, it is normally preferable to use the *LMF* rather than the *LM* statistic.

The second of the causality tests described here has its origins in a paper by Sims (1972) who cleverly used the feature of the general concept of causality that the future cannot cause the present. The test was developed by Geweke, Meese and Dent (1983) and is called here the Sims–GMD test. Suppose, as before, that we wish to test whether x is a Granger cause for y (in our notation $x \to y$). Instead of equation (6.13), consider the following equation explaining x_t:

$$x_t = A_0 D_t + \sum_{j=1}^{k} \gamma_j x_{t-j} + \sum_{j=-m}^{k} \delta_j y_{t-j} + v_t. \qquad (6.14)$$

Equation (6.14) looks like the part of a *VAR* model describing x_t, apart from the fact that it contains *leading* values of y_t; note the negative lower summation limit for the variable y_{t-j} which means that in equation (6.14), the variables y_{t+1}, y_{t+2} ,..., y_{t+m} appear as well as lagged values of y_t ($j = 0$ must be excluded from the summation of the y_{t-j} terms). Evidently, if the coefficients of the leading ys are all zeros, that is if $\delta_{-1} = \delta_{-2} = ... = \delta_{-m} = 0$, we have a typical *VAR* equation for x_t.

But what if the hypothesis that $\delta_{-1} = \delta_{-2} = ... = \delta_{-m} = 0$ is rejected? Since the future cannot cause the present, future *y*s cannot cause the current *x*. Indeed, a necessary condition for *x* not to cause *y* is that the leading y_t terms in equation (6.14) have zero coefficients (see Greenberg and Webster (1983, pp. 149–151)). Thus the logical conclusion of finding nonzero coefficients on leading y_t terms, that is if $\delta_{-1}, \delta_{-2}, ..., \delta_{-m}$ are not jointly equal to zero, is that *x is a Granger cause for y*.

The technique for computing the Lagrange Multiplier test in this case is analogous to that described for the Granger test. The 'omitted variables' are now leading *y*s , y_{t+1} , $y_{t+2}, ..., y_{t+m}$:

1. Regress x_t on all the explanatory variables in equation (6.14) with the exception of $y_{t+1}, y_{t+2}, ..., y_{t+m}$;
2. Calculate residuals v_t^* ;
3. Regress v_t^* on the full set of explanatory variables, inclusive of $y_{t+1}, y_{t+2}, ..., y_{t+m}$;
4. Compute the coefficient of determination of the above regression;
5. Using this coefficient of determination, compute the *LM* or *LMF* statistic, as described above.

It is difficult to say which of these two tests is better. Some Monte Carlo experiments (Guilkey and Salemi (1982)) show the Granger test to be superior. Also, the Sims–GMD test is more costly in terms of the loss of degrees of freedom, since for a given lag length there are more parameters to estimate (we also have leading variables in this case) and the number of observations used for estimation is smaller, since observations for the most recent periods of time are taken by the leading variables. Nevertheless, because of the different philosophical background of the tests, it seems advisable to use both rather than to choose one of them.

It should be stressed that these tests are strictly appropriate only where the variables are stationar͜ʸ. For nonstationary variables they are valid only approximately or, in some cases, may not be valid at all (see Lütkepohl (1991, p.379)). It has been pointed out by Geweke (1984, pp. 1139–1140) that these causality tests may still be valid if the form of nonstationarity of the variables can be captured by the inclusion of deterministic trends and/or logarithmic transformations.

As with any other method of statistical modelling, the validity of the tests and their interpretation in a *VAR* model depends on a proper specification, so that all relevant information is included in the model. This specification would involve the absence of autocorrelation in the error terms, and might imply the need for prior filtering or prewhitening of the data series (see Vandaele (1983, Chapter 11) or Greenberg and Webster (1983, pp. 149–155)). If autocorrelation is present, the Lagrange Multiplier statistics do not have the required distributions. One way of tackling the problem of autocorrelated errors is to ensure that the lag length adopted in the *VAR* model is long enough to approximate the possible autocorrelation, although Granger and Newbold (1986, p.252) suggest that this practice can lead to disappointing forecasts. As with any statistical tests, causality tests have to be viewed with caution.

One area in which these causality tests have been widely used is in the testing of monetarist and Keynesian theories of income determination and inflation, some examples of which are included in the further reading at the end of this chapter.

6.4   Cointegration Inference

In this section we will outline the linkage of cointegration analysis with *VAR* modelling. This linkage gives cointegration analysis an entirely new dimension and allows the analysis to be applied in a more general way than that described in Chapter 5. However, the analysis becomes computationally (and also conceptually) more complicated. Because of this complexity, we present only an introductory and highly simplified account of cointegration inference in a *VAR* model.

Consider the unrestricted *VAR* model, introduced in Section 6.2:

$$Z_t = \sum_{i=1}^{k} A_i Z_{t-i} + \mathcal{E}_t, \qquad (6.9)$$

where Z_t contains all n variables of the model and $\mathcal{E}_t$ is a vector of random errors. We will use a straightforward vector generalization of the notation of integration and cointegration introduced in Chapter 5. The operator Δ in the expression of the type ΔW_t will denote first differencing of all the variables in a vector of variables W_t. Analogously, the notation $W_t \sim I(1)$ means that all the variables which constitute the vector of variables W_t are integrated of order one, that is their first differences are stationary. Notation '$W_t \sim CI(1, 1)$ with cointegrating vector γ' means that the linear combination $\gamma' W_t \sim I(0)$. There might be more than one cointegrating vector; vectors $\gamma_1, \gamma_2, ..., \gamma_l$ may constitute a matrix γ such that $\gamma' W_t \sim I(0)$.

We will assume throughout this section that all the variables in Z_t are integrated of the same order, and that this order of integration is either zero or one. This assumption is in fact not very restrictive. If some variables which are integrated of order higher than one are of interest, we may consider their appropriate differences, which themselves are integrated of order one, to be included in the *VAR* model. For simplicity, the deterministic part of the *VAR* model (intercepts, deterministic trends, seasonals, etc.) are excluded.

The *VAR* model (6.9) can also be represented in the form:

$$\Delta Z_t = \sum_{i=1}^{k-1} \Gamma_i \Delta Z_{t-i} + \Pi Z_{t-k} + \mathcal{E}_t, \qquad (6.15)$$

where:

$$\Gamma_i = -I + A_1 + \ldots + A_i \quad (I \text{ is a unit matrix}),$$

$$\Pi = -(I - A_1 - \ldots - A_k).$$

The equality of models (6.9) and (6.15) may be confirmed by adding Z_{t-1}, Z_{t-2},..., Z_{t-k} and $A_1 Z_{t-2}$, $A_2 Z_{t-3}$,..., $A_{k-1} Z_{t-k}$ to both sides of (6.9) and rearranging. We will call the transformation of a *VAR* model into the form of (6.15) a *cointegrating transformation*. (We are using notation consistent with that used in the literature on this subject. Please note, however, that in Section 6.1 the symbols Γ and Π have a different meaning from that here.)

We will focus our attention on matrix Π of (6.15) and particularly on its rank. Since there are n variables which constitute the vector Z_t, the dimension of Π is $n \times n$ and its rank can be at most equal to n. It follows from the *Granger Representation Theorem* (see Engle and Granger (1987), or Johansen (1989)) that under some general conditions:

(*i*)   If the rank of matrix Π is equal to n, that is equal to the total number of variables explained in the *VAR* model, the vector process Z_t is stationary (that is all the variables in Z_t are integrated of order zero);

(*ii*)   If the rank of matrix Π is equal to $r < n$, there exists a representation of Π such that:

$$\Pi = \alpha \cdot \beta', \qquad (6.16)$$

where α and β are both $n \times r$ matrices.

Matrix β is called the *cointegrating matrix* and has the property that $\beta' Z_t \sim I(0)$, while $Z_t \sim I(1)$. If the definition of cointegration is recalled from Chapter 5, the straightforward conclusion is that the variables in Z_t are cointegrated, with the cointegrating vectors β_1, β_2,..., β_r being particular columns of the cointegrating matrix β. Hence, in a *VAR* model explaining n variables there can be at most $r = n - 1$ cointegrating vectors.

We may note that model (6.15) can be regarded as a multivariate generalization of a model in differences with an error correction mechanism such as was discussed in Chapter 5. If the hypothesis concerning cointegration holds, that is if in (6.15) $\Pi = \alpha \cdot \beta'$, the matrix $\beta' Z_{t-k}$ constitutes a set of r error correction mechanisms separating out the long and short run responses in the model.

For empirical analysis, the essential problems are in the determination of r, that is in identifying the number of cointegrating vectors, and in estimating the cointegrating matrix β. The procedure outlined below is that of Johansen (1988, 1989). It is numerically quite complicated and we only describe the general principles. It consists of the following steps:

STEP 1: Regress ΔZ_t on ΔZ_{t-1} , ΔZ_{t-2} , ΔZ_{t-k+1} . Since there are n variables to explain in the VAR model, this is equivalent to performing n separate regressions. Construct the n x 1 vector from the residual from each of these regressions at time t, and denote it by R_{0t}. Also, regress Z_{t-k} on ΔZ_{t-1} , ΔZ_{t-2} , ΔZ_{t-k+1} . Construct the n x 1 vector of the residual from each of these regressions at time t, and denote it by R_{kt}.

STEP 2: Compute the four n x n matrices S_{00}, S_{0k}, S_{k0}, and S_{kk} from the second moments and crossproducts of R_{0t} and R_{kt} as:

$$S_{ij} = T^{-1} \sum_{t=1}^{T} R_{it} R'_{jt} , \quad i,j = 0, k. \ (T = \text{sample size}).$$

STEP 3: Solve the equation:

$$| \mu S_{kk} - S_{k0} S_{00}^{-1} S_{0k} | = 0 .$$

That is, find the roots or eigenvalues of the polynomial equation in μ obtained from the determinant above. This is a non–standard form of the eigenvalue problem. The solution yields the eigenvalues $\hat{\mu}_1 > \hat{\mu}_2 > ... > \hat{\mu}_n$ (ordered from the largest to the smallest) and associated eigenvectors $\hat{v}_i$ which may be arranged into the matrix $\hat{V} = [\ \hat{v}_1\ \ \hat{v}_2\ ...\ \hat{v}_n]$. The eigenvectors are normalized such that $\hat{V}' S_{kk} \hat{V} = I$. Hall (1989, pp. 216–217) provides some guidance on the computational aspects of these calculations.

If the cointegrating matrix β is of rank $r < n$, the first r eigenvectors $\hat{v}_1, \hat{v}_2, ..., \hat{v}_r$ are the cointegrating vectors, that is they are the columns of matrix β .

STEP 4: For each μ_i compute the LR statistic:

$$LR = -T \cdot \sum_{i=r+1}^{n} ln(1 - \hat{\mu}_i) , \qquad (6.17)$$

which, under the null hypothesis that there are at most r cointegrating vectors, has an asymptotic distribution whose quantiles are tabulated by Johansen (1988) and Osterwald-Lenum (1990). Normally testing starts from $r = 0$, that is from the hypothesis that there are no cointegrating vectors in a *VAR* model. If this cannot be rejected, the procedure stops since no confirmation of the existence of cointegrating vectors has been found. If it is rejected, it is possible to examine sequentially the hypotheses that $r \leq 1$, $r \leq 2$, etc. If the null hypothesis cannot be rejected for, say $r \leq r_0$, but it has been rejected for $r \leq r_0 - 1$, the straightforward conclusion is that the number of cointegrating vectors or, in other words, the rank of β, is r_0 . Johansen (1989) has shown that the first r

estimated eigenvectors $\hat{v}_1$, $\hat{v}_2$,..., $\hat{v}_r$ are the maximum likelihood estimates of the columns of β, the cointegrating
vectors.

So far, we have concentrated on the elements of the
matrix β in (6.16), since the columns of β have an economic
interpretation as cointegrating vectors. That is, after normalization, they may be interpreted as long run parameters.
The elements of α in (6.16) are straightforward to obtain once
the matrix β is known, as the first r columns in the matrix
$S_{0k}\hat{V}$. These elements also have an economic interpretation.

In general, they measure the speed of adjustment of particular variables with respect to a disturbance in the equilibrium
relation (see Johansen (1989, p.16)). Quite appropriately, the
matrix α is called the *adjustment matrix* or, since we are
dealing with a *VAR* model where the lagged values of the
left–hand side variables enter the error correction
mechanism, the *feedback matrix*.

In empirical applications of the Johansen method a major
problem can be establishing the maximum lag length, that is
k in (6.9). If an empirical analysis is concerned exclusively
with the estimation and identification of a cointegrating
vector, the problem is relatively simple. Since in (6.9), the
random errors ε_t have to be free from autocorrelation, the

usual practice is to allow for relatively long lags, since these
might approximate the possible autocorrelation structure of
the error terms. This argument parallels that used to justify
the role of the length of augmentation in the augmented
Dickey–Fuller test (see Chapter 5). However, if the aim is to
use the estimated cointegrating vector(s) for further analysis
of the *VAR* model in the form of model (6.15), using long lags
may be inconsistent with economic sense. In (6.15), the lag
length corresponds to the length of response (adjustment) to
a deviation from a long run path, according to the interpretation of an error correction mechanism. It is usually assumed
(and sometimes tested) that these corrections occur after a
relatively short period of time. Since model (6.15) defines the
error correction mechanism as $\beta' X_{t-k}$, in order to interpret

the adjustment matrix α sensibly, the value of k cannot be large. On the other hand, a low k increases the possibility of autocorrelation in the error terms and this may affect the validity of the entire estimation process.

A simple solution to this problem seems to be to compare estimates of model (6.15) for both small and large k. Intuitively, for a properly formulated model, the estimates of the long run relationship $\beta' X_{t-k}$ should not depend on k, but analogously, the estimates of the adjustment matrix α *should* depend on k. Hence, if the estimated cointegrating vectors are similar for two *VAR* models with a different lag length, we may choose the model with a shorter lag length if we feel that the economic interpretation of α is more sensible.

Testing and analyzing cointegration in a *VAR* model is often regarded as superior to the Engle–Granger single equation method described in Chapter 5. The statistical properties of the Johansen procedure are generally better and the power of the cointegration test is higher. However, it should be stressed that the Engle–Granger and Johansen procedures are grounded within different econometric methodologies and therefore cannot be directly compared. Most notably, in the Engle–Granger modelling approach, the endo–exogenous division of variables is assumed (and therefore there might be only one cointegrating relation) while in the Johansen approach, based on *VAR* modelling, there are no exogenous variables. It seems that the Johansen procedure can be used for single equation modelling as an auxiliary tool, checking the validity of the endo–exogenous variable division. Suppose, for instance, that the Johansen procedure indicates the existence of only one cointegrating vector. If the estimated cointegrating coefficients have, after normalization, economically sensible signs and are roughly similar in size to those estimated by the Engle–Granger method, this could be regarded as some confirmation of the single equation model to which the Engle–Granger method was applied. If, on the other hand, the number of cointegrating vectors found by the Johansen procedure is greater than one, it is likely that the endo–exogenous division of variables in this model is imperfect and that the model under consideration should consist of not one but two or more equations (see also the discussion of exogeneity in Chapter 7).

6.5   *VAR* Alternatives to the *DHSY* Model

(a) Forecasting

Following the claim made in Section 2 of this chapter on the convenience of using a *VAR* model for *ex ante* forecasting, consider the formulation of a *VAR* analogue to the *DHSY* model of aggregate consumption. The unrestricted *VAR* model is in the form of model (6.9), with a deterministic component D_t, namely:

$$Z_t = A_0 D_t + \sum_{i=1}^{k} A_i Z_{t-i} + \varepsilon_t , \qquad (6.18)$$

where $Z_t = [\ cons_t\ \ inc_t\ \ inf_t\ ]$. The deterministic component in this case is only an intercept term. Since the model is to be used for an *ad hoc* mechanistic forecast, no adjustment to the data has been made, though from the results of Chapter 5 we know that the data are nonstationary. The length of lag (the order of the *VAR* process) is assumed to be five (so that $k = 5$). This gives 48 parameters to be estimated in the *VAR*: three as elements of the 3×1 vector A_0 (we have only one deterministic component in the model), and nine in each of the five 3×3 A_i matrices. The forecasts made are one–step ahead forecasts where values for the periods up to and including period t are used for making predictions for period $t + 1$. The model is estimated by multivariate least squares. A selection from the computer output (from the *PC–FIML* part of the *PC–GIVE* package which is used for multi equation analysis) relating to the parameter estimates and the forecasts is shown in Section 6.6 under the heading

MODEL 6.1. (In the *PC–GIVE* output a *VAR* model is called an *Unrestricted Reduced Form (URF)* or *system* and the
multivariate least squares estimates are called the *direct
estimates*.) The goodness of fit measures reported here for
the unrestricted reduced form estimates are the loglikelihood
value (see Hendry (1989, p.66)), denoted as *likelihood* and the
logarithm of the determinant of Ω , denoted as *log det* Ω (Ω
stands for the covariance matrix of the multivariate error
term). The model is estimated using quarterly data from
1958 (1st quarter) to 1970 (4th quarter) and forecasts from
this model have been made for the period from 1971 (1st
quarter) to 1975 (4th quarter) which are the same as were
used by *DHSY* for evaluating the forecasting performance of
the *DHSY* model.

Two types of forecasts have been made. The first are
one–step ahead forecasts, conditional on the observed values
of lagged variables (that is, under the assumption that the
forecaster making a forecast for period $t+1$ knows the realized
values of the variables in period t).

The second type of forecasts for the next period ahead are
dynamic or multi–step forecasts, where it is assumed that
until the last quarter of 1970, the values of the variables are
known, but after that period the forecasted values of the
variables are used instead of the realizations of the particular
variables. For instance, the forecasts for 1971 (1st quarter),
denoted as $cons_{t+1}^{f}$, inc_{t+1}^{f}, inf_{t+1}^{f} are conditional on ($cons_{t}$,
$cons_{t-1}$, $cons_{t-2}$, $cons_{t-3}$, $cons_{t-4}$, inc_{t} , inc_{t-1} , inc_{t-2} ,
inc_{t-3} , inc_{t-4} , inf_{t} , inf_{t-1} , inf_{t-2} , inf_{t-3} , inf_{t-4}), where
$t \equiv 1970$ (4th quarter). For 1971 (2nd quarter), the forecasts
$cons_{t+2}^{f}$, inc_{t+2}^{f}, inf_{t+2}^{f} are conditional on ($cons_{t+1}^{f}$, $cons_{t}$,
$cons_{t-1}$, $cons_{t-2}$, $cons_{t-3}$, inc_{t+1}^{f} , inc_{t} , inc_{t-1} , inc_{t-2} ,
inc_{t-3} , inf_{t+1}^{f} , inf_{t} , inf_{t-1} , inf_{t-2} , inf_{t-3}), for 1971 (3rd
quarter) on ($cons_{t+2}^{f}$, $cons_{t+1}^{f}$, $cons_{t}$, $cons_{t-1}$, $cons_{t-2}$,

inc_{t+2}^{f} , inc_{t+1}^{f} , inc_{t} , inc_{t-1} , inc_{t-2} , inf_{t+2}^{f} , inf_{t+1}^{f} , inf_{t} , inf_{t-1} , inf_{t-2}) , and so on.

Figures 6.1 to 6.3 show the one–step ahead forecasts for consumption, income and inflation, together with realizations and forecast confidence intervals (equal to ($\overset{+}{\cdot}$) two standard errors of forecast) whilst Figures 6.4 to 6.6. depict the dynamic or multi–step forecasts.

For interest, the two sets of forecasts obtained from the *VAR* model may be compared with those generated by a multivariate deterministic trend model with seasonal components, that is by:

$$Z_t = B_0 T_t + \xi_t , \qquad\qquad (6.19)$$

where $T_t = [$ intercept , TREND , $Q1_t$, $Q2_t$, $Q3_t]$.

TREND $= 1 , 2, ... , T$, the variables $Q1_t$, $Q2_t$, and $Q3_t$ are seasonal dummy variables, and ξ_t is a vector of error terms.

Estimates of equations (6.19) are summarized in Section 6.6 under MODEL 6.2. Figures 6.7 to 6.9 show the forecasts and realizations for this model for the same forecast period as the *VAR* model.

An inspection of the time paths of forecasts and realizations shows that none of the forecasts is fully admissible. In every figure some realizations lie outside the forecast confidence interval, with a tendency for all models to underpredict the series from 1973 onwards. The one–step *VAR* forecast is the only forecasting method which does not completely miss the huge rise in inflation which started from the beginning of 1974, a finding which is unsurprising given the nature of these forecasts. A comparison of aggregate forecast error measures shows some superiority of the one–step *VAR* forecasts over those from the multivariate trend model. The forecast F statistic of 2.566 is computed jointly for the entire model (6.18) so that it has the number of degrees of freedom in the numerator of 3 equations × 20 forecasts or 60. This forecast F statistic is substantially smaller than the value of 10.549 for

One-Step Forecasts, *VAR*

Fig. 6.1: Consumption

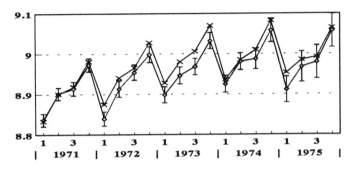

Fig. 6.2: Income

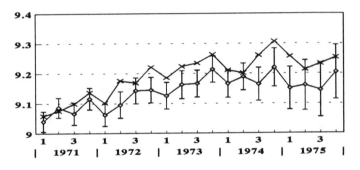

Fig. 6.3: Inflation

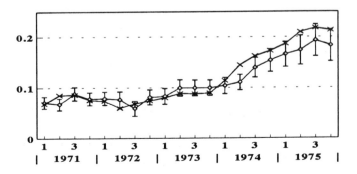

Multi-Step Forecasts, *VAR*

Fig. 6.4: Consumption

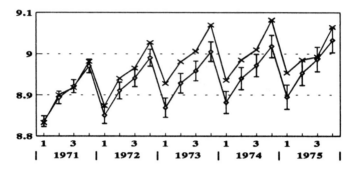

Fig. 6.5: Income

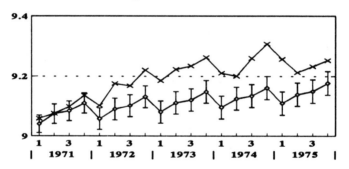

Fig. 6.6: Inflation

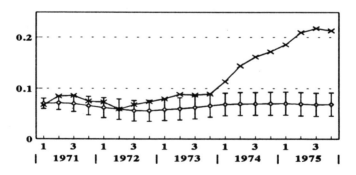

Multivariate Trend Forecasts

Fig. 6.7: Consumption

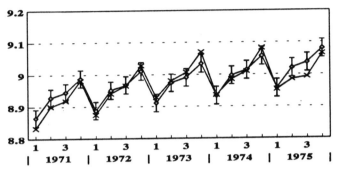

Fig. 6.8: Income

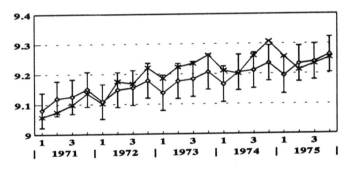

Fig. 6.9: Inflation

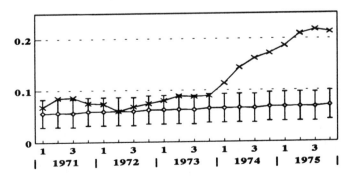

model (6.19), though both values are statistically significant at the 0.05 level of significance. A similar pattern may be observed for the cumulative χ^2 test (see Hendry (1989, p.68) for these forecast tests). Also, a comparison of the forecast standard errors is in favour of one–step VAR forecasting, especially for inflation. However, it is worth noting that mean forecast errors (showing the average bias) for both consumption and income are smaller in absolute value for the multivariate trend than for the VAR forecast.

The multi–step forecasts are not significantly better than either the one–step or multivariate trend models (for reasons of space, we do not report full output for this model). As with the other methods, realizations are within the confidence intervals at the start of the forecast period, but substantially underpredict both income and inflation towards the end (see Figures 6.4 to 6.6).

The forecasting diagnostics for the one–step VAR forecast for consumption are not as good as those computed for the $DHSY$ model for the same period (see Chapter 3). However, it could be considered unfair to compare the multi–step VAR and $DHSY$ forecasts directly as they are made under totally different assumptions. In particular, the forecasts analysed for the $DHSY$ model in Chapter 3 were made under the rather unrealistic assumption that the time series of income and inflation were known for the forecasting period. Hence, this test was more a test for parameter constancy rather than a forecasting exercise. The multi–step VAR forecasts have been made under the more realistic assumption that values of income and inflation are unknown for the forecasting period and have to be predicted simultaneously with consumption.

(b) Causality

A VAR model may be used as the basis for testing causality (in the Granger sense) between consumption and inflation. As was mentioned in Chapter 3, the existence of a causal relation running from inflation to real consumption ($inf \rightarrow cons$) might result either from the existence of an unanticipated inflation effect or from a 'money illusion' effect. On the other hand, there could be a causal relation from real consumption to inflation ($cons \rightarrow inf$), if there is demand–pull inflation in the economy. Thus both types of causal relations might appear simultaneously, creating a feedback relation $inf \overset{\rightarrow}{\leftarrow} cons$.

We have used two alternative *VAR* models to illustrate the testing of causality, both formulated for a three-dimensional vector autoregressive process for the variables $cons_t$, inc_t, inf_t. Both of the models are *VAR*(5) models, incorporating up to five lags for each of the variables. The first model is formulated in seasonal differences and with the deterministic part reduced to an intercept, or:

$$\Delta_4 Z_t = A_0 D_t + \sum_{i=1}^{5} A_i \Delta_4 Z_{t-i} + \mathcal{E}_t \,, \qquad (6.20)$$

where $D_t = [\, \text{intercept} \,]$.

The second model is formulated in levels of the variables with a more fully developed deterministic part (constant, trend and seasonals):

$$Z_t = A_0 D_t + \sum_{i=1}^{5} A_i Z_{t-i} + \mathcal{E}_t \,, \qquad (6.21)$$

where $D_t = [\, \text{intercept} \,, \text{TREND} \,, Q1_t \,, Q2_t \,, Q3_t \,]$. It is worth emphasizing that testing for Granger causality in a model in levels is, for the case where variables are nonstationary, a popular but problematic exercise (see Harvey (1990, p.83)).

Model (6.20) corresponds to the assumption that the seasonal components of the entire system are stochastic, while in (6.21) it is assumed that both trend and seasonal components are deterministic. Since our interest is in testing causality between consumption and inflation and the causality tests disregard covariances of the error terms, it is sufficient to base the analysis on the ordinary least squares estimates of the first and third equation of each model. Thus for model (6.20) we consider:

$$\Delta_4 cons_t = \alpha_{c0} + \sum_{i=1}^{5} \alpha_{ci} \Delta_4 cons_{t-i} + \sum_{i=1}^{5} \beta_{ci} \Delta_4 inc_{t-i}$$

$$+ \sum_{i=1}^{5} \gamma_{ci} \Delta_4 inf_{t-i} + \epsilon_{ct}, \tag{6.22}$$

$$\Delta_4 inf_t = \alpha_{p0} + \sum_{i=1}^{5} \alpha_{pi} \Delta_4 cons_{t-i} + \sum_{i=1}^{5} \beta_{pi} \Delta_4 inc_{t-i}$$

$$+ \sum_{i=1}^{5} \gamma_{pi} \Delta_4 inf_{t-i} + \epsilon_{pt}, \tag{6.23}$$

and for model (6.21) we consider:

$$cons_t = \alpha_{c0} + \sum_{i=1}^{5} \alpha_{ci} cons_{t-i} + \sum_{i=1}^{5} \beta_{ci} inc_{t-i} + \sum_{i=1}^{5} \gamma_{ci} inf_{t-i} +$$

$$\sum_{i=1}^{3} \delta_{ci} Qi_t + \delta_{c0} TREND + \epsilon_{ct}, \tag{6.24}$$

$$inf_t = \alpha_{p0} + \sum_{i=1}^{5} \alpha_{pi} cons_{t-i} + \sum_{i=1}^{5} \beta_{pi} inc_{t-i} + \sum_{i=1}^{5} \gamma_{pi} inf_{t-i} +$$

$$\sum_{i=1}^{3} \delta_{pi} Qi_t + \delta_{p0} TREND + \epsilon_{pt}. \tag{6.25}$$

For stationary variables, the Granger tests of the causal relations $inf \rightarrow cons$ or $\Delta_4 inf \rightarrow \Delta_4 cons$ consist of testing the hypothesis that in (6.24) or respectively in (6.22), $\gamma_{c1} = \gamma_{c2} = \gamma_{c3} = \gamma_{c4} = \gamma_{c5} = 0$. Analogously, the hypothesis that *cons → inf* is equivalent to testing whether $\alpha_{p1} = \alpha_{p2} = \alpha_{p3}$ $= \alpha_{p4} = \alpha_{p5} = 0$ in (6.25) or (for $\Delta_4 inf \to \Delta_4 cons$) in (6.23). Hence, the Granger test is simply a Lagrange Multiplier test for testing zero restrictions (see Chapter 5). Technically, this test can be computed in three different ways:

i)   By estimating *an unrestricted* equation, with lags of particular variables formulated individually for each equation and then testing the (joint) *significance of each variable.* For instance, for the estimated equation (6.22) (MODEL 6.3 in Section 6.6) the *LMF* test statistic for significance of the variable *d4inf1* (that is all the lagged inflation variables) is equal to 3.485. (Technical note: The transformation of variables and associated notation which appears above the output for Model 6.3 in Section 6.6 is one way of estimating an unrestricted *VAR* model using *PC–GIVE*. This transformation avoids the problem of the inclusion of current values of variables when a lag polynomial is specified in *PC–GIVE*, and allows for joint tests of significance of each variable directly.)

ii)   By estimating a restricted equation, that is an equation with all the zero restrictions discussed above imposed, and then testing the omitted variables as *missing variables.* MODEL 6.4 is the restricted version of equation (6.22), with the variables $\Delta_4 inf_{t-1}$, $\Delta_4 inf_{t-2}$, $\Delta_4 inf_{t-3}$, $\Delta_4 inf_{t-4}$ and $\Delta_4 inf_{t-5}$ eliminated. Then the *F* test *for adding* these five variables is 3.48, which is the same as the *LMF* statistic above.

iii)   By performing a *model reduction* sequence in the way described in Chapter 4 as *general to specific* modelling. Regarding MODEL 6.3 as *general* and MODEL 6.4 as *specific* gives the same *F* statistic as before as the reduction from MODEL 6.3 to 6.4 produces an *F* statistic of 3.48.

Although the reported F statistics are identical, the corresponding number of degrees of freedom are not. The F test for the significance of each variable (that is the test computed as i) above) has the reported number of the degrees of freedom equal to [5, 52]. Here, 5 is the number of the restrictions imposed, and 52 is equal to the sample size (63) plus the observations retained for the lags (5) less the total number of estimated parameters (16) in the unrestricted equation (6.22). The F statistics computed in ii) and iii) have degrees of freedom equal to [5, 47], where 47 is the difference between the sample size (63) and the total number of parameters (16), so that the observations retained to form the lagged values are disregarded. For the purpose of testing causality we are testing the restrictions within an already reduced sample, and therefore we will take the number of the degrees of freedom for the Granger test as [5, 47].

MODELS 6.3 and 6.4 in Section 6.6 show the results of estimating equation (6.22) for testing $\Delta_4 inf \rightarrow \Delta_4 cons$ and MODELS 6.5 and 6.6 for testing the causality relation $\Delta_4 cons \rightarrow \Delta_4 inf$ from equation (6.23). The F statistics have been computed using all three approaches described above, i), ii) and iii). For testing causality by the Granger test in the second model (6.21), only the computationally simplest method i) is illustrated by the computer output of MODELS 6.7 and 6.8.

For testing causality with the use of Sims–GMD method the approach described in i) cannot be implemented directly using *PC–GIVE* since *PC–GIVE* does not allow for formulation of leads in the process of developing an equation. Consequently, leads have to be constructed prior to modelling and are regarded by *PC–GIVE* as separate variables. Therefore, for testing causality by the Sims–GMD method, only methods ii) and iii) for computing the F statistic have been used. The techniques parallel those described above, but it should be noted that for *VAR* model (6.20), the regression of $\Delta_4 inf_t$ on lagged $\Delta_4 inf_t$s , lagged $\Delta_4 cons_t$s and lagged $\Delta_4 inc_t$s is now run and *leading* $\Delta_4 cons_t$ variables (that is $\Delta_4 cons_{t+1}$, $\Delta_4 cons_{t+2}$, $\Delta_4 cons_{t+3}$, $\Delta_4 cons_{t+4}$) are tested as missing variables for testing the hypothesis that $\Delta_4 inf \rightarrow \Delta_4 cons$ (MODEL 6.9). MODEL 6.10 shows the analogous results for testing the hypothesis that $\Delta_4 cons \rightarrow \Delta_4 inf$. Note that in the Sims–GMD test the sample finishes in 1974 (fourth quarter) and not 1975 (fourth quarter). The last four observations are discarded to allow for the formulation of leads in the variables. Similar computations for *VAR* model (6.21) are shown in the computer output as MODELS 6.11 and 6.12. It should be noted that all the Durbin–Watson statistics computed for the above models are reasonably close to two. Although one must be aware of the possible bias of the Durbin–Watson statistic towards two in models containing lagged dependent variables, this is at least an indication that first order autocorrelation of the residuals is not likely to affect the validity of these Lagrange Multiplier statistics. It is interesting to note that the Sims–GMD method regards the equations of the *VAR* models as the restricted ones, while in the Granger method these are regarded as unrestricted. The unrestricted equations for the Sims–GMD method are those with the leading variables explicitly included, so that for (6.20) these are:

$$\Delta_4 Z_t = A_0 D_t + \sum_{i=-4}^{5} A_i \Delta_4 Z_{t-i} + \mathcal{E}_t, \quad i \neq 0,$$

and for (6.21):

$$Z_t = A_0 D_t + \sum_{i=-4}^{5} A_i Z_{t-i} + \mathcal{E}_t, \quad i \neq 0.$$

The *LMF* statistics for testing causality between inflation and consumption are as follows:

For model (6.20):

$\Delta_4 inf \rightarrow \Delta_4 cons$: 3.48 (Granger) , 2.69 (Sims–GMD)

$\Delta_4 cons \rightarrow \Delta_4 inf$ 1.92 (Granger) , 6.35 (Sims–GMD)

For model (6.21):

$inf \rightarrow cons$: 2.92 (Granger) , 3.93 (Sims–GMD)

$cons \rightarrow inf$ 1.57 (Granger) , 6.48 (Sims–GMD)

The 5% critical values of the F distribution are 2.40 for $F(5 , 47)$ and 2.63 for $F(4 , 38)$. All the F statistics given above are significant apart from those for the Granger tests for $cons \rightarrow inf$ and $\Delta_4 cons \rightarrow \Delta_4 inf$. Conclusions cannot be very strong (especially for model (6.21)) since the assumption of stationarity for the variables in the model is, even in the presence of a deterministic trend and seasonals, a rather heroic one. Nevertheless, the results suggest the possibility of a feedback relation between inflation and consumption.

(c) Cointegration

In estimating cointegrating vectors and undertaking short run analysis in a VAR model describing consumption, income and inflation, one immediately encounters the problem of establishing the order of integration for the variables. It was suggested in Section 6.4 that cointegration analysis could be performed using the transformed model (6.15) and the Johansen procedure if all the variables which constitute the vector Z_t are integrated of order one. As was discovered in Chapter 5, however, this is not the case for the data we are using. The variables are seasonally integrated, so that they become stationary after both seasonal differencing and first differencing. The discussion in Chapter 5 pointed out that seasonal cointegration analysis is still relatively undeveloped and complicated. For simplicity we have decided only to investigate long run cointegration. We also simplify the problem by assuming that the stochastic seasonality is approximated by deterministic seasonality and that the variables are integrated of order one conditionally on the presence of an intercept term and seasonal dummy variables in the non-stochastic part of the *VAR* model. Such a procedure has been used in practice in *VAR* cointegration analysis in models estimated with quarterly data by Johansen and Juselius (1990) and by Hendry, Muellbauer and Murphy (1990). Since we are interested not only in estimating and testing long run cointegrating vectors but also in analyzing the speed of adjustment, we would prefer to keep the lag length *k* relatively small. On the other hand, as was pointed out above, this may result in the dynamic misspecification of the model. Therefore, for comparison, we have estimated the *VAR* model for both $k = 1$, denoted as *VAR*(1), and for $k = 2$, denoted as *VAR*(2). The results of a similar exercise for a *VAR*(5) model but using a slightly different data sample are given in Hendry, Muellbauer and Murphy (1990, p.315).

The *VAR*(1) model is:

$$Z_t = A_0 D_t + A_1 Z_{t-1} + \mathcal{E}_t , \qquad (6.26)$$

where $D_t = [$ intercept, $Q1_t, Q2_t, Q3_t]$, and $Z_t = [$ $cons_t$, inc_t, $inf_t]$. After the cointegrating transformation, this *VAR*(1) model can be written as:

$$\Delta Z_t = A_0 D_t + \Pi Z_{t-1} + \mathcal{E}_t , \qquad (6.27)$$

The initial problem is the estimation of the number of cointegrating vectors and their elements. That is, one needs to decide on the order and elements of β in $\Pi = \alpha \cdot \beta'$. The results of applying the Johansen procedure for testing the order of the matrix β and estimating the elements of α and β for model (6.26) are given in Section 6.6 under MODEL 6.13. Three eigenvalues μ_i , $i = 1, 2, 3$, are printed at the beginning of this output. The *LR* statistics in the form of equation (6.17) for testing the hypothesis that there are at most *r* cointegrating vectors are given below. The figures in brackets are the critical values for a 5% significance test produced by Osterwald–Lenum (1990) which differ slightly from those originally reported by Johansen (1988, 1989), and Johansen and Juselius (1990). (The Osterwald–Lenum tables are said to be more accurate than the original Johansen tables):

$$
\begin{array}{lll}
\text{for } r \leq 2 : & 0.00 & (\ 8.18) \\
\text{for } r \leq 1 : & 6.56 & (17.95) \\
\text{for } r = 0 : & 38.58 & (31.52)
\end{array}
$$

The results above suggest that the null hypothesis that there is no cointegrating vector should be rejected, since $38.58 > 31.52$. The next hypothesis, that the number of the cointegrating vectors is at most equal to one cannot be rejected, since 6.56 is not in the rejection region, that is $6.56 < 17.95$. The conclusion is that there is precisely one cointegrating vector in the estimated model and that the rank of the matrix Π is one. The first row of the β' matrix is:

$$74.009 \quad -59.133 \quad 7.819$$

which can be standardized (divided by 74.009), so that its first element will correspond to the dependent variable ($cons_t$) in the first equation. This gives the following long run relationship:

$$cons_t = 0.799 inc_t - 0.106 inf_t .$$

The long run income elasticity of consumption is below unity, which is in line with findings concerning the market for nondurables in the UK by Bollerslev and Hylleberg (1985). The negative sign of the inflation variable is consistent with the hypothesis of an unanticipated inflation effect (see Chapter 3). The first element in the first row of the matrix α is negative, which is consistent with the hypothesis of an error correction mechanism given by the deviations from the long run consumption path.

Estimates of the $VAR(2)$ model are given as MODEL 6.14 in Section 6.6. The comparison of the eigenvalues computed for this model by the Johansen method with the 0.05 critical values reveals that the hypothesis that $r \leq 0$

cannot be rejected (30.36 < 31.52). Consequently, we do not have statistical confirmation of the existence of a single cointegrating vector in the $VAR(2)$ model. Moreover, even if there is one cointegrating vector in this model, the first element of the first row of matrix α is positive, which conflicts with the interpretation of this cointegrating vector as elements of an error correction mechanism for consumption. Also, one should consider the differences between the estimated elements of the first row of β' from those of the $VAR(1)$ model. For the income variable, the estimated long run coefficient from the $VAR(1)$ model is 0.799 and from the $VAR(2)$ model is 0.831. For the inflation variable, the estimates are respectively −0.106 ($VAR(1)$) and −0.192 ($VAR(2)$). Since the long run coefficients should not be dependent on the lag of the corresponding variables, these differences, although not large, do indicate the need to exercise caution in interpreting the estimation results of the $VAR(1)$ model. This conclusion is strengthened when the results of Hendry, Muellbauer and Murphy (1990) are considered. The $VAR(5)$ model they adopted yielded long run coefficients of 0.93 for the income variable and −0.66 for the inflation variable. Their results suggest that the proper lag length for the VAR model adopted may be greater than two, in which case both the VAR(1) and VAR(2) models are misspecified.

6.6 Stylized Computer Output (*PC–GIVE*)

Forecasting

MODEL 6.1: (*VAR* model (6.18) in text)

Present Sample Dates are: 1959 (2) to 1975 (4) less 20 Forecasts

DIRECT UNRESTRICTED SYSTEM ESTIMATES

	INCPT	lc 1	li 2	inf 1	lc 2
lc	.1328	−.288	.2953	−.240	.0701
li	−.639	−.267	.4788	−.839	.2064
inf	−.513	.3698	−.068	1.003	−.024

	li 2	inf 2	lc 3	li 3	inf 3	lc 4
lc	−.138	−.043	−.002	.0203	−.339	1.081
li	−.193	.6227	.0567	.0502	−.562	.4082
inf	.0794	−.160	−.018	.0693	.3531	−.008

	li 4	inf 4	lc 5	li 5	inf 5
lc	−.114	.3386	.2535	−.186	.1587
li	.3152	.3611	.1855	−.109	−.068
inf	.0163	−.485	−.298	.0594	.0153

DIRECT UNRESTRICTED SYSTEM STANDARD ERRORS

	INCPT	lc 1	li 1	inf 1	lc 2
lc	.2644	.1855	.0864	.1740	.0493
li	.5797	.4068	.1896	.3817	.1080
inf	.2026	.1422	.0662	.1334	.0378

	li 2	inf 2	lc 3	li 3	inf 3	lc 4
lc	.0752	.1701	.0489	.0757	.1570	.0481
li	.1649	.3729	.1072	.1659	.3443	.1055
inf	.0576	.1303	.0375	.0580	.1203	.0369

	li 4	inf 4	lc 5	li 5	inf 5
lc	.0712	.1502	.1888	.0837	.1431
li	.1561	.3294	.4123	.1834	.3138
inf	.0545	.1151	.1441	.0641	.1097

LOG DET Ω = −29.813293
LIKELIHOOD = 2977654.64

CUMULATIVE TEST: $\chi^2(60)/60$ $= 3.891$
Forecast Test F–FORM: F(60, 31) $= 2.566$

MEAN FORECAST ERRORS

lc	li	inf
.01972	.05293	.00765

FORECAST STANDARD ERRORS

lc	li	inf
.01415	.0309	.01684

MODEL 6.2: Multivariate trend model (Model (6.19) in text)

Present Sample Dates are: 1958 (1) to 1975 (4) less 20 Forecasts

DIRECT UNRESTRICTED SYSTEM ESTIMATES

	INCPT	Q1	Q2	Q3	TREND
lc	8.64	−.105	−.048	−.037	.00578
li	8.72	−.048	−.016	−.016	.00709
inf	0147	−.001	−.001	−.002	.00074

DIRECT UNRESTRICTED SYSTEM STANDARD ERRORS

	INCPT	Q1	Q2	Q3	TREND
lc	.0051	.0049	.0049	.0049	.000117
li	.0109	.0105	.0105	.0105	.000248
inf	.0051	.0049	.0049	.0049	.000117

LOG DET Ω $= -26.123792$
LIKELIHOOD $= 470662.21$

CUMULATIVE TEST: $\chi^2(60)/60$ $= 11.671$

Forecast Test F–FORM: F(60, 47) $= 10.549$

MEAN FORECAST ERRORS

lc	li	inf
−.00568	.01775	.05472

FORECAST STANDARD ERRORS

lc	li	inf
.0212	.0356	.05137

Causality analysis

Initial transformations of variables:

d4lc1	=	LAG[1](d4lc)
d4li1	=	LAG[1](d4li)
d4inf1	=	LAG[1](d4inf)

Granger test for $\Delta_4 inf \rightarrow \Delta_4 cons$ (*VAR* model (6.20) in text), method *i*)

MODEL 6.3: Modelling d4lc by OLS (equation (6.22) in text)

The Sample is 1960 (2) to 1975 (4) less 0 Forecasts

VARI	COEF	STD ERR	t−VALUE
d4lc1	.03478	.19932	.17447
d4lc1 1	−.2819	.21159	−1.332
d4lc1 2	−.1176	.20545	−.5727
d4lc1 3	−.0296	.20220	−.1465
d4lc1 4	.12367	.18371	.67320
INCPT	.01562	.00576	2.7116
d4li1	.32437	.08411	3.8566
d4li1 1	.06761	.09518	.71032
d4li1 2	.03631	.09046	.40137
d2li1 3	−.0967	.09057	−1.068
d4li1 4	.19179	.09186	2.0877
d4inf1	−.2329	.11680	−1.994
d4inf1 1	−.0429	.14307	−.3000

d4infl 2	−.1332	.13425	−.9922
d4infl 3	−.0423	.12680	−.3342
d4infl 4	.09100	.10725	.84843

$R^2 = .723968$ $\sigma = .009344$ $F(15, 47) = 8.22$ DW = 1.959
RSS = .0041041   for 16 Variables and 63 Observations

Tests on the Significance of each Variable

Variable	F[NUM,DENOM]	=	Value
d4lc1	F[5, 52]		0.460
INCPT	F[1, 52]		7.353
d4li1	F[5, 52]		3.641
d4infl	**F[5, 52]**		**3.485**

Granger test for $\Delta_4 inf \rightarrow \Delta_4 cons$, (*VAR* model (6.20) in text), methods *ii*) and *iii*)

MODEL 6.4: Modelling d4lc by OLS

The Sample is 1960 (2) to 1975 (4) less 0 Forecasts

VARI	COEF	STD ERR	t−VALUE
d4lc 1	.48827	.18342	2.6619
d4lc 2	.18333	.18854	.97239
d4lc 3	.20924	.19254	1.0867
d4lc 4	.04559	.20075	.22709
d4lc 5	−.0817	.18715	−.4369
INCPT	.00507	.00366	1.3836
d4li1	.22010	.08785	2.5055
d4li1 1	−.1310	.08887	−1.474
d4li1 2	−.0945	.08684	−1.088
d4li1 3	−.1846	.09125	−2.023
d4li1 4	.11524	.09736	1.1836

$R^2 = .621639$ $\sigma = .010401$ $F(10, 52) = 8.54$ DW = 1.971
RSS = .0056256   for 11 Variables and 63 Observations

F–TEST for Adding:
d4infl   d4infl 1   d4infl 2   d4infl 3   d4infl 4

F[5, 47]   = 3.48

PROGRESS TO DATE:

MODEL	PARAMETERS	RSS	σ
1	16	.0041041	.00934468
2	11	.0056256	.01040120

TESTS OF MODEL REDUCTION

From Model 1 to Model 2
Model 1: F(5, 47)   = 3.48

Granger test for $\Delta_4 cons \rightarrow \Delta_4 inf$, (*VAR* model (6.20) in text), method *i*)

MODEL 6.5: Modelling d4inf by OLS (equation (6.23) in text)

The Sample is 1960 (2) to 1975 (4) less 0 Forecasts

VARI	COEF	STD ERR	t–VALUE
d4inf 1	1.0728	.12479	8.5971
d4inf 2	−.0897	.15287	−.5872
d4inf 3	.09083	.14344	.63318
d4inf 4	.47134	.13549	−3.478
d4inf 5	.43004	.11460	3.7525
INCPT	−.0118	.00615	−1.929
d4lc1	−.2575	.21297	−1.209
d4lc1 1	.21027	.22608	.93010
d4lc1 2	.11503	.21953	.52399
d4lc1 3	.55112	.21605	2.5508
d4lc1 4	.19226	.19629	.97946
d4li1	.08165	.08987	.90856
d4li1 1	.07898	.10169	.77668
d4li1 2	.01766	.09666	.18275

d4li1 3	−.0809	.09677	−.8366
d4li1 4	−.3083	.09815	−3.141

$R^2 = .88746$ $\sigma = .009984$ $F(15, 47) = 24.71$ $DW = 2.008$
$RSS = .0046855$ for 16 Variables and 63 Observations

Tests on the Significance of each Variable

Variable	F[NUM,DENOM]	=	Value
d4inf	F[5, 52]		25.788
INCPT	F[1, 52]		3.724
d4lc1	F[5, 52]		**1.923**
d4li1	F[5, 52]		2.635

Granger test for $\Delta_4 cons \to \Delta_4 inf$, (*VAR* model (6.20) in text), methods *ii*) and *iii*)

MODEL 6.6: Modelling d4inf by OLS

The Sample is 1960 (2) to 1975 (4) less 0 Forecasts

VARI	COEF	STD ERR	t–VALUE
d4inf 1	1.0818	.12161	8.8958
d4inf 2	−.1030	.15611	−.6603
d4inf 3	.11801	.14444	.81699
d4inf 4	−.5347	.13548	−3.947
d4inf 5	.34566	.11181	3.0915
INCPT	−.0026	.00316	−.8451
d4li1	.01367	.06308	.21667
d4li1 1	.07583	.07166	1.0582
d4li1 2	.11761	.07183	1.6374
d4li1 3	.08187	.07351	1.1138
d4li1 4	−.1513	.07029	−2.153

$R^2 = .864435$ $\sigma = .010418$ $F(10, 2) = 33.16$ $DW = 1.823$
$RSS = .00564421$ for 11 Variables and 63 Observations

F–TEST for Adding:
d4lc1 d4lc1 1   d4lc1 2   d4lc1 3   d4lc1 4

F[5, 47]   = 1.92

PROGRESS TO DATE:

MODEL	PARAMETERS	RSS	σ
1	16	.00468557	.00998464
2	11	.00564422	.01041838

TESTS OF MODEL REDUCTION

From Model 1 to Model 2
Model 1: F(5, 47)   = 1.92

Granger test for *inf→ cons*, (*VAR* model (6.21) in text),
method *i*)

Basic transformations:
lc1   =   LAG[1](lc)
li1   =   LAG[1](li)
inf1   =   LAG[1](inf)

MODEL 6.7: Modelling lc by OLS (equation (6.24) in text)

The Sample is 1959 (2) to 1975 (4) less 0 Forecasts

VARI	COEF	STD ERR	t–VALUE
lc 1	−.0189	.21967	−.0861
lc 2	−.4354	.20866	−2.086
lc 3	−.3214	.20441	−1.572
lc 4	.44372	.20280	2.1879
lc 5	−.1274	.19542	−.6522
INCPT	7.1200	2.6708	2.6658
Q1	−.0397	.02305	−1.724
Q2	.00748	.01792	.41713
Q3	−.0164	.02261	−.7294
TREND	.00409	.00151	2.7079
lin1	.33745	.09334	3.6152

lin1 1	.11427	.10761	1.0619
lin1 2	.12962	.10069	1.2872
lin1 3	.06952	.10066	.69068
lin1 4	−.0250	.10390	−.2409
infl	−.2532	.15185	−1.667
infl 1	.14400	.20533	.70129
infl 2	−.3734	.18709	−1.995
infl 3	.13840	.18535	.74668
infl 4	.03818	.15414	.24772

$R^2 = .99550$ $\sigma = .009226$ $F(19, 47) = 547.27$ $DW = 2.032$
$RSS = .0040005$ for 20 Variables and 67 Observations

Tests on the Significance of each Variable

Variable	F[NUM,DENOM]	= Value
lc	F[5, 52]	4.050
INCPT	F[1, 52]	7.107
Q1	F[1, 52]	2.976
Q2	F[1, 52]	0.174
Q3	F[1, 52]	0.532
TREND	F[1, 52]	7.333
lin1	F[5, 52]	2.991
infl	**F[5, 52]**	**2.922**

Granger test for *cons → inf*, (*VAR* model (6.21) in text), method *i*)

MODEL 6.8: Modelling inf by OLS (equation (6.25) in text)

The Sample is 1959 (2) to 1975 (4) less 0 Forecasts

VARI	COEF	STD ERR	t–VALUE
inf 1	1.2771	.12773	9.9986
inf 2	−.2081	.17272	−1.205
inf 3	.25826	.15737	1.6410
inf 4	−.4626	.15591	−2.967
inf 5	.28469	.12965	2.1958
INCPT	−5.063	2.2465	−2.254

Q1	.01848	.01938	.95350
Q2	−.0103	.01508	−.6866
Q3	.03174	.01902	1.6689
TREND	−.0028	.00127	−2.248
lcl	.07694	.18478	.41638
lcl 1	.48162	.17552	2.7439
lcl 2	.07702	.17194	.44795
lcl 3	.27698	.17058	1.6237
lcl 4	.05019	.16438	.30535
lil	.03895	.07851	.49606
lil 1	−.0485	.09052	−.5360
lil 2	−.0427	.08470	−.5048
lil 3	−.0915	.08467	−1.081
lil 4	−.2264	.08739	−2.591

$R^2 = .98266$ $\sigma = .00776$ $F(19, 47) = 140.21$ DW = 2.161
RSS = .0028304 for 20 Variables and 67 Observations

Tests on the Significance of each Variable

Variable	F[NUM,DENOM]	=	Value
inf	F[5, 52]		53.977
INCPT	F[1, 52]		5.081
Q1	F[1, 52]		0.909
Q2	F[1, 52]		0.471
Q3	F[1, 52]		2.785
TREND	F[1, 52]		5.054
lcl	F[5, 52]		**1.573**
lil	F[5, 52]		1.566

Sims–GMD test for $\Delta_4 inf \to \Delta_4 cons$, (*VAR* model (6.20)) in text), methods *ii*) and *iii*)

MODEL 6.9: Modelling d4inf by OLS

The Sample is 1960 (2) to 1974 (4) less 0 Forecasts

VARI	COEF	STD ERR	t–VALUE
d4inf 1	1.0193	.14566	6.9981
d4inf 2	−.0972	.15708	−.6190
d4inf 3	.12232	.14891	.82142
d4inf 4	−.4305	.14017	−3.071
d4inf 5	.40137	.11864	3.3830
INCPT	−.0107	.00639	−1.674
d4lc1	−.3385	.22380	−1.512
d4lc1 1	.22069	.23648	.93321
d4lc1 2	.11230	.22217	.50548
d4lc1 3	.55821	.22308	2.5022
d4lc1 4	.16986	.21792	.77947
d4li1	.05912	.09176	.64436
d4li1 1	.08550	.10455	.81780
d4li1 2	.06102	.10488	.58186
d4li1 3	−.0329	.10627	−.3103
d4li1 4	−.3487	.10956	−3.183

$R^2 = .86413$ $\sigma = .01006$ $F(15, 43) = 18.23$ $DW = 2.029$
$RSS = .0043583$ for 16 Variables and 59 Observations

F–TEST for Adding:
d4lc +1   d4lc +2   d4lc +3   d4lc +4

$F(4, 39)$ $= 2.692$

PROGRESS TO DATE:

MODEL	PARAMETERS	RSS	σ
1	20	.0034153	.009358
2	16	.0043583	.010067

TESTS OF MODEL REDUCTION

From Model 1 to Model 2
Model 1: $F(4, 39)$ $= 2.69$

Sims–GMD test for $\Delta_4 cons \to \Delta_4 inf$, (*VAR* model (6.20) in text), methods *ii*) and *iii*)

MODEL 6.10: Modelling d4lc by OLS

The Sample is 1960 (2) to 1974 (4) less 0 Forecasts

VARI	COEF	STD ERR	t–VALUE
d4lc 1	.03506	.21002	.16692
d4lc 2	−.2311	.22192	−1.041
d4lc 3	−.0957	.20849	−.4591
d4lc 4	−.0031	.20935	−.0150
d4lc 5	−.0054	.20450	−.0268
INCPT	.01623	.00600	2.7048
d4li1	.32461	.08611	3.7698
d4li1 1	.06340	.09811	.64619
d4li1 2	.06818	.09842	.69276
d4li1 3	−.1318	.09972	−1.321
d4li1 4	.18977	.10281	1.8458
d4infl	−.2008	.13669	−1.469
d4infl 1	−.0137	.14741	−.0931
d4infl 2	−.0851	.13974	−.6096
d4infl 3	−.0416	.13154	−.3169
d4infl 4	.08035	.11134	.72170

$R^2 =$ .65421　$\sigma =$ .0094477　$F(15, 43) =$ 5.42　DW = 1.946
RSS = .0038381 for 16 Variables and 59 Observations

F–TEST for Adding:
d4inf +1　d4inf +2　d4inf +3　d4inf +4

$F(4, 39)$　　　　　= 6.349

PROGRESS TO DATE:

MODEL	PARAMETERS	RSS	σ
1	20	.0023244	.007720
2	16	.0038381	.009447

TESTS OF MODEL REDUCTION

From Model 1 to Model 2
Model 1: F(4, 39)   =   6.35

Sims–GMD test for *inf* → *cons*, (*VAR* model (6.21) in text), methods *ii*) and *iii*)

MODEL 6.11: Modelling inf by OLS

The Sample is 1959 (3) to 1974 (4) less 0 Forecasts

VARI	COEF	STD ERR	t–VALUE
inf 1	1.2198	.13814	8.8308
inf 2	−.1569	.19965	−.7862
inf 3	.19892	.18048	1.1021
inf 4	−.4083	.16688	−2.447
inf 5	.26344	.13613	1.9351
INCPT	−4.419	2.4043	−1.838
Q1	.01790	.02217	.80772
Q2	−.0206	.01786	−1.153
Q3	.02160	.02037	1.0606
TREND	−.0024	.00136	−1.802
lcl	.04425	.19598	.22581
lcl 1	.44811	.19304	2.3213
lcl 2	.12957	.18703	.69279
lcl 3	.24209	.17895	1.3528
lcl 4	−.0081	.18609	−.0440
lil	.01711	.08398	.20378
lil 1	−.0614	.09603	−.6398
lil 2	−.0228	.09741	−.2345
lil 3	−.0353	.09434	−.3747
lil 4	−.2356	.09628	−2.447

$R^2 =$ .96281 $\sigma =$ .007867 F(19, 42) = 57.23 DW = 2.058
RSS = .0025996 for 20 Variables and 62 Observations

F–TEST for Adding:
lc +1   lc +2   lc +3   lc +4

F(4, 38)   =   3.932

PROGRESS TO DATE:

MODEL	PARAMETERS	RSS	σ
1	24	.0018386	.006955
2	20	.0025996	.007867

TESTS OF MODEL REDUCTION

From Model 1 to Model 2
Model 1: F(4, 38)   =   3.93

Sims–GMD test for *cons* → *inf*, (*VAR* model (6.21) in text), methods *ii*) and *iii*)

MODEL 6.12: Modelling lc by OLS

The Sample is 1959 (3) to 1974 (4) less 0 Forecasts

VARI	COEFF	STD ERR	t–VALUE
lc 1	−.0549	.22187	−.2476
lc 2	−.2935	.21854	−1.343
lc 3	−.3027	.21173	−1.429
lc 4	.49368	.20259	2.4365
lc 5	−.1818	.21067	−.8632
INCPT	6.6144	2.7219	2.4300
Q1	−.0370	.02509	−1.476
Q2	−.0083	.02022	−.4137
Q3	−.0137	.02306	−.5951
TREND	.00364	.00154	2.3581
li1	.31464	.09507	3.3094
li1 1	.09202	.10871	.84643
li1 2	.18609	.11027	1.6875
li1 3	.01707	.10680	.15980
li1 4	−.0445	.10900	−.4084

infl	−.1587	.15638	−1.015
infl 1	.05111	.22602	.22615
infl 2	−.1945	.20432	−.9522
infl 3	.10992	.18893	.58179
infl 4	.09425	.15412	.61152

$R^2 = .99550 \quad \sigma = .00890 \quad F(19, 42) = 489.68 \quad DW = 1.935$
RSS $= .0033317$ for 20 Variables and 62 Observations

F–TEST for Adding:
inf +1   inf +2   inf +3   inf +4

$F(4, 38) \qquad\qquad = 6.477$

PROGRESS TO DATE:

MODEL	PARAMETERS	RSS	σ
1	24	.0019811	.007220
2	20	.0033317	.008906

TESTS OF MODEL REDUCTION

From Model 1 to Model 2
  Model 1: $F(4, 38) \qquad = 6.48$

MODEL 6.13: *VAR*(1) with intercepts and seasonal variables (*VAR* model (6.26) in text)

Present Sample Dates are: 1958 (2) to 1975 (4) less 0 Forecasts

EIGENVALUES μ_i are:

.000005   .088248   .363019

There are 3 valid eigenvalues $\mu_i \in (0,1)$ out of 3

$$-T \cdot \text{Log}(1-\mu_i) \qquad\qquad -T \cdot \Sigma \text{Log}(1-\mu_i)$$

.000365	.000365
6.55950	6.55986
32.0220	38.5819

NORMALIZED EIGENVECTOR MATRIX E*

.96199	.27295	.00833
−.1939	.70425	−.6829
−.1922	.65539	.73041

β' EIGENMATRIX [largest μ_i first]:

Variable	lc	li	inf
lc	74.008	−59.1329	7.81881
li	20.998	−9.18903	−2.1370
inf	.64063	−7.32108	34.4372

STANDARDIZED β' EIGENVECTORS

Variable	lc	li	inf
lc	1.0000	−.79900	.10565
li	−2.285	1.00000	.23257
inf	.01860	−.21259	1.0000

STANDARDIZED α COEFFICIENTS

Variable	lc	li	inf
lc	−.0384	.01445	−.00083
li	.79743	.00251	−.00103
inf	−.1677	−.0269	−.00005

DIRECT UNRESTRICTED SYSTEM ESTIMATES

	lc 1	li 1	inf 1
lc	.9285	.0453	−.001
li	.7917	.3656	.0838
inf	−.106	.1070	.9760

DIRECT UNRESTRICTED SYSTEM STANDARD ERRORS

	lc 1	li 1	inf 1
lc	.1080	.0846	.0497
li	.1777	.1393	.0817
inf	.0906	.0710	.0417

$$\text{LOG DET } \Omega \quad = \quad -26.52069$$
$$\text{LIKELIHOOD} \quad = \quad 573978.36$$

SYSTEM SEASONALS

	INCPT	Q1	Q2	Q3
lc	.2732	−.1524	.0072	−.0328
li	−1.26	−.0892	.0400	−.0096
inf	−.022	.00326	−.001	−.0012

STANDARD ERRORS OF SYSTEM SEASONALS

	INCPT	Q1	Q2	Q3
lc	.2384	.00499	.00632	.00407
li	.3924	.00822	.01045	.00671
inf	.2000	.00419	.00530	.00342

COVARIANCE MATRIX OF UNRESTRICTED SYSTEM RESIDUALS

	lc	li	inf
lc	.0001		
li	.0001	.0004	
inf	−.000	−.000	.0001

STANDARD DEVIATIONS OF EQUATION RESIDUALS

lc	.01183
li	.01947
inf	.00992

CORRELATION MATRIX OF SYSTEM RESIDUALS

	lc	li	inf
lc	1.000		
li	.5887	1.0000	
inf	−.329	−.2198	1.0000

MODEL 6.14: *VAR*(2) with constant and seasonal variables

Present Sample Dates are: 1958 (3) to 1975 (4) less 0 Forecasts

EIGENVALUES μ_i are:

.000039	.092597	.285601

There are 3 valid eigenvalues $\mu_i \in (0,1)$ out of 3

$-T \cdot \text{Log}(1-\mu_i)$	$-T \cdot \Sigma \text{Log}(1-\mu_i)$
.002698	.002698
6.80181	6.80451
23.5419	30.3464

NORMALIZED EIGENVECTOR MATRIX E*

.89520	.44565	.00340
−.4043	.81546	−.4141
−.1873	.36935	.91021

β' EIGENMATRIX [largest μ_i first]

Variable	lc	li	inf
lc	84.846	−70.5852	16.31277
li	42.238	−24.4277	−10.0438
inf	.32204	−4.61437	35.68388

STANDARDIZED β' EIGENVECTORS

Variable	lc	li	inf
lc	1.0000	−.83191	.19226
li	−1.729	1.00000	.41116
inf	.00902	−.12931	1.0000

STANDARDIZED α COEFFICIENTS

Variable	lc	li	inf
lc	.02662	.03086	−.0024
li	.66849	−.0438	−.0030
inf	−.3232	−.0553	.00011

DIRECT UNRESTRICTED SYSTEM ESTIMATES

	lc 1	li 1	inf 1	lc 2	li 2	inf 2
lc	.7812	.0267	−.1705	.1920	−.017	.1859
li	.8401	.3431	−.0760	−.095	.0572	.1834
inf	−.180	.0753	1.0301	−.047	.1383	−.114

DIRECT UNRESTRICTED SYSTEM STANDARD ERRORS

	lc 1	li 1	inf 1	lc 2	li 2	inf 2
lc	.1570	.0896	.1481	.1591	.0905	.1573
li	.2630	.1501	.2481	.2665	.1516	.2635
inf	.1256	.0717	.1185	.1273	.0724	.1259

LOG DET Ω = −26.69639
LIKELIHOOD = 626684.96

SYSTEM SEASONALS

	INCPT	Q1	Q2	Q3
lc	.2075	−.1478	−.012	−.0241
li	−1.15	−.0895	.0469	−.0125
inf	.0961	.00692	−.009	−.0017

STANDARD ERRORS OF SYSTEM SEASONALS

	INCPT	Q1	Q2	Q3
lc	.2705	.0060	.0167	.0075
li	.4533	.0102	.0279	.0127
inf	.2165	.0048	.0133	.0060

6.7   Suggestions for Further Reading

The seminal papers on *VAR* modelling are those of Sims
(1980, 1982). An important development was made by Doan,
Litterman and Sims (1984), where simple Bayesian priors
were adopted for *VAR* modelling (see also Todd (1990)).
Evaluation of the forecasting results from *VARs* has not been
consistent. Litterman (1986) found the results good, but Fair
(1988) was less impressed. The best known sophisticated
applications of *VAR* models for policy analysis are those of
Bernanke (1986) and Blanchard and Watson (1986). *VAR*
models may be generalized to include moving average error
terms, in which case they are described as *VARMA* models.
Models of this type are discussed in Kendall and Ord (1990,
Chapter 14) and Granger and Newbold (1986, Chapter 8). A
comparison of *VAR* models with traditional macroeconometric models has been given by McNees (1986). Critic-
isms of *VAR* modelling are contained in Darnell and Evans
(1990, Chapter 7), Epstein (1987, Chapter 7), Leamer (1985),
Runckle (1987) and Pagan (1987). A recent development in
VAR modelling is in their relationship to structural models as
illustrated by Monfort and Rabemanjara (1990). VAR
modelling was extended for use with panel (cross section and
time series) data by Holtz–Eakin, Newey and Rosen (1988).
A thorough statistical inquiry to the *VAR* approach,
including cointegrated *VAR* models, is given by Lütkepohl
(1991).

Causality analysis was developed prior to that of *VAR*
modelling. Following the seminal paper of Granger (1969), a
great amount of theoretical and empirical analysis was
carried out. Apart from those mentioned in the text,

noteworthy theoretical contributions are the papers of Geweke (1984), Wu (1983) and Zellner (1979). Conceptual difficulties of causality were discussed by Jacobs, Leamer and Ward (1979) and Spohn (1984). Various causality tests are compared in Geweke, Meese and Dent (1983) and Guilkey and Salemi (1982).

Among various applications of causality testing which are relatively straightforward are the following. Price–wage causality has been analysed by Shannon and Wallace (1985-86), Fosu and Huq (1988) and Charemza (1989). Causality between public expenditure and national income was evaluated by Singh and Sahni (1984), between velocity and growth of money by Fisher and Serletis (1989), and money and income by Hsiao (1981), Stock and Watson (1989), Williams, Goodhart and Gowland (1976) and Sims (1972). An example of a time series approach for investigating money and price causality is that of Deadman and Ghatak (1989). Published applications of the Johansen method are still scarce, though one may note those of Johansen and Juselius (1990), Hall (1989), Hall and Henry (1988), and Hendry, Muellbauer and Murphy (1990). There is also a number of (as yet) unpublished papers in circulation (for example Clements (1989), Jacobson and Ohlsson (1991), Charemza (1990a) and Podvinsky (1990)) which suggests that a more extensive range of published work in this area will soon be available. The relationship between causation and cointegration has been investigated by Granger (1988).

Chapter 7

Exogeneity
and Structural Invariance

7.1   Data Generating Processes

In Chapter 6 we outlined the principal assumptions of multi-equation modelling within the Cowles Commission framework, and introduced in greater detail, the 'atheoretical' VAR approach. We stated that the two principal assumptions of structural modelling, namely the endo–exogenous division of the variables and the zero restrictions imposed on a model's parameters, are abandoned in VAR modelling. There are no exogenous variables in the system and, due to the lack of zero restrictions, there is nothing like a 'structural form' of the model.

The VAR approach is quite difficult to apply in the real world. In practice, VAR modelling for more than four variables is rarely feasible. An investigator has to include many lags on many variables in each equation. The number of parameters to be estimated becomes large and even a single equation may become impossible to estimate, due to the shortage of observations. Moreover, the fact that the VAR approach is 'atheoretical' makes the development of an economically sensible model from a VAR system a quite difficult task (although, as shown in Chapter 6, not necessarily impossible).

The method of multi–equation modelling presented in this chapter, which we will call *exogeneity modelling*, can be thought of as a compromise in some respects between the need to keep the size of the model manageable and consistent with economic theory on the one hand, and the properties of the statistical data used for the modelling on the other. Generally speaking, exogeneity modelling still allows for some *a priori* zero restrictions to be imposed and therefore for control over the size of the model, but the endo–exogenous division between variables is not given *a priori* any more. This division constitutes a testable hypothesis and because of this it is, to some extent, connected with the former problem of zero restrictions. If a certain variable is not exogenous, it should be modelled within the system and therefore some of the hypothetical zero restrictions may not be valid.

Exogeneity modelling can be envisaged as bringing together elements from both structural and *VAR* modelling. It bears some resemblance to the concept of recursive systems (for example, see Wold (1954)), which were regarded in the 1950s as a criticism of simultaneous equation structural modelling. According to Wold, simultaneity does not exist in the economy as there is always a time lag between a cause and an outcome. Hence, models represented by the general form of equations (6.6) do not make sense.

However, exogeneity modelling is not as extreme as the early Wold theories would require. A system of simultaneous equations can be a valid part of the model, provided it is the result of a general to specific modelling exercise and survives the tests described in Chapters 3 and 4. Adapting slightly the notation of equation (6.7) in Chapter 6, this structural model may be written as:

$$y'_t \Gamma = z'_t B_0 + \sum_{i=1}^{k} y'_{t-i} B_i + u'_t \,.\qquad(7.1)$$

In structural modelling, the model specification stops here. In exogeneity modelling, however, the variables z_t can also be modelled, creating something like a recursive part of the system, as:

$$z_t = \sum_{i=1}^{g} C_i y_{t-i} + \sum_{i=1}^{l} D_i z_{t-i} + v_t \,.\qquad(7.2)$$

The problem is to separate the parts of the model describing

y_t and z_t in such a way that y_t can be modelled independently (but conditionally) on z_t. That is, no knowledge about the process generating z_t will be required for the modelling of y_t. Evidently for this to be the case, there should be no relation between the error terms u_t and v_t and no cross–restrictions between the parameters of the two parts of the model.

Exogeneity modelling can also be regarded as a method of inference in a *VAR* model. In the unrestricted *VAR* model, where the entire set of contemporaneous variables is denoted as $\mathbb{L}_t$:

$$\mathbb{L}_t = \sum_{i=1}^{k} A_i \mathbb{L}_{t-i} + \epsilon_t,$$

the problem is in the partitioning of $\mathbb{L}_t$ into two sets of variables, say $[\mathbb{L}_t^1 \quad \mathbb{L}_t^2]$, whose error terms are not correlated between the two sets. The part corresponding to $\mathbb{L}_t^1$ is then the *VAR* equivalent to (7.1), while the part corresponding to $\mathbb{L}_t^2$ is the *VAR* equivalent to (7.2).

Hence, the problem of distinguishing which variables should enter the vectors y_t and z_t plays a central role in exogeneity modelling. Before we move to the problems of establishing the partition between y_t and z_t, that is defining and testing for exogeneity, it will be useful to introduce the concept of a data generating process.

We start with some rather involved notation. Let x_t^* denote a vector of observations on n^* random variables at time t ($t = 1,2,..,T$). The matrix X_t^* denotes all observations on the n^* variables up to and including time t, that is $X_t^* = [x_1^* \ x_2^* \ ... \ x_t^*]$. The joint density function of the entire set of observations, current and past, is denoted herein as $D(x_1^* \; x_2^* \; ... \; x_t^* \mid \theta^*)$ or $D(X_t^* \mid \theta^*)$, where θ^* is the vector of parameters of the joint density function. This joint density function is called the *Data Generating Process* (*DGP*). A working definition of this concept has been given by Spanos (1986, p.20) as 'the mechanism underlying the observable phenomena of interest'. An important decomposition of a *DGP* can be derived by representing it as a process of generating the data conditionally on the past, that is as:

$$D(X_T^* \mid \theta^*) = \prod_{t=1}^{T} D(x_t^* \mid X_{t-1}^* \; ; \; \theta^*) . \qquad (7.3)$$

The notation of the type $D(\bullet \mid \bullet)$ used here bears a strong resemblance to that used for joint, conditional and marginal probability density functions. In fact, there are some formal differences between the analysis of probability distributions and *DGP*s, which we will ignore for simplicity. However, in order to avoid confusion when we use these concepts below, we will refer to 'processes' rather than to 'density functions'.

It is known from the foundations of probability theory (for example see Freund and Walpole (1987, pp. 102–127) or, at a more advanced level, Spanos (1986, pp. 78–95)) that if a *joint probability density* function of two continuous random variables, X and Y is $f(x, y)$, where x is a realization of X and y is a realization of Y, the *marginal distribution* of X has a density function:

$$g(x) = \int_y f(x, y) \, dy ,$$

where the range of integration is the range of values of Y. Note that as this integration is with respect to y, the marginal distribution of x will not involve y (loosely, the variable y has been 'integrated out' of the joint probability distribution of x and y). The *conditional distribution* of y *given* x has its density function denoted as $f(y \mid x)$ and can be interpreted as the probability distribution of the random variable Y given that a realization of X is known to be x. The relationship between the joint, conditional and marginal distributions is:

$$f(x, y) = g(x) \cdot f(y \mid x) .$$

As an example (adapted later in the text as EXAMPLE 7.1) consider the bivariate normal random variables (X, Y), that is random variables with a joint density function:

$$f(x, y) =$$

$$\frac{1}{\sqrt{1-\rho^2} \cdot 2 \cdot \pi \cdot \sigma_1 \sigma_2} \, exp \left\{ -\frac{1}{2 \cdot (1-\rho^2)} \left(\left[\frac{x - \mu_1}{\sigma_1} \right]^2 \right. \right.$$

$$\left. \left. -2 \cdot \rho \left[\frac{x - \mu_1}{\sigma_1} \right] \left[\frac{y - \mu_2}{\sigma_2} \right] + \left[\frac{y - \mu_2}{\sigma_2} \right]^2 \right) \right\} ,$$

for $-\infty \le x \le \infty$, $-\infty \le y \le \infty$, $\sigma_1 > 0$, $\sigma_2 > 0$, and $-1 < \rho < 1$.
The density function above has five parameters. In order to keep the notation conformable with most of the literature, we will denote the variance of x (that is σ_1^2) by σ_{11}, the variance of y (that is σ_2^2) by σ_{22} and the covariance of x and y by σ_{12}. In the case of the bivariate normal distribution this covariance is equal to $\rho \cdot \sigma_1 \cdot \sigma_2$. The random variables having the above density function will be denoted in an abbreviated form as $(X, Y) \sim N_2(\mu_1, \mu_2, \sigma_{11}, \sigma_{22}, \rho)$.

The marginal density function for X can be derived from the bivariate distribution $N_2(\mu_1, \mu_2, \sigma_{11}, \sigma_{22}, \rho)$ by integrating it with respect to Y, giving:

$$g(x) = \frac{1}{\sqrt{2\cdot\pi\cdot\sigma_1}} exp\left\{-\frac{1}{2}\left[\frac{x-\mu_1}{\sigma_1}\right]^2\right\}$$

(see Spanos (1986, p.88)). Hence, the marginal distribution for X is nothing more than a univariate normal distribution with parameters μ_1 , σ_{11} , or in conventional notation, $X \sim N(\mu_1, \sigma_{11})$.

Tedious but not particularly complicated algebra will lead to the following density function for the conditional distribution of Y on X (see Spanos (1986, p.93)):

$$f(y\mid x) = \frac{1}{\sqrt{1-\rho^2}\cdot\sqrt{2\cdot\pi}\cdot\sigma_2} exp\left\{-\frac{1}{2\cdot(1-\rho^2)\cdot\sigma_{22}}\left[\left[y-\mu_2-\rho\cdot\frac{\sigma_2}{\sigma_1}\cdot(x-\mu_1)\right]^2\right\}\right.,$$

which is in fact a density function for a univariate normal distribution with mean equal to $\mu_2 + \rho\cdot\frac{\sigma_2}{\sigma_1}\cdot(x-\mu_1)$ and variance $\sigma_{22}\cdot(1-\rho^2)$. Hence, the conditional distribution of Y on X can be denoted as:

$$Y\mid X \sim N(\mu_2 + \rho\cdot\frac{\sigma_2}{\sigma_1}\cdot(x-\mu_1), \sigma_{22}\cdot(1-\rho^2)).$$

This result will be used in further examples throughout this chapter.

If we are dealing with three rather than two random

variables, say X, Y and Z, the joint density function can be factorized as:

$$f(x, y, z) = s(z) \cdot h(y \mid z) \cdot f(x \mid y, z),$$

where $s(z)$ is the marginal density of z (that is, it is equal to $\int_x \int_y f(x, y, z) dy dx$) and $h(y \mid z)$, $f(x \mid y, z)$ are conditional densities. Equation (7.3) above can be thought of as an application and generalization of this result.

Having returned to the DGP and its representation, it is also interesting to note that the right–hand side conditional density processes $D(x_t^* \mid X_{t-1}^* ; \theta^*)$ bear a resemblance to a VAR model in that all the current observations are conditional on all the information from the past. However, for exogeneity modelling this is only the beginning. The size and complexity of (7.3) is in practical cases so big that any sensible inference on it is not possible. Hence, we would like to reduce (strictly speaking, to decompose) the DGP by distinguishing between the *redundant (irrelevant) variables* (w_t), which can be eliminated from (7.3) without affecting its entire structure, the *variables of interest* (y_t), which are subject to our economic inference, and the *extraneous variables* (z_t), which are in some sense not conditioned upon the variables of interest. Let us partition the vector of observations x_t^* into these three sets of variables $(w_t\, y_t\, z_t)$, and analogously let us partition X_t^* into $(W_t\, Y_t\, Z_t)$ and θ^* into $(\lambda_0\, \lambda_1\, \lambda_2)$. The idea of such notation is that variables denoted by lower case letters $(w_t\, y_t\, z_t)$ represent *contemporaneous* values of these variables at time t, while the capital letters $(W_t\, Y_t\, Z_t)$ correspond to *all past* values of particular variables *and* the contemporaneous ones. Generally, we may represent each factor on the right–hand side of (7.3) as:

$$D(x_t^* \mid X_{t-1}^* ; \theta^*) =$$
$$D_0(w_t \mid W_{t-1}, Y_t, Z_t; \lambda_0) \cdot D_1(y_t \mid W_{t-1}, Y_{t-1}, Z_t; \lambda_1) \cdot$$
$$D_2(z_t \mid W_{t-1}, Y_{t-1}, Z_{t-1}; \lambda_2) .$$

However, if the variables w_t are redundant or irrelevant in relation to the remaining variables, they *may* depend on Y_t and Z_t, but y_t and z_t *may not* depend on W_t. The partition between the variables y_t and z_t is such that y_t depends on its own lagged values and the contemporaneous and lagged values of z_t, while z_t may depend on its own lagged values but only on lagged and not contemporaneous values of y_t. Hence, we may write (7.3) as (see Gilbert (1986)):

$$D(x_t^* \mid X_{t-1}^* ; \theta^*) =$$
$$D_0(w_t \mid W_{t-1}, Y_t, Z_t; \lambda_0) \cdot D_1(y_t \mid Y_{t-1}, Z_t; \lambda_1) \cdot$$
$$D_2(z_t \mid Y_{t-1}, Z_{t-1}; \lambda_2) . \qquad (7.4)$$

From now on we will ignore the redundant variables. The *general to specific* modelling approach, described in Chapter 4, shows one way of eliminating redundant variables from a model. Let us say that this has already been done and we are left with n variables (that is $n^* - n$ variables have been eliminated), which constitute the vector $x_t = (y_t, z_t)$. Analogously, there is now a matrix X_t partitioned as (Y_t, Z_t), and the factorization in (7.4) can be simplified to:

$$D(x_t \mid X_{t-1} ; \theta) = D_1(y_t \mid Y_{t-1}, Z_t; \lambda_1) \cdot D_2(z_t \mid Y_{t-1}, Z_{t-1}; \lambda_2).$$
$$(7.5)$$

where θ denotes that part of θ^* which corresponds to X_t.

The factor $D_1(\bullet \mid \bullet)$ in (7.5) is called a *conditional process* while the factor $D_2(\bullet \mid \bullet)$ is called, rather imprecisely, a *marginal process*. In general, the econometrician is particularly interested in obtaining the estimates of the parameters of the conditional process $D_1(\bullet \mid \bullet)$, especially its mean and variance, rather than the estimates of the marginal process for z_t.

It has to be stressed that a *DGP* itself is *not* an econometric model. As its name implies, it describes the way the data are generated, which does not necessarily correspond to any particular economic theory. An econometric model derived on the basis of a *DGP* might correspond either to its marginal or conditional process, depending on which is consistent with an economic theory.

One of the simplest examples of a model described by conditional and marginal processes is the case of two variables , z_t and y_t, which do not depend on any extraneous information and have no dynamics (EXAMPLE 7.1) . They constitute bivariate normal random variables, that is:

$$z_t = \mu_1 + \epsilon_{1t} \, ,$$
$$y_t = \mu_2 + \epsilon_{2t} \, ,$$

where $E(\epsilon_{1t}) = E(\epsilon_{2t}) = 0$, $Var(\epsilon_{1t}) = \sigma_{11}$, $Var(\epsilon_{2t}) = \sigma_{22}$, and $Cov(\epsilon_{1t} \epsilon_{2t}) = \sigma_{12}$. Recalling the previously given result, in this example the joint process of z_t , y_t is $N_2(\mu_1$, μ_2, σ_{11} , σ_{22} , ρ) where $\rho = \sigma_{12}/(\sigma_{11} \cdot \sigma_{22})^{0.5}$ and N_2 stands for a bivariate normal distribution. The marginal processes of z_t , y_t are univariate normal processes, $N(\mu_1$, $\sigma_{11})$ and $N(\mu_2$, $\sigma_{22})$ respectively. The conditional process can be either that of y_t conditional on z_t , that is:

$$y_t \mid z_t \sim N(\,\alpha + \beta z_t\,,\,\sigma_y\,),$$

where $\alpha = \mu_2 - \beta \cdot \mu_1$, $\beta = \sigma_{12}/\sigma_{11}$, $\sigma_y = \sigma_{22} - \sigma_{12}^2/\sigma_{11}$, or analogously, that of z_t conditional on y_t. Returning to the general notation, $x_t = (\,z_t\ y_t\,)$, and, assuming the variable of interest is y_t, then $y_t = (\,y_t\,)$, $z_t = (z_t)$, $Y_t = (\,y_1\ y_2 \cdots y_t\,)$, $Z_t = (\,z_1\ z_2 \cdots z_t\,)$, $X_t = (\,Y_t\ Z_t\,)$ and $\theta = (\,\mu_1, \mu_2, \sigma_{11}, \sigma_{22}, \rho\,)$. Hence, the *DGP* is given by:

$$D(X_T \mid \theta) = \prod_{t=1}^{T} D(x_t \mid X_{t-1}\,;\,\theta)$$

$$= \prod_{t=1}^{T} f_1(y_t \mid z_t;\ \alpha,\ \beta,\ \sigma_y) \cdot f_2(z_t \mid \mu_1,\ \sigma_{11}),$$

where $f_i(\bullet)$, $i = 1, 2$, denotes a density function of a normal random variable.

A straightforward extension of the above example is represented by a two equation model, consisting of two simple regression equations with contemporaneously correlated errors (EXAMPLE 7.2):

$$z_t = \alpha \cdot q_{1t} + \epsilon_{1t},$$
$$y_t = \beta \cdot q_{2t} + \epsilon_{2t},$$

where q_{1t} and q_{2t} are nonstochastic variables, and where, as before, $E(\epsilon_{1t}) = E(\epsilon_{2t}) = 0$, $Var(\epsilon_{1t}) = \sigma_{11}$, $Var(\epsilon_{2t}) = \sigma_{22}$, and $Cov(\epsilon_{1t}\ \epsilon_{2t}) = \sigma_{12}$. The analysis is virtually the same as for EXAMPLE 7.1, with the only difference being that the mean of each marginal process, for z_t and y_t, is not constant but equal to $\alpha \cdot q_{1t}$ and $\beta \cdot q_{2t}$ respectively. The joint process of z_t, y_t is $N_2(\alpha \cdot q_{1t}, \beta \cdot q_{2t}, \sigma_{11}, \sigma_{22}, \rho)$ for each t where ρ $= \sigma_{12}/(\sigma_{11} \cdot \sigma_{22})^{0.5}$. The conditional process of y_t on z_t is:

$$y_t \mid z_t \sim N(\beta \cdot q_{2t} - \gamma \cdot \alpha \cdot q_{1t} + \gamma \cdot z_t, \sigma_y),$$

where $\gamma = \sigma_{12}/\sigma_{11}$, and $\sigma_y = \sigma_{22} - \sigma_{12}^2/\sigma_{11}$. In the general notation introduced above, $x_t = (z_t \ y_t \ q_{1t} \ q_{2t})$, $y_t = (y_t)$, $z_t = (z_t \ q_{1t} \ q_{2t})$, $Y_t = (y_1 \ y_2 \cdots y_t)$, $Z_t = (z_1 \ z_2 \cdots z_t)$, $X_t = (Y_t \ Z_t)$ and $\theta = (\alpha, \beta, \sigma_{11}, \sigma_{22}, \rho)$. Here, for convenience, we are regarding the q_{it} variables as random variables rather than complicate the notation even further by introducing another set of (nonrandom) variables. The *DGP* is:

$$D(X_T \mid \theta) = \prod_{t=1}^{T} D(x_t \mid X_{t-1}; \theta) =$$

$$\prod_{t=1}^{T} f_1(y_t \mid z_t, q_{1t}, q_{2t}; \alpha, \beta, \gamma, \sigma_y) \cdot f_2(z_t, q_{1t}, q_{2t} \mid \alpha, \sigma_{11}).$$

To stress the generality of exogeneity modelling, we will show that the 'orthogonalization' of a *VAR* model, as discussed in Chapter 6, can also be regarded as a case of conditioning and marginalization of a *DGP*. For EXAMPLE 7.3, consider a two dimensional *VAR* model with two lags and contemporaneously correlated error terms, that is:

$$\begin{bmatrix} z_t \\ y_t \end{bmatrix} = \begin{bmatrix} a_1 & b_1 \\ c_1 & d_1 \end{bmatrix} \begin{bmatrix} z_{t-1} \\ y_{t-1} \end{bmatrix} + \begin{bmatrix} a_2 & b_2 \\ c_2 & d_2 \end{bmatrix} \begin{bmatrix} z_{t-2} \\ y_{t-2} \end{bmatrix} + \begin{bmatrix} \epsilon_{1t} \\ \epsilon_{2t} \end{bmatrix},$$

with $E(\epsilon_{1t}) = E(\epsilon_{2t}) = 0$, $Var(\epsilon_{1t}) = \sigma_{11}$, $Var(\epsilon_{2t}) = \sigma_{22}$, and $Cov(\epsilon_{1t}\,\epsilon_{2t}) = \sigma_{12}$. In order to develop a conditional process of y_t on z_t we may condition y_t on z_t, that is we multiply the first row of the above matrix by $\delta = \sigma_{12}/\sigma_{11}$ and subtract the result from the second row. As shown in Chapter 6, the result is:

$$
\begin{bmatrix} z_t \\ y_t - \delta z_t \end{bmatrix} = \begin{bmatrix} a_1 & b_1 \\ c_1^* & d_1^* \end{bmatrix} \begin{bmatrix} z_{t-1} \\ y_{t-1} \end{bmatrix} + \begin{bmatrix} a_2 & b_2 \\ c_2^* & d_2^* \end{bmatrix} \begin{bmatrix} z_{t-2} \\ y_{t-2} \end{bmatrix} + \begin{bmatrix} \epsilon_{2t} \\ \epsilon_{2t}^* \end{bmatrix},
$$

where
$$ c_i^* = (c_i - \delta a_i) \,; \quad d_i^* = (d_i - \delta b_i) \,; \quad \epsilon_{2t}^* = (\epsilon_{2t} - \delta\epsilon_{1t}) \,, \quad i = 1,2 \,. $$

Note that the expression for z_t does not involve the current value of y_t. In addition, there is no contemporaneous correlation between the error terms in this 'orthogonalized' form of the equations.

Hence, the factorization of the *DGP* is given by:

$$
D(X_T \mid \theta) = \prod_{t=1}^{T} D(x_t \mid X_{t-1}; \theta) =
$$

$$
\prod_{t=1}^{T} f_1(y_t \mid z_t, z_{t-1}, y_{t-1}, z_{t-2}, y_{t-2}; c_1^*, c_2^*, d_1^*, d_2^*, \delta)
$$

$$
\cdot f_2(z_t \mid z_{t-1}, y_{t-1}, z_{t-2}, y_{t-2}; a_1, a_2, b_1, b_2, \sigma_{11}).
$$

In Examples 7.1 and 7.2 we have shown that simple statistical bivariate models can be represented by a *DGP*. EXAMPLE 7.3 shows the factorization of a *VAR* model. Finally we present an example (EXAMPLE 7.4) of a typical structural (Cowles–Commission type) model, often used to illustrate the so–called 'cobweb effect' in economic dynamics.

$$y_t = \alpha \cdot z_t + \epsilon_{1t}, \tag{7.6a}$$

$$z_t = \beta \cdot y_{t-1} + \epsilon_{2t}, \tag{7.6b}$$

where, as before, it is assumed that ϵ_{1t}, ϵ_{2t} constitute a bivariate normal error process with $E(\epsilon_{1t}) = E(\epsilon_{2t}) = 0$, $Var(\epsilon_{1t}) = \sigma_{11}$, $Var(\epsilon_{2t}) = \sigma_{22}$, and $Cov(\epsilon_{1t} \epsilon_{2t}) = \sigma_{12}$. The marginal process of z_t is defined by (7.6b), being $N(\beta \cdot y_{t-1}, \sigma_{22})$, while the marginal process for y_t is a derived 'reduced form' equation for y_t, that is by a process for an equation derived from (7.6a) after the substitution for z_t from (7.6b):

$$y_t = \alpha \cdot \beta \cdot y_{t-1} + \nu_t, \tag{7.7}$$

where $\nu_t = \epsilon_{1t} + \alpha \cdot \epsilon_{2t}$. The expected value of ν_t is zero and its variance is equal to:

$$E[(\epsilon_{1t} + \alpha \cdot \epsilon_{2t})^2] = \sigma_{11} + 2\alpha \cdot \sigma_{12} + \alpha^2 \sigma_{22},$$

since $E[(\epsilon_{1t} \cdot \epsilon_{2t}) = \sigma_{12}$. Hence, the covariance between the error terms of the marginal distributions, that is between ν_t and ϵ_{2t}, is equal to $\sigma_{12} + \alpha \cdot \sigma_{22}$. By analogy to the previous examples, the conditional process of y_t for z_t can be derived from (7.7) and (7.6b) by defining $\delta = Cov(\nu_t \epsilon_{2t}) / \sigma_{22} = \sigma_{12}/\sigma_{22} + \alpha$, multiplying (7.6b) by δ and subtracting the result from (7.7). This gives:

$$y_t = \delta \cdot z_t - (\sigma_{12}/\sigma_{22}) \cdot \beta \cdot y_{t-1} + u_t, \tag{7.8}$$

where $u_t = \epsilon_{1t} - (\sigma_{12}/\sigma_{22}) \cdot \epsilon_{2t}$. The variance of u_t (say σ^2) is equal to $\sigma_{11} - (\sigma_{12}^2/\sigma_{22})$. In fact (7.8) can be regarded as a regression equation:

$$y_t = a \cdot z_t + b \cdot y_{t-1} + u_t, \qquad (7.9)$$

where $a = (\alpha + \sigma_{12}/\sigma_{22})$ and $b = -(\sigma_{12}/\sigma_{22}) \cdot \beta$. It is easy to check that the error terms in the conditional equation (7.9) and the marginal equation (7.6b), that is u_t and ϵ_{2t}, are orthogonal. Finally, the *DGP* for (7.6a – 7.6b) can be written as:

$$D(X_T \mid \theta) = \prod_{t=1}^{T} D(x_t \mid X_{t-1}; \theta)$$

$$= \prod_{t=1}^{T} f_1(y_t \mid y_{t-1}, z_t; a, b, \sigma^2) \cdot f_2(z_t \mid y_{t-1}; \beta, \sigma_{22}).$$

7.2   Weak and Strong Exogeneity

The arguments and examples in the previous section illustrate the idea of the division of the variables between those for which the conditioning is made (that is those which constitute the set y_t) and those for which the marginal processes are evaluated (that is z_t). This is connected with the much wider question of what are really the dependent and independent parts of the model.

Structural (Cowles Commission) econometrics distinguishes between the *endogenous* and *exogenous* variables of an econometric model. Generally, but not very precisely, the endogenous variables are those which are explained by the structure of the model and all the remaining variables are the exogenous variables. In so–called *full* econometric models (nearly all known structural econometric models are full) the number of endogenous variables is equal to the number of equations. As an illustration, recall the two structural models discussed in Chapter 6. The first one is a simple Keynesian model:

$$C_t = \alpha + \beta Y_t + \epsilon_t ,$$
$$Y_t = C_t + I_t ,$$

where C_t is the level of consumption, Y_t is aggregate income, I_t is the level of investment, ϵ_t is an error term, and α and β are coefficients. In Chapter 6 it was postulated that the variables C_t and Y_t are endogenous and I_t exogenous. Since this model does not contain any lagged variables, the endogenous variables are also *jointly dependent* and the exogenous variable is *predetermined*. For estimation purposes, it is necessary to assume that the exogenous variable is not correlated with current (and indeed lagged) error terms.

The second example given in Chapter 6 is a supply-demand equilibrium model:

$$Q_t = \alpha_0 + \alpha_1 P_t + \alpha_2 r_t + u_{1t} ,$$
$$Q_t = \beta_0 + \beta_1 P_t + \beta_2 P_{t-1} + u_{2t} ,$$

where Q_t denotes the quantity transacted, P_t is the price, r_t is the interest rate and u_{1t}, u_{2t} are the error terms, assumed to be mutually and serially independent. In the above model the *current* endogenous variables are Q_t and P_t, which are also *jointly dependent*. P_{t-1} is the *lagged* endogenous variable which, together with r_t (the exogenous variable) creates the set of *predetermined* variables.

The above distinction between endogenous and exogenous variables is not sufficient for all purposes. For model estimation, some of the endogenous variables sometimes have to be treated more akin to exogenous rather than to endogenous variables. For instance, in the model discussed as EXAM-PLE 7.4 in the previous section of this chapter, that is in:

$$y_t = \alpha \cdot z_t + \epsilon_{1t} \, , \qquad\qquad (7.6a)$$

$$z_t = \beta \cdot y_{t-1} + \epsilon_{2t} \, , \qquad\qquad (7.6b)$$

z_t and y_t are regarded as the jointly dependent or non–lagged endogenous variables, no matter whether the covariance of the error terms is zero or not. However, if the error terms are not contemporaneously correlated, the first of these equations can be consistently estimated by the ordinary least squares method, since z_t is not correlated with ϵ_{1t} . However, if ϵ_{1t} and ϵ_{2t} are contemporaneously correlated, z_t becomes correlated with ϵ_{1t} and ordinary least squares estimates of the equation for y_t are not consistent. Hence, the 'jointly dependent' variable z_t may be treated in the first case as an exogenous variable, and in the second case as an endogenous variable.

Further confusion arises when the model in EXAMPLE 7.4 is to be used for a dynamic enquiry (that is forecasting) for y_t. To make the example more interesting let us add an autoregressive process to the formation of z_t, so that the model becomes:

$$y_t = \alpha \cdot z_t + \epsilon_{1t} \, , \qquad\qquad (7.10a)$$

$$z_t = \beta \cdot y_{t-1} + \gamma \cdot z_{t-1} + \epsilon_{2t} \, . \qquad\qquad (7.10b)$$

Suppose, to keep things simple, that the error terms are neither serially nor contemporaneously correlated. If $\beta = 0$, the forecast values of y_t are simply conditional upon the set of observations for z_t . If $\beta \neq 0$, forecast values for y_t cannot be evaluated so straightforwardly from z_t since z_t depends on the lagged value of y_t and consequently, on the lagged ϵ_{1t}. Hence, despite the fact that y_t and z_t are formally endogenous, they have been treated differently, depending whether $\beta = 0$ or not.

Some of the problems encountered above may be dealt with by using the concepts of *predeterminedness* and *strict exogeneity*. It is said that a variable is predetermined in an equation of interest if it is independent of the *current* and *future* errors of that equation, while it is strictly exogenous if it is independent of the current, future and *past* errors of that equation. According to this, in model (7.10a) and (7.10b) the variable z_t is predetermined in equation (7.10a) if $\beta \neq 0$ (since it does depend on ϵ_{1t-1} through y_{t-1}) and is strictly endogenous if $\beta = 0$, since then it does not depend on the lagged errors of the equation (7.10a).

Although the concepts of predeterminedness and strict exogeneity are more precise than the traditional division of variables into endogenous and exogenous, it is still not precise enough to deal with all the potential ambiguities in defining econometric variables. In particular, it does not explicitly describe, *for what* an examining variable is to be exogenous. It can be easily shown that one's view of a variable can alter drastically, depending on which parameters of a model are of interest. (For a discussion of the concept of *parameters of interest* see Spanos (1986, pp. 418–421)). Returning to EXAMPLE 7.4 above (and retaining for the time being, the assumption that the error terms are independent), it is clear that if interest is in the estimation of the parameters of (7.6b), the role of the variable y_t is completely different from the case where interest is in the estimation of the parameters of (7.6a). This point may be exemplified by a problem posed by Pratt and Schlaifer (1984), which has subsequently been widely discussed in the literature. The model presented in this example is:

$$y_t = b \cdot z_t + u_t \, ,$$

where $E(u_t \mid z_t) = 0$. Evidently, if this is a full model, z_t meets any of the criteria of exogeneity given above. However, suppose that the same model is rewritten as:

$$y_t = b^* \cdot z_t + u_t^* \, ,$$

where $b^* = b + 1$ and $u_t^* = u_t - z_t$. Now the question of exogeneity of z_t looks much more complicated, since $E(u_t^* \mid z_t) \neq 0$. The problem becomes clearer if we decide whether our parameter of interest is b or b^*. If it is b, z_t is indeed exogenous (in the light of all the above definitions of exogeneity), but if the parameter of interest is b^*, z_t is not exogenous.

The idea of defining exogeneity for a given set of parameters of interest is central for the concepts of exogeneity proposed by Engle, Hendry and Richard (1983). They consider the following distinctions:

1. Between the variables which contain all necessary information for efficient estimation (static inference) of the parameters of interest conditionally on the values of these variables, and the remaining variables;
2. Between the variables whose values have to be known (be observed) in order to make a dynamic inference (forecast) from the estimated model using the parameters of interest, and those whose values may not be known;
3. Between the variables which do not alter the parameters of interest in a policy analysis experiment, and those which do.

The first of these divisions is connected with the concept of *weak exogeneity*, the second one with that of *strong exogeneity*, and the third with *superexogeneity*. In this section we will discuss the first two of these concepts. Superexogeneity will be discussed in Section 7.3 below.

The concept of weak exogeneity is related to the problem of static inference in an econometric model, that is estimation. Generally, a variable z_t can be regarded as weakly exogenous for a set of parameters of interest, say ψ, if the marginal process for z_t contains no useful information for the estimation of ψ, that is if an inference for ψ can be efficiently made conditionally on z_t alone and its marginal process contains no relevant information. The concept can also be formulated in reverse. That is, z_t is weakly exogenous for the parameters of interest ψ, if knowledge of ψ is not required for inference on the marginal process of z_t (see Spanos (1986, pp. 376 and 421–422)).

A slightly simplified (and therefore not entirely precise, but nevertheless sufficient for most practical purposes) definition of weak exogeneity is the following. The variable z_t is said to be weakly exogenous for ψ (the parameters of interest) if it is possible to write the *DGP* in terms of conditional and marginal processes as in (7.5), that is:

$$D(x_t \mid X_{t-1} ; \theta) = D_1(y_t \mid Y_{t-1}, Z_t; \lambda_1) \cdot D_2(z_t \mid Y_{t-1}, Z_{t-1}; \lambda_2):$$

and if:

1. ψ is a function of the parameters of the conditional process λ_1 alone (note that λ_1 itself *can* be a function of the parameters of the marginal process, that is of λ_2);

2. λ_1 and λ_2 are *variation free*, which means that, in particular, there cannot be any cross–restrictions between λ_1 and λ_2. In this case it is still possible for λ_1 to be a function of λ_2, whilst λ_2 is not a function of λ_1.

Let us examine the existence of weak exogeneity for particular sets of parameters in the examples of *DGPs* introduced in Section 7.1. EXAMPLE 7.1 analyses the bivariate normal process:

$$z_t = \mu_1 + \epsilon_{1t} \, ,$$

$$y_t = \mu_2 + \epsilon_{2t} \, ,$$

where $E(\epsilon_{1t}) = E(\epsilon_{2t}) = 0$, $Var(\epsilon_{1t}) = \sigma_{11}$, $Var(\epsilon_{2t}) = \sigma_{22}$, and $Cov(\epsilon_{1t} \, \epsilon_{2t}) = \sigma_{12}$. The conditional process of y_t on z_t is:

$$y_t \mid z_t \sim N(\alpha + \beta z_t \, , \, \sigma_y) \, ,$$

where $\alpha = \mu_2 - \beta \cdot \mu_1$, $\beta = \sigma_{12} / \sigma_{11}$, and $\sigma_y = \sigma_{22} - \sigma_{12}^2 / \sigma_{11}$. The *DGP* is given by:

$$D(X_T \mid \theta) = \prod_{t=1}^{T} D(x_t \mid X_{t-1} \, ; \, \theta)$$

$$= \prod_{t=1}^{T} f_1(y_t \mid z_t; \, \alpha \, , \, \beta \, , \, \sigma_y) \cdot f_2(z_t \mid \mu_1 \, , \, \sigma_{11}) \, .$$

Let us say that the parameters of interest are those of the conditional process, so that $\psi \equiv \lambda_1 = (\alpha \, , \, \beta \, , \, \sigma_y)$. Although the parameters in λ_1 are functions of the parameters in the marginal process $\lambda_2 = (\mu_1 \, , \, \sigma_{11})$, the parameters in λ_2 are not functions of those in λ_1, and there are no cross–restrictions between λ_1 and λ_2. Hence, z_t is weakly exogenous for $(\alpha \, , \, \beta \, , \, \sigma_y)$. In other words, the econometric model:

$$y_t = \alpha + \beta \cdot z_t + u_t \, ,$$

can be sensibly derived from the *DGP* and consistently estimated, without any need for further inference concerning z_t.

Note that formally the above equation is a part of a two equation model, since it should be accompanied by:

$$z_t = \mu_1 + \epsilon_{1t} \, .$$

EXAMPLE 7.2 is very similar to the above. The difference is that means of the processes are not constant and are functions of external variables q_{1t} and q_{2t}:

$$z_t = \alpha \cdot q_{1t} + \epsilon_{1t} \, ,$$
$$y_t = \beta \cdot q_{2t} + \epsilon_{2t} \, ,$$

where $E(\epsilon_{1t}) = E(\epsilon_{2t}) = 0$, $Var(\epsilon_{1t}) = \sigma_{11}$, $Var(\epsilon_{2t}) = \sigma_{22}$, and $Cov(\epsilon_{1t} \, \epsilon_{2t}) = \sigma_{12}$. The conditional process of y_t on z_t is:

$$y_t \mid z_t \sim N(a \cdot q_{1t} + b \cdot q_{2t} + c \cdot z_t \, , \, \sigma_y) \, ,$$

where $b = \beta$, $a = -(\sigma_{12} / \sigma_{22}) \cdot \alpha$, $c = \sigma_{12} / \sigma_{11}$, $\sigma_y = (\sigma_{22} - \sigma_{12}^2 / \sigma_{11})$ and the *DGP* is:

$$D(X_T \mid \theta) = \prod_{t=1}^{T} D(z_t \mid X_{t-1} \, ; \, \theta) =$$

$$\prod_{t=1}^{T} f_1(y_t \mid z_t \, , \, q_{1t}, \, q_{2t}; \, a \, , \, b \, , \, c \, , \, \sigma_y) \cdot f_2(z_t \, , \, q_{1t}, \, q_{2t} \mid \alpha \, , \, \sigma_{11}) \, .$$

If the parameters of interest are $(a \, , \, b \, , \, c \, , \, \sigma_y)$, then z_t is weakly exogenous for them, since there are no cross–restrictions between $(a \, , \, b \, , \, c \, , \, \sigma_y)$ and $(\alpha \, , \, \sigma_{11})$. Hence, the suggested econometric model is:

$$y_t = a \cdot q_{1t} + b \cdot q_{2t} + c \cdot z_t + u_t \, ,$$

$$z_t = \alpha \cdot q_{1t} + \epsilon_{1t} \, .$$

The problem of weak exogeneity becomes more complicated in the two remaining examples. In EXAMPLE 7.3 the
DGP is a straightforward *VAR* process:

$$\begin{bmatrix} z_t \\ y_t \end{bmatrix} = \begin{bmatrix} a_1 & b_1 \\ c_1 & d_1 \end{bmatrix} \begin{bmatrix} z_{t-1} \\ y_{t-1} \end{bmatrix} + \begin{bmatrix} a_2 & b_2 \\ c_2 & d_2 \end{bmatrix} \begin{bmatrix} z_{t-2} \\ y_{t-2} \end{bmatrix} + \begin{bmatrix} \epsilon_{1t} \\ \epsilon_{2t} \end{bmatrix} ,$$

$$(7.11)$$

where $E(\epsilon_{1t}) = E(\epsilon_{2t}) = 0$, $Var(\epsilon_{1t}) = \sigma_{11}$, $Var(\epsilon_{2t}) = \sigma_{22}$, and $Cov(\epsilon_{1t} \, \epsilon_{2t}) = \sigma_{12}$. The conditional process of y_t
on z_t together with the marginal process of z_t is:

$$\begin{bmatrix} z_t \\ y_t - \delta z_t \end{bmatrix} = \begin{bmatrix} a_1 & b_1 \\ c_1^* & d_1^* \end{bmatrix} \begin{bmatrix} z_{t-1} \\ y_{t-1} \end{bmatrix} + \begin{bmatrix} a_2 & b_2 \\ c_2^* & d_2^* \end{bmatrix} \begin{bmatrix} z_{t-2} \\ y_{t-2} \end{bmatrix} + \begin{bmatrix} \epsilon_{1t} \\ \epsilon_{2t}^* \end{bmatrix} ,$$

where:
$c_i^* = (c_i - \delta \cdot a_i)$, $\delta = \sigma_{12}/\sigma_{11}$, $d_i^* = (d_i - \delta \cdot b_i)$ and $\epsilon_{2t}^* = (\epsilon_{2t} - \delta \cdot \epsilon_{1t})$, $i = 1,2$.

After reading EXAMPLES 7.1 and 7.2 it should be easy
to check that z_t is weakly exogenous for the parameters of the
conditional process of y_t on z_t, that is for c_i^* and d_i^* ($i = 1,2$).
Suppose, however, that interest is in a short run model for y_t
with a cointegrated error correction mechanism developed
from a *VAR*. Recalling the general results from Chapter 6,
for a *VAR* model:

$$\mathit{l}_t = \sum_{i=1}^{k} A_i \mathit{l}_{t-i} + \mathcal{E}_t,$$

where l_t contains all n variables of the model and $\mathcal{E}_t$ is a vector of random errors, the Johansen decomposition is:

$$\Delta\mathit{l}_t = \sum_{i=1}^{k-1} \Gamma_i \Delta\mathit{l}_{t-i} + \Pi\mathit{l}_{t-k} + \mathcal{E}_t,$$

where:
$\Gamma_i = -I + A_1 + ... + A_i$ (I is a unit matrix),
$\Pi = -(I - A_1 - ... - A_k)$.

If there are r cointegrating vectors, the above equation can be rewritten as:

$$\Delta\mathit{l}_t = \sum_{i=1}^{k-1} \Gamma_i \Delta\mathit{l}_{t-i} + \alpha \cdot \beta' \cdot \mathit{l}_{t-k} + \mathcal{E}_t,$$

where β is a $n \times r$ matrix of cointegrating vectors and α is a $n \times r$ matrix of adjustment coefficients. For a two dimensional VAR process with $k = 2$ we have:

$$\begin{bmatrix} \Delta z_t \\ \Delta y_t \end{bmatrix} = \begin{bmatrix} \bar{a}_1 & \bar{b}_1 \\ \bar{c}_1 & \bar{d}_1 \end{bmatrix} \begin{bmatrix} \Delta z_{t-1} \\ \Delta y_{t-1} \end{bmatrix} + \begin{bmatrix} \bar{a}_2 & \bar{b}_2 \\ \bar{c}_2 & \bar{d}_2 \end{bmatrix} \begin{bmatrix} z_{t-2} \\ y_{t-2} \end{bmatrix} + \begin{bmatrix} \epsilon_{1t} \\ \epsilon_{2t} \end{bmatrix},$$

$$(7.12)$$

where:

$$\bar{a}_1 = a_1 - 1, \quad \bar{d}_1 = d_1 - 1, \quad \bar{a}_2 = a_1 + a_2 - 1, \quad \bar{b}_2 = b_1 + b_2,$$
$$\bar{c}_2 = c_1 + c_2, \quad \bar{d}_2 = d_1 + d_2 - 1.$$

Suppose now that there is a cointegrating vector in the VAR (as may be recalled from Chapter 6, in a two dimensional VAR there cannot be more than one cointegrating vector), $\beta' = [\beta_1 \quad \beta_2]$, and a corresponding vector of adjustment coefficients $\alpha' = [\alpha_1 \quad \alpha_2]$, so that the elements of matrix $\Pi = \alpha \cdot \beta'$ become:

$$\bar{a}_2 = \alpha_1 \cdot \beta_1, \quad \bar{b}_2 = \alpha_1 \cdot \beta_2,$$
$$\bar{c}_2 = \alpha_2 \cdot \beta_1, \quad \bar{d}_2 = \alpha_2 \cdot \beta_2.$$

If we derive a conditional process for Δy_t on Δz_t (by multiplying the first equation by $\delta = \sigma_{12}/\sigma_{11}$ and subtracting the result from the second equation) the marginal process for Δz_t and the conditional process for Δy_t given Δz_t are:

$$
\begin{bmatrix} \Delta z_t \\ \Delta y_t - \delta \Delta z_t \end{bmatrix} = \begin{bmatrix} \bar{a}_1 & \bar{b}_1 \\ \bar{c}_1^* & \bar{d}_1^* \end{bmatrix} \begin{bmatrix} \Delta z_{t-1} \\ \Delta y_{t-1} \end{bmatrix} + \begin{bmatrix} \bar{a}_2 & \bar{b}_2 \\ \bar{c}_2^* & \bar{d}_2^* \end{bmatrix} \begin{bmatrix} z_{t-2} \\ y_{t-2} \end{bmatrix}
$$

$$
+ \begin{bmatrix} \epsilon_{1t} \\ \epsilon_{2t}^* \end{bmatrix},
$$

where:

$$\bar{c}_1^* = \bar{c}_1 - \delta \cdot \bar{a}_1, \quad \bar{d}_1^* = \bar{d}_1 - \delta \cdot \bar{b}_1, \quad \bar{c}_2^* = \bar{c}_2 - \delta \cdot \bar{a}_2, \quad \bar{d}_2^* = \bar{d}_2 - \delta \cdot \bar{b}_2, \quad \text{and} \quad \epsilon_{2t}^* = (\epsilon_{2t} - \delta \cdot \epsilon_{1t}).$$

As before, ϵ_{1t} and ϵ_{2t}^* are orthogonal, so that their covariance is zero. This does not mean, however, that z_t is weakly exogenous if the parameters of interest are those of the conditional process of Δy_t.   The parameters of the conditional process are $\bar{c}_1^*$, $\bar{d}_1^*$, $\bar{c}_2^*$ and $\bar{d}_2^*$, and those of the marginal process are $\bar{a}_1$, $\bar{b}_1$, $\bar{a}_2$ and $\bar{b}_2$.   If there is one cointegrating vector in the process, it is clear that the parameters of the conditional and marginal processes are not variation free. Specifically:

$$\bar{a}_2 = \alpha_1 \cdot \beta_1 \; ; \quad \bar{c}_2^* = \alpha_2 \cdot \beta_1 - \delta \cdot \alpha_1 \cdot \beta_1 \; ,$$

and:

$$\bar{b}_2 = \alpha_1 \cdot \beta_2 \; ; \quad \bar{d}_2^* = \alpha_2 \cdot \beta_2 - \delta \cdot \alpha_1 \cdot \beta_2 \; .$$

Hence, there are two cross–restrictions between the parameters of the marginal and conditional distributions. It is not possible to alter the cointegrating coefficients β_1 and β_2 and the adjustment coefficient α_1 without affecting the coefficients of the marginal process.   Only α_2 can be changed freely, since it does not enter the marginal process.   It is important to note that z_t becomes weakly exogenous for δ,

$\bar{c}_1^*$, $\bar{d}_1^*$, $\bar{c}_2^*$ and $\bar{d}_2^*$ if $\alpha_1 = 0$ since in that case there are no cross–restrictions between the parameters of the marginal and conditional distributions.

There is some simple intuition behind the above example. There are two equations and only one error correction mechanism. If this mechanism enters both equations simultaneously, it is not possible to enquire about one of the equations separately from the other.   The only possibility of separate inference is when one of the adjustment coefficients is equal to zero, so that the error correction mechanism enters only one of the equations. This exogeneity analysis in an error correction model is derived from the more general approach of Urbain (1991); a similar problem is briefly discussed by

Hendry, Muellbauer and Murphy (1990).

EXAMPLE 7.4 analyses a *DGP* which corresponds to a cobweb model:

$$y_t = \alpha \cdot z_t + \epsilon_{1t}, \tag{7.6a}$$

$$z_t = \beta \cdot y_{t-1} + \epsilon_{2t}, \tag{7.6b}$$

where $E(\epsilon_{1t}) = E(\epsilon_{2t}) = 0$, $Var(\epsilon_{1t}) = \sigma_{11}$, $Var(\epsilon_{2t}) = \sigma_{22}$, and $Cov(\epsilon_{1t} \epsilon_{2t}) = \sigma_{12}$. The reduced form equation (marginal process) for y_t is:

$$y_t = \alpha \cdot \beta \cdot y_{t-1} + \nu_t, \tag{7.7}$$

where $\nu_t = \epsilon_{1t} + \alpha \cdot \epsilon_{2t}$, $Var(\nu_t) = E[(\epsilon_{1t} + \alpha \cdot \epsilon_{2t})^2] = \sigma_{11} + 2\alpha \cdot \sigma_{12} + \alpha^2 \sigma_{22}$, and $Cov(\nu_t \epsilon_{2t}) = \sigma_{12} + \alpha \cdot \sigma_{22}$. These results have been derived in Section 7.1 above, where it was also shown that the conditional process of y_t on z_t is:

$$y_t = \delta \cdot z_t - (\sigma_{12}/\sigma_{22}) \cdot \beta \cdot y_{t-1} + u_t, \tag{7.8}$$

where $\delta = Cov(\nu_t \epsilon_{2t})/ \sigma_{22} = \sigma_{12}/\sigma_{22} + \alpha$, $u_t = \epsilon_{1t} - (\sigma_{12}/\sigma_{22}) \cdot \epsilon_{2t}$, and $Var(u_t) = \sigma_{11} - (\sigma_{12}^2/\sigma_{22}) = \sigma^2$, or:

$$y_t = a \cdot z_t + b \cdot y_{t-1} + u_t, \tag{7.9}$$

where $a = \alpha + (\sigma_{12}/\sigma_{22})$ and $b = -(\sigma_{12}/\sigma_{22}) \cdot \beta$.

Suppose that the parameter of interest is the regression coefficient on z_t in equation (7.6a), that is α. The parameters of the conditional process of y_t on z_t are (a, b, σ^2) and those of the marginal process for z_t are (β, σ_{22}). It is not possible to recover α solely from the parameters of the conditional process since:

$$\alpha = a - (\sigma_{12}/\sigma_{22}),$$

that is, additional knowledge on the parameter σ_{22} of the marginal process is required. We may relate this result to our earlier definition of weak exogeneity since the marginal process of z_t contains relevant information for the estimation of the parameter of interest. Hence, z_t is not weakly exogenous for the parameter of interest α. The condition for z_t to become weakly exogenous for α is that the covariance between ϵ_{1t} and ϵ_{2t} is zero. If $\sigma_{12} = 0$, then $\alpha = a$ and no knowledge on the marginal process is needed for an enquiry concerning α.

The above examples suggest that testing for weak exogeneity is, in many cases, equivalent to testing for zero covariance of the error terms. In EXAMPLE 7.2 the *DGP* is:

$$z_t = \alpha \cdot q_{1t} + \epsilon_{1t},$$
$$y_t = \beta \cdot q_{2t} + \epsilon_{2t},$$

where $E(\epsilon_{1t}) = E(\epsilon_{2t}) = 0$, $Var(\epsilon_{1t}) = \sigma_{11}$, $Var(\epsilon_{2t}) = \sigma_{22}$ and $Cov(\epsilon_{1t}, \epsilon_{2t}) = \sigma_{12}$. If the null that $\sigma_{12} = 0$ is rejected, the next step is to move to a model where one of the variables is conditioned upon the other, for example to:

$$y_t = a \cdot q_{1t} + b \cdot q_{2t} + c \cdot z_t + u_t,$$
$$z_t = \alpha \cdot q_{1t} + \epsilon_{1t}.$$

However, we still do not know whether the above equations constitute a *DGP* (and hence the covariance between u_t and ϵ_{1t} is nonzero), or a marginal process for z_t and a conditional process for y_t (in this case the covariance between u_t and ϵ_{1t} is zero). A straightforward generalization of EXAMPLE 7.4 shows that if $Cov(u_t, \epsilon_{1t}) \neq 0$, z_t is not weakly exogenous for a, b and c. Hence the hypothesis of zero covariance between u_t and ϵ_{1t} has to be tested.

Technically, testing for zero covariance can be performed by the use of the Lagrange Multiplier test once again. We simply estimate the equation we think represents the marginal process by the method of ordinary least squares, compute the residuals and test these residuals as a missing variable in what we think is the conditional process. Since there is only one 'variable' (that is, the computed residuals) added to the regression, the traditional Student–t significance test is equivalent to the Lagrange Multiplier test. Such a procedure for testing weak exogeneity was originally suggested by Engle (1984, pp. 815–816).

EXAMPLE 7.3 shows, however, that in some cases the problem of weak exogeneity is more complex than this. If our interest is in the parameters of a short run equation with an error correction mechanism, it is essential that the marginal processes for the variables which appear in this short run equation do not contain the same error correction mechanism. If the equation for y_t is, for instance, a simple model with an error correction mechanism of the form introduced in Chapter 3, namely:

$$\Delta y_t = \alpha_1 \Delta z_t + \alpha_2 (y_{t-1} - \beta \cdot z_{t-1}) + \epsilon_{1t},$$

it is important in order for z_t to be weakly exogenous for the parameters in this equation that an equation explaining z_t (i) has its errors uncorrelated with ϵ_{1t} and (ii) does not contain the term $(y_{t-1} - \beta \cdot z_{t-1})$. If β is not specified *a priori*, it may be taken as having been estimated by the Engle–Granger (Chapter 5) or Johansen (Chapter 6) method. In any case, the testing procedure is more complex and consists firstly of testing (ii) in an equation for z_t, that is by an ordinary Student–t test. If the hypothesis of a zero regression coefficient for $(y_{t-1} - \beta \cdot z_{t-1})$ in the equation for z_t cannot be rejected, then the residuals of the equation for z_t with this term omitted may be computed and their significance in the equation for y_t may be tested. In the general case, the error correction terms may appear in the marginal model with various lags $(t-1, t-2,$ and so on) so that the first stage in the testing procedure would be a joint test on the coefficients of the lagged error correction variables.

    While the concept of weak exogeneity is primarily of a static nature, in that it deals with problems of static enquiry in a model (particularly estimation), the concept of *strong exogeneity* widens the issue by adding a dynamic aspect to it. Thus in forecasting, in order to avoid any feedback problems between the endogenous variables to be forecast and an 'exogenous' variable z_t, it would be necessary for the variable z_t not to be influenced by either the contemporaneous value of the endogenous variables or by the past or lagged values of these variables. Thus in EXAMPLE 7.4 above, forecast values of y_t outside of the sample period cannot be made conditionally on the values of z_t for these forecast periods, as these values of z_t will themselves depend upon lagged forecast values of y_t. Returning to our general notation, z_t should not be influenced either by the parameters of the conditional distribution of an endogenous variable y_t, or by the past values, y_{t-1}, y_{t-2}, etc. In other words, in this case, z_t is both weakly exogenous and is not preceded by any of the endogenous variables in the model. This suggests the following definition of strong exogeneity (see Engle, Hendry and Richard (1983) or Spanos (1986, p.505)):

Definition: A vector of variables z_t is strongly exogenous with respect to y_t for the parameters of interest ψ if:

1. z_t is weakly exogenous for ψ;
2. Y_{t-1} is not a Granger cause for z_t.

The definition of Granger causality as given in Section 6.3 states that y is a Granger cause for z if z_t can be predicted better with the use of information on past y (Y_{t-1}) rather than by not doing so, other information being identical. As a consequence, the Granger test for causality consists of testing that the coefficients of all lagged y_ts in equations explaining z_t are jointly zero.

Returning to the factorization of a *DGP* as (7.5):

$$D(x_t | X_{t-1} ; \theta) = D_1(y_t | Y_{t-1}, Z_t; \lambda_1) \cdot D_2(z_t | Y_{t-1}, Z_{t-1}; \lambda_2),$$

z_t is strongly exogenous with respect to y_t for the parameters of interest ψ if:

a) ψ is a function of λ_1 and not of λ_2,

b) λ_1 and λ_2 are variation free,

c) $D_2(z_t | Y_{t-1}, Z_{t-1}; \lambda_2) = D_2(z_t | Z_{t-1}; \lambda_2)$; that is Y_{t-1} is excluded from the set of variables explaining z_t.

Conditions a) and b) are that of weak exogeneity and condition c) defines Granger noncausality of y_t for z_t.

In EXAMPLES 7.1 and 7.2, the distinction between weak and strong exogeneity is irrelevant, since the processes are static. Granger causality does not appear and what is weakly exogenous is, at the same time, strongly exogenous. In EXAMPLE 7.3 when considering the exogeneity of z_t with respect to y_t with the parameters of interest being those of the conditional distribution, δ, c_1, c_2, d_1, d_2 in:

$$
\begin{bmatrix} z_t \\ y_t - \delta z_t \end{bmatrix} = \begin{bmatrix} a_1 & b_1 \\ c_1^* & d_1^* \end{bmatrix} \begin{bmatrix} z_{t-1} \\ y_{t-1} \end{bmatrix} + \begin{bmatrix} a_2 & b_2 \\ c_2^* & d_2^* \end{bmatrix} \begin{bmatrix} z_{t-2} \\ y_{t-2} \end{bmatrix} + \begin{bmatrix} \epsilon_{1t} \\ \epsilon_{2t}^* \end{bmatrix}
$$

weak exogeneity requires that $Cov(\epsilon_{1t}\ \epsilon_{2t}^*) = 0$ and strong exogeneity requires, additionally, that $b_1 = b_2 = 0$, so that y_t does not Granger cause z_t.

In EXAMPLE 7.4 , that is for the model:

$$y_t = \alpha \cdot z_t + \epsilon_{1t} , \tag{7.6a}$$

$$z_t = \beta \cdot y_{t-1} + \epsilon_{2t} , \tag{7.6b}$$

where the parameter of interest is α, the weak exogeneity requirement for z_t is that $Cov(\epsilon_{1t}\ \epsilon_{2t}) = 0$ and, additionally, for strong exogeneity, that $\beta = 0$. Obviously, if $\beta = 0$, the model can no longer be interpreted as a 'cobweb model'.

Testing for Granger causality has been described in detail in Chapter 6. Testing for strong exogeneity consists in testing for weak exogeneity as described above, and then separately for Granger causality. The difficulty with this is the fact that weak exogeneity in most cases is tested through estimation of an equation representing the conditional process while Granger causality requires inference on the marginal process. Since these processes are represented by two separate regression equations, estimated in most cases by ordinary least squares, both hypotheses cannot be tested jointly, but rather sequentially. As it is well known, this increases the probability of rejecting the true null hypothesis which is, in this case, the hypothesis of strong exogeneity.

7.3 Structural Invariance, Superexogeneity and the Lucas Critique

In the previous sections of this chapter it was assumed that 'structure' of the model (that is the parameters of interest) are constant, both over time and with respect to changes in particular variables. Changes of parameters over time are not considered here as we have already outlined some methods of evaluating time constancy of parameters in Chapter 3 above. Instead, our interest is focused on the problem of possible variability in the parameters of a model generated by changes in variables. If there is no such variability in a model it is said that the model is *structurally invariant*. In particular, our interest is with evaluating the possibility of such changes with respect to variables likely to be used as 'policy instruments', that is variables whose changes depend on the decisions of policy makers (for instance, a central bank interest rate, the rate of *VAT*, or the level of import duties).

A simple illustration of the problem of structural invariance can be made with the use of a single equation model:

$$y_t = \alpha \cdot z_t + \epsilon_t \, ,$$

where ϵ_t is an error term with $E(\epsilon_t) = 0$, so that $E(y_t | z_t) = \alpha \cdot z_t$ where y_t and z_t are observed variables. Let us assume that this model represents all our economic knowledge (strictly speaking, that the marginal process of z_t is deterministic) and that the problem is to evaluate the expected response (output) of y_t if, in period T, z_t (the input) is changed from z_T to $z_T^\dagger$. We may say that by changing an input, in our case by changing z_T to $z_T^\dagger$, we are making *an intervention* in the model. If:

$$E(y_T \mid z_T^\dagger) = \alpha \cdot z_T^\dagger \, ,$$

that is:

$$E(y_T \mid z_T^\dagger) - E(y_T \mid z_T) = \alpha \cdot (z_T^\dagger - z_T) \, ,$$

then the model is structurally invariant. The structure (in this case, the parameter α) can be successfully used for evaluating the expected response of the dependent variable in a 'what if' type exercise (simulation, or policy analysis). If, however:

$$E(y_T \mid z_T^\dagger) = \alpha^* \cdot z_T^\dagger \, ,$$

and $\alpha^* \neq \alpha$, the model is *not* structurally invariant. Since the lack of structural invariance of the model is reflected in the change of the parameter α with respect to a change in z_t, we say that the parameter α *is not structurally invariant with respect to* z_t . The lack of structural invariance is usually a sad message to a policy analyst. If a model intended for use is structurally invariant and data on y_t and z_t are available, the parameter α can be estimated by, say, ordinary least squares and the estimate can safely be used in a policy simulation experiment. If it is not structurally invariant, no knowledge can be retrieved from the sample relevant to α^* .

Generally, as described above the problem of structural invariance of an economic model is purely academic. Nobody would seriously argue that a model describing an economic phenomenon would be absolutely robust for changes in an input, irrespective of the size of these changes. If in the above model y_t represents consumption of non–durables and

z_t is income, it is clear that the marginal propensity to consume *must* change if income changes by, say, 1,000% . We can make the problem of structural invariance operational if we narrow the class of potential changes in z_t. We may, for instance, say that although the structure of a model is not absolutely robust for *any* change in input, it is structurally invariant if such a change is relatively small. We may therefore narrow the concept of structural invariance to a *given class of input changes (interventions)*.

In an econometric model, we are interested in identifying variables which can be used safely as instruments in policy analysis, that is which are at least weakly exogenous (without any feedback relations or cross–restrictions with the variable representing output) and whose changes (policy interventions) do not affect the parameters of interest. If these two conditions are fulfilled, that is if a variable x_t is weakly or strongly exogenous and the parameters of interest are structurally invariant with respect to z_t, then z_t is said to be *super-exogenous*.

For a more formal definition of superexogeneity, recall the factorization of the data generating process (see equation (7.5) in Section 7.1):

$$D(x_t|X_{t-1}; \theta) = D_1(y_t|Y_{t-1}, Z_t; \lambda_1) \cdot D_2(z_t|Y_{t-1}, Z_{t-1}; \lambda_2).$$

Following Hendry, Muellbauer and Murphy (1990), z_t may be defined as being superexogenous for λ_1 (the parameters of interest) if:

a) it is weakly exogenous,
b) λ_1 is invariant to changes in λ_2.

It is worth noting that if z_t is to be regarded as a policy instrument and is represented by a proper non–degenerate marginal process, the policy interventions are represented by changes in the parameters of that marginal process, λ_2, rather than in z_t itself. For example, a change in the value of a variable can be seen as a change in the mean or variance of that process.

EXAMPLE 7.1 was that of the bivariate normal distribution:

$$z_t = \mu_1 + \epsilon_{1t},$$
$$y_t = \mu_2 + \epsilon_{2t},$$

where $E(\epsilon_{1t}) = E(\epsilon_{2t}) = 0$, $Var(\epsilon_{1t}) = \sigma_{11}$, $Var(\epsilon_{2t}) = \sigma_{22}$ and $Cov(\epsilon_{1t}\,\epsilon_{2t}) = \sigma_{12}$.

The parameters of the conditional process of y_t on z_t are: $\lambda_1 = (\alpha, \beta, \sigma_y)$, where $\alpha = \mu_2 - \beta \cdot \mu_1$, $\beta = \sigma_{12}/\sigma_{11}$, $\sigma_y = \sigma_{22} - \sigma_{12}^2/\sigma_{11}$, and of the marginal process for z_t are: $\lambda_2 = (\mu_1, \sigma_{11})$. It has already been noted that z_t is weakly exogenous for the parameters of interest λ_1, since λ_1 and λ_2 are variation free. Nevertheless, z_t may not be super-exogenous for λ_1, since the parameters of the conditional process α, β and σ_y are functions of the parameters of the marginal process for z_t. Hence, if a policy analyst wants to perform an intervention on z_t by changing either μ_1 or σ_{11}, then provided that σ_{12} remains constant, the parameters of the conditional process will also change.

The problem of structural invariance and its relevance for policy analysis is the essence of what is called the *Lucas critique* of policy evaluation. Lucas (1976) questioned the appropriateness of using econometric models for policy simulation experiments by arguing that the structure of a model can be altered by the impact of expectations concerning the policy. Hence, even if a model is perfectly estimated and remarkably stable within the sample period, its structure may change once expectations concerning the policy become formulated. What is even more important, the Lucas critique states that in such a case, when a policy experiment is performed, the parameters of the marginal process must change, and often in a way unexpected to the policy maker. The Lucas critique is widely regarded as an important explanation of the failure of structural econometric models in policy simulation experiments.

To illustrate the Lucas critique, recall EXAMPLE 7.4. The *DGP* considered in that example was the following:

$$y_t = \alpha \cdot z_t + \epsilon_{1t},\tag{7.6a}$$

$$z_t = \beta \cdot y_{t-1} + \epsilon_{2t},\tag{7.6b}$$

where $E(\epsilon_{1t}) = E(\epsilon_{2t}) = 0$, $Var(\epsilon_{1t}) = \sigma_{11}$ and $Var(\epsilon_{2t}) = \sigma_{22}$. It was shown in Section 7.2 that if $Cov(\epsilon_{1t}\ \epsilon_{2t}) = \sigma_{12} \neq 0$, z_t is not a weakly exogenous variable for the parameter of interest α. If, however, $\sigma_{12} = 0$ then z_t becomes weakly exogenous *and* superexogenous, since the relationship between the parameters of the conditional process of y_t for z_t, namely

a, b and σ^2 and these of the marginal distribution of z_t, are:

$$a = \alpha + (\sigma_{12}/\sigma_{22})\ ,\ b = -(\sigma_{12}/\sigma_{22}) \cdot \beta\ ,\ \sigma^2 = \sigma_{11} - (\sigma_{12}^2/\sigma_{22})\ .$$

Hence, if $\sigma_{12} = 0$, $a = \alpha$, $b = 0$ and $\sigma^2 = \sigma_{11}$. This means that whatever change is made in the marginal distribution of z_t (that is alterations to either β or σ_{22}), the structure of the conditional distribution is unaffected. The variable z_t can be safely used as a policy instrument (if, of course, it makes economic sense).

Suppose, however, that it is not z_t which enters equation (7.6a), but rather its expected value conditional on relevant information available at time t. This 'relevant information' will be denoted by Ω_t. Hence:

$$y_t = \alpha \cdot E(z_t \mid \Omega_t) + \epsilon_{1t} . \qquad (7.6c)$$

What we will show below is that now, even when the covariance between the error terms of equations (7.6b – 7.6c) is zero, z_t is no longer superexogenous for α. According to (7.6b), the 'relevant information available at time t' is nothing but y_{t-1} and hence we have:

$$E(z_t \mid \Omega_t) = \beta \cdot y_{t-1} , \qquad (7.6d)$$

or:

$$z_t = E(z_t \mid \Omega_t) + \epsilon_{2t} .$$

It is easy to discover that if the model consists of equations (7.6b), (7.6c) and (7.6d), z_t is not superexogenous for α. If in (7.6c), $E(z_t \mid \Omega_t)$ is replaced by $z_t - \epsilon_{2t}$ from (7.6d), orthogonalization of the equations:

$$y_t = \alpha \cdot z_t + \xi_t ,$$

where $\xi_t = \epsilon_{1t} - \alpha \cdot \epsilon_{2t}$, and (7.6b) gives:

$$y_t = \alpha \cdot \beta \cdot y_{t-1} + \eta_t , \qquad (7.6e)$$

where $\eta_t = (\xi_t + \alpha \cdot \epsilon_{2t}) = \epsilon_{1t}$. Although $Cov(\eta_t \epsilon_{2t}) = 0$, z_t does not appear in (7.6e). Consequently, (7.6e) is a marginal process for y_t (strictly speaking, a process conditional on y_{t-1}) rather than a conditional process of y_t on z_t. Despite lacking z_t, it does contain parameters from the marginal process of z_t. Therefore z_t is not superexogenous for the parameter of interest α.

The example below shows the difficulty in using an econometric model for policy analysis in the light of the Lucas critique. We again consider a consumption function with an unanticipated inflation effect. In contrast to the *DHSY* consumption function, we now assume that consumers can, at least to some extent, foresee a future inflation and are able to adjust their decisions accordingly. In simplified notation the consumption function is the following:

$$cons_t = \mu_t + \alpha \cdot (inf_t - E(inf_t|\ \Omega_t)) + u_{1t}, \qquad (7.13a)$$

where μ_t represents all the elements of the consumption function apart from the Deaton effect and u_{1t} is an error term. Hence, if consumers foresee the inflation correctly, there is no unanticipated inflation effect. The consumers' expectations of inflation at time t are assumed to be formed in a rational expectations fashion using all information available at time $t - 1$. For simplicity we assume that all the relevant information at time $t - 1$ is represented by a single variable g_{t-1}, so that:

$$E(inf_t|\ \Omega_t) = \beta \cdot g_{t-1}. \qquad (7.13b)$$

or:

$$inf_t = \beta \cdot g_{t-1} + u_{2t},$$

where $E(u_{2t}) = 0$. Equations (7.13a $-$ 7.13b) can be combined to eliminate the unobserved expectations variable as:

$$cons_t = \mu_t + \alpha \cdot inf_t - \alpha \cdot \beta \cdot g_{t-1} + u_{1t}. \qquad (7.14)$$

Suppose now that an econometrician is not aware of the model (7.13a)–(7.13b). He or she estimates the model:

$$cons_t = \mu_t + a \cdot inf_t + b \cdot g_{t-1} + v_t . \qquad (7.15)$$

Not surprisingly, if the true model is (7.13a − 7.13b), the ordinary least squares estimates of (7.15) are likely to be highly accurate. In fact $a = \alpha$, $b = -\alpha \cdot \beta$, and $v_t = u_{1t}$, and it is easy to check that for the parameters of interest a, b and $Var(v_t)$, inf_t is weakly exogenous. Suppose, however, that the econometrician wants to evaluate the expected response of consumption to a change of inf_t, from inf_t to $inf_t^\dagger$ by an amount δ_t. The intervention is:

$$inf_t^\dagger = \beta \cdot g_{t-1} + u_{2t} + \delta_t .$$

The econometrician expects consumption to change by $a \cdot \delta_t$, that is he or she expects the simulated consumption to be:

$$cons_t^{sim} = \mu_t + a \cdot (inf_t + \delta_t) + b \cdot g_{t-1} .$$

This, however, is not going to happen. According to (7.13b):

$$E((inf_t + \delta_t) | \Omega_t) = \beta^* \cdot g_{t-1} ,$$

that is, if inf_t changes and g_{t-1} remains unchanged, the parameter β must change, otherwise (7.13b) will no longer be the expected value. Consequently, the true outcome of the simulation, in terms of its expected value, is:

$$cons_t^{true} = \mu_t + \alpha \cdot (inf_t + \delta_t) - \alpha \cdot \beta^* \cdot g_{t-1} ,$$

and this is not what the econometrician would expect.

Testing for structural invariance and superexogeneity is generally not a simple task, since, as was stated before, the assertion of structural invariance is, in absolute terms, never valid. It can only be tested to some extent, assuming that the class of the interventions is known and usually equivalent to that of the variability of the exogenous variable or its predictions. Tests for superexogeneity are not yet firmly established in the econometric literature; nevertheless some guidance can be given.

Hendry, Muellbauer and Murphy (1990) assumed that 'historical' interventions (in other words the variation of the tested variable within a sample) affect the parameters of interest if there is no structural invariance. Hence, if there is a structural break in the conditional model, it should correspond to a structural break in the marginal model. The straightforward procedure is to test for structural breaks in both conditional and marginal processes (for example by examining one–step recursive residuals as described in Chapter 3) and to compare the eventual occurrences of structural breaks. If there are some structural breaks, it means that the parameters of the processes are not constant within the sample. If the structural breaks for the conditional and marginal processes coincide in time, that is they appear for the same time period, it is likely that the structural break in the conditional model has been caused by variability in the parameters of the marginal model. If this is the case, the hypothesis of structural invariance (or, if weak exogeneity holds, the hypothesis of superexogeneity) can be rejected.

Slightly more general tests can be developed by assuming that the parameter of interest can be regarded as a linear function of the variable tested for structural invariance. In the simplest case of a linear model with one weakly exogenous variable z_t:

$$y_t = \alpha \cdot z_t + \epsilon_t, \qquad (7.16)$$

the parameter α can be expressed as:

$$\alpha = \alpha_0 + \alpha_1 z_t. \qquad (7.17)$$

If the superexogeneity hypothesis holds, $\alpha_1 = 0$, so that $\alpha = \alpha_0 = $ constant. If it does not hold, (7.16) can be tested for heteroscedasticity due to the omitted squares of the variable z_t. Substituting (7.17) into (7.16) gives:

$$y_t = \alpha_0 \cdot z_t + \alpha_1 \cdot z_t^2 + \epsilon_t ,$$

which means that in the model:

$$y_t = \alpha \cdot z_t + \zeta_t ,$$

where $\zeta_t = \alpha_1 \cdot z_t^2 + \epsilon_t$, there are heteroscedastic errors, proportional to the squares of z_t.

Alternatively, one may assume that variability in α is not due to the changes in z_t itself, but rather to the deviations of z_t from its conditional expected value (that is from the mean of its marginal process). Hence, it is assumed that:

$$\alpha = \alpha_0 + \alpha_1 (z_t - \mu_t) , \tag{7.18}$$

where μ_t is the conditional expected value of the marginal process of z_t. If we combine (7.18) with (7.16), we get:

$$y_t = \alpha_0 \cdot z_t + \alpha_1 (z_t - \mu_t) \cdot z_t + \epsilon_t .$$

The expected value of $(z_t - \mu_t) \cdot z_t$ is the same as $E(z_t - \mu_t)^2$, which is the variance of the marginal process of z_t. This suggests testing the squared residuals $(\hat{u}_t^2)$ from the marginal process of z_t as an omitted variable in (7.16). If the null hypothesis that $\alpha_1 = 0$ is rejected in the regression:

$$y_t = \alpha_0 \cdot z_t + \alpha_1 \cdot \hat{u}_t^2 + \epsilon_t,$$

the variable z_t cannot be regarded as superexogenous (see Engle and Hendry (1990)). The above procedure can be easily extended, for instance for allowing for a dynamic process in (7.18), that is:

$$\alpha = \alpha_0 + \sum_{i=0}^{k} \alpha_{i+1}(z_{t-i} - \mu_{t-i}),$$

which eventually leads to testing the hypothesis that in the equation:

$$y_t = \alpha_0 \cdot z_t + + \sum_{i=0}^{k} \alpha_{i+1} \hat{u}_{t-i}^2 + \epsilon_t,$$

$\alpha_1 = \alpha_2 = \dots = \alpha_k = 0$. This can be done with the use of a Lagrange Multiplier test (note, however, that some additional degrees of freedom are required, since the residuals of the marginal process are not known and have to be estimated).

Charemza and Király (1991) assumed that the set of 'admissible interventions' is that generated not by the variability of z_t, but rather by prediction errors made from the conditional process. Hence, if the variable z_t is not superexogenous and predictions (for instance one–step ahead recursive forecasts) have been made from the model with invariant parameters, the prediction errors are likely to be correlated with z_t. This suggests regressing the prediction errors on current and/or lagged z_t and testing their significance. If the hypothesis that the regression coefficients are equal to zero in such a regression is rejected, z_t is not superexogenous.

7.4   Exogeneity in the *DHSY* Model

In this section we will illustrate the use of the tests outlined above to investigate the exogeneity properties of the inflation variable included in the *DHSY* formulation of UK aggregate consumption (see Chapter 3). A similar analysis could also be performed for the income variable which appears in this model, but we do not pursue this here (see Hendry, Muellbauer and Murphy (1990) for such an analysis).

Irrespective of whether one is testing for weak, strong, or superexogeneity, the initial step is the formulation of a marginal model for inflation. There is no unique way of doing this, but from the arguments already presented in this book, one way would be to start from an equation for inflation from a quite general *VAR* representation of the variables appearing in the *DHSY* model. Chapter 5 considered the level of integration of the variables appearing in the *DHSY* model. From this it seems reasonable to use a differenced form of these variables, rather than their levels. Accordingly, estimation is started from a *VAR*(3, 5, 5) equation for Δinf_t, $\Delta_4 cons_t$ and $\Delta_4 inc_t$ respectively, that is from an equation with three lags for Δinf_t, and five lags for both $\Delta_4 cons_t$ and $\Delta_4 inc_t$. The ordinary least squares estimates of this *VAR* equation are given in Section 7.5 under MODEL 7.1. It is immediately apparent from this estimated model that at the 5% level of significance, no individual consumption or income coefficients are statistically significant, nor are the consumption or income coefficients taken together (the *F* test values for these joint tests are only 0.476 and 1.153). This *VAR* equation was successively reduced to a simple autoregressive model of order one (an *AR*(1) model) by a sequence of model reduction tests. (Full computer output of this sequence is not given in Section 7.5 to preserve space.) First one can test whether an autoregressive model of order three (that is, the regression of Δinf_t on Δinf_{t-1}, Δinf_{t-2} and Δinf_{t-3}) can be rejected as a specific case of the general *VAR*(3, 5, 5) equation. The computer output under MODEL 7.2 in Section 7.5 shows that the $F(10, 54)$ value for this model reduction is 2.04 which is right on the borderline of statistical significance (the 5% critical value for $F(10, 50)$ is 2.026). As the null hypothesis that the $AR(3)$ is a specific case of the $VAR(3, 5, 5)$ equation could not be clearly rejected, model reduction proceeded by first omitting the seemingly insignificant term Δinf_{t-2} from MODEL 7.2 (the $F(1, 64)$ value for this reduction is only 0.32) and then omitting Δinf_{t-3} from the resulting model (the $F(1, 64)$ value for this final reduction being 3.14 compared with a critical value for an $F(1, 60)$ of 4.001). Compared with the general $VAR(3, 5, 5)$ equation, the simple $AR(1)$ model has the value for a model reduction $F(12, 54)$ test of 2.03 which is just significant at the 5% significance level, whereas the autoregressive model with both first and third order lagged variables has an $F(11, 54)$ value of 1.89 which is not significant. Hence, both the simple $AR(1)$ model and the model containing both first and third order lagged variables are candidates for adoption as the marginal process for inflation (the conclusions drawn from either are identical). For simplicity (and to maximize the degrees of freedom available) we have chosen to give the results stemming from the estimation of the simple first order autoregressive model given as MODEL 7.3 in Section 7.5. This $AR(1)$ model has been taken to represent the marginal process for the inflation variable in the exogeneity testing which follows.

An important aspect of this marginal process is that it contains neither lagged consumption nor lagged income terms. This has some immediate consequences for both the concepts of exogeneity one may test for, and for the tests themselves. So far as weak exogeneity is concerned, despite the fact that the *DHSY* model contains an error correction mechanism, the absence of consumption and income in the marginal process means that there is no question as to whether error correction terms appear in the marginal process. Clearly they cannot. Hence, for testing weak exogeneity, one may simply investigate the possible covariance between the residuals of the marginal process (termed *unif* in the computer output) and the residuals of the conditional process, namely the *DHSY* model. However, since there are no lagged consumption terms in the marginal process, such a test is simultaneously a test for the strong exogeneity of inflation.

The *DHSY* model estimated for the same sample period as the $AR(1)$ model for the first difference of inflation is reported as MODEL 7.4 in Section 7.5. The test for the strong exogeneity of inflation may be carried out by a standard Student–t test or equivalent F test on the residuals from the marginal process included as a variable in the *DHSY* model. This $F(1, 62)$ value reported in MODEL 7.4 is very small (0.013) and is clearly not significant. One can conclude that inflation may be taken as strongly exogenous for the parameters of interest of the conditional model, which in this case are the parameters of the *DHSY* model.

Let us now consider testing for the structural invariance of the *DHSY* model. Both the marginal process for inflation and the *DHSY* model were re–estimated by recursive least squares (see Chapter 3) and the one–step recursive residuals for each were calculated. Figures 7.1 and 7.2 are graphs of these residuals. Inspection of these graphs reveals no cases in which structural breaks in the marginal process coincide with breaks in the conditional or *DHSY* model. This is consistent with the *DHSY* model being structurally invariant, and with inflation being superexogenous in this model. The other tests for superexogeneity outlined in Section 7.3 above have also been carried out. MODEL 7.4 reports the F test value for testing for heteroscedastic errors due to the omission of the squares of the regressors. This $F(10, 51)$ value (0.6681) is not significant, a finding consistent with the previous test. MODEL 7.5 reports the results of testing the significance of current and lagged squared residuals in the *DHSY* model. The $F(2, 60)$ value for adding these squared residuals is 1.06 which, like the preceding test statistic, is not significant at the 5% level of significance. MODEL 7.6 reports the results of the Charemza–Király test. The prediction errors from the *DHSY* model (designated as *icons* in the computer output in Section 7.5) are regressed on the first difference of inflation and its lag. The low $F(2, 74)$ value for the joint significance of these regressors is in line with the previous test results which all point towards the structural invariance of the *DHSY* model and the superexogeneity of inflation.

One-Step Residuals

Fig. 7.1: Consumption

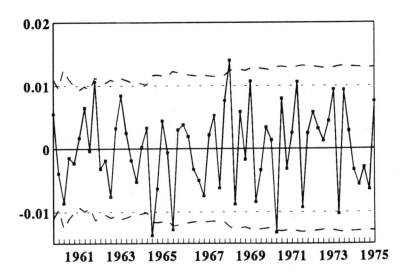

Fig. 7.2: Inflation

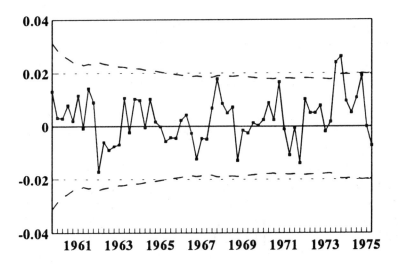

7.5   Stylized Computer Output (*PC–GIVE*)

Initial transformations of variables:
d4cl1 = LAG[1](d4lc)
d4li1 = LAG[1](d4li)

MODEL 7.1: VAR equation; Modelling dinf by OLS

The Sample is 1959 (2) to 1975 (4) less 0 Forecasts

VARI	COEFF	STD ERR	t–VALUE
dinf 1	.29351	.14874	1.9733
dinf 2	.01959	.13871	.14124
dinf 3	.32444	.13699	2.3684
d4lc1	−.1716	.16784	−1.022
d4lc1 1	.07065	.16718	.42262
d4lc1 2	.00129	.16181	.00796
d4lc1 3	.20808	.16388	1.2697
d4lc1 4	−.0791	.14500	−.5458
d4li1	.10391	.07306	1.4222
d4li1 1	.06526	.08186	.79720
d4li1 2	.03058	.07569	.40398
d4li1 3	−.0416	.07541	−.5525
d4li1 4	−.1243	.07938	−1.566

σ = .00852   F(13, 54) = 3.34   DW = 1.889
RSS = .0039275 for 13 Variables and 67 Observations

Solved STATIC LONG RUN Equation

dinf   =   .081·d4lc1   +   .093·d4li1
S.E.   (.60279)   (.39936)

Tests on the Significance of each Variable

Variable	F[NUM,DENOM]	Value
dinf	F[3, 63]	3.426
d4lc1	F[5, 63]	0.476
d4li1	F[5, 63]	1.153

Tests on the Significance of each LAG

LAG	F[NUM,DENOM]	= Value
4	F[2, 63]	3.478
3	F[3, 63]	0.571
2	F[3, 63]	1.549
1	F[3, 63]	0.470

MODEL 7.2: AR(3); Modelling dinf by OLS

The Sample is 1959 (2) to 1975 (4) less 0 Forecasts

VARI	COEF	STD ERR	H.C.S.E.	t–VALUE
dinf 1	.4149	.11499	.13675	3.60861
dinf 2	−.063	.11309	.12991	−.56327
dinf 3	.2025	.10978	.11003	1.84521

$\sigma =$ .009196 F(3, 64) = 6.60 DW = 1.988
RSS = .005412 for 3 Variables and 67 Observations

TESTS Of MODEL REDUCTION

From Model 1 to Model 2
Model 1: F(10, 54)   = 2.04

MODEL 7.3: AR(1); Modelling dinf by OLS

The Sample is 1959 (1) to 1975 (4) less 0 Forecasts

VARI	COEF	STD ERR	H.C.S.E.	t–VALUE
dinf 1	.3385	.10991	.15223	3.08002

$\sigma =$ .009869 F(1, 67) = 9.49 DW = 1.678
RSS = .0065262 for 1 Variable and 68 Observations

uinfsq   = uinf   *   uinf

MODEL 7.4: *DHSY* ; Modelling d4lc by OLS

The Sample is 1959 (1) to 1975 (4) less 0 Forecasts

VARI	COEF	STD ERR	H.C.S.E.	t–VALUE
d4linc	.4956	.03063	.02977	16.17811
dd4linc	−.217	.04098	.03703	−5.30928
lc_li 4	−.086	.01282	.01303	−6.72365
inf	−.109	.02395	.02497	−4.57980
dinf	−.294	.09757	.10645	−3.01697

$\sigma = .00646$ F(5, 63) = 236.97 DW = 2.283
RSS = .0026359 for 5 Variables and 68 Observations

F–Test for adding uinf
F(1, 62)   = .013

TEST FOR HETEROSCEDASTIC ERRORS
F(10, 51)   = .6681

MODEL 7.5: *DHSY*; Modelling d4lc by OLS

The Sample is 1959 (2) to 1975 (4) less 0 Forecasts

VARI	COEF	STD ERR	t–VALUE
d4li	.49379	.03087	15.9937
dd4li	−.2243	.04160	−5.3924
lc_li 4	−.0860	.01340	−6.4207
inf	−.1140	.02433	−4.688
dinf	−.2865	.10430	−2.7470
uinfsq	−4.302	6.884	−0.6249
uinfsq 1	7.7818	5.4642	1.42414

$\sigma = .00651$ F(7, 60) = 165.84 DW = 2.297
RSS = .0025454 for 7 Variables and 67 Observations

F–TEST for adding:
uinfsq   uinfsq 1
F[2, 60]   = 1.06

MODEL 7.6: Modelling icons by OLS

The Sample is 1966 (4) to 1975 (4) less 0 Forecasts

VARI	COEFF	STD ERR	H.C.S.E.	t–VALUE
dinf	.0069	.12572	.14436	.05511
dinf 1	.0347	.12593	.12151	.27591

$\sigma = $ .006976 F(2, 35) = .07 DW = 2.616
RSS = .0017035 for 2 Variables and 37 Observations

Tests on the Significance of each Variable
Variable	F[NUM,DENOM]	= Value
dinf	F[2, 74]	.074

Tests on the Significance of each LAG
LAG	F[NUM,DENOM]	= Value
1	F[1, 74]	.076

7.6   Suggestions for Further Reading

Relatively little has been published on exogeneity analysis. Apart from the seminal paper of Engle, Hendry and Richard (1983), concepts of exogeneity have been considered by Wu (1983), Leamer (1985), Eichenbaum (1985), and Cooley and LeRoy (1985), mostly in relation to the concept of causality (also see Geweke (1984)). A survey of tests which can be useful for the testing of weak exogeneity is given by Pesaran and Smith (1990). An historical account of the development of the concept of exogeneity has been provided by Epstein (1987), and an enquiry into the origins of the concept of autonomy or structural invariance by Aldrich (1989). Spanos (1986) provides a systematic formalization of the use of Data Generating Processes in econometric modelling.

Some advances in exogeneity analysis have been made within a Bayesian framework, for example by Lubrano, Pierse and Richard (1986), Steel (1987, 1989), and Steel and Richard (1989). Theoretical papers on superexogeneity and structural invariance which are as yet unpublished include Engle and

Hendry (1990), and Charemza (1988). Applications of weak and strong exogeneity testing include Charemza and Király (1990) and Hendry, Muellbauer and Murphy (1990). Theoretical and empirical works concerning the Lucas critique have mainly been conducted within the framework of encompassing analysis and therefore are referred to in Chapter 8.

Chapter 8

Non–Nested Models, Encompassing and Model Selection

8.1 Problems in Choosing Between Models

In the earlier chapters we have suggested various methods of deriving an econometric model which, for one reason or another, may be regarded as 'good' practice. For instance, use of the general to specific methodology (Chapter 4) can result in a single equation model derived from an autoregressive distributed lag model in a systematic way, in that it survives a series of Lagrange Multiplier tests for various linear and/or nonlinear restrictions. On the other hand, one may construct a model using, say, the Engle–Granger approach (Chapter 5). In the multi–equation case, a model may be formulated from a Cowles Commission type structural model, a vector autoregressive model (Chapter 6), or a system of equations based on the principle of exogeneity modelling (Chapter 7). If it is not clear which is the best modelling approach on *a priori* grounds and various methodologies are applied to derive an empirical model, it is unlikely that one would finish up with identical models. An obvious question which arises in this context is: how can one select the best model?

The answer to the model selection problem is not necessarily obvious even if there is no question as to the modelling methodology believed to be appropriate. Suppose, for instance, that one starts from a simple autoregressive distributed lag model of order one which is regarded as a general model (see Chapter 4):

$$y_t = \alpha_1 y_{t-1} + \beta_0 x_t + \beta_1 x_{t-1} + \epsilon_t. \tag{8.1}$$

Imagine that one model derived from (8.1) through applying the general to specific methodology turns out to be a first order autoregressive process:

$$y_t = \alpha_1 y_{t-1} + \epsilon_t .$$ (8.2)

It was said in Chapter 4 that the general model (8.1) becomes the specific model (8.2), if it satisfies the restrictions:

$$\beta_0 = \beta_1 = 0 .$$

Alternatively, from the same general *ADL* model (8.1) and using the same methodology, one may develop another specific form, for instance a finite distributed lag model:

$$y_t = \beta_0 x_t + \beta_1 x_{t-1} + \epsilon_t .$$ (8.3)

The restriction required to derive (8.3) from (8.1) is:

$$\alpha_1 = 0 .$$

Evidently, both models (8.2) and (8.3) are special cases of (8.1). However, (8.2) is not a special case of (8.3), nor is (8.3) a special case of (8.2). We may write down the hypotheses concerning (8.1) and (8.2) in a way typical of traditional testing of statistical 'null' (H_0) and 'alternative' (H_A) hypotheses, as:

H_0 :　it is true that $\beta_0 = \beta_1 = 0$, or model (8.2) is true ;

H_A :　it is *not* true that $\beta_0 = \beta_1 = 0$, or model (8.1) is true.

Similarly, the corresponding hypotheses concerning models (8.1) and (8.3) can be formulated. Hypothesis H_A above is a *composite* hypothesis, and as it covers all other possible values of the parameters other than those specified in H_0, it may be said to complement H_0 to the set of all *admissible* values of the parameters β_0 and β_1. The parameter space (the set of all admissible values of the parameters) has been effectively partitioned or divided by the null and alternative hypotheses into a rejection and a non–rejection region. Rejection of the null hypothesis in this case automatically implies acceptance of the alternative hypothesis. As model (8.2) is a special case of model (8.1) in that it can be derived from (8.1) by means of parametric restrictions, the testing of the null hypothesis that $\beta_0 = \beta_1 = 0$ is also an example of the testing of *nested* hypotheses. More generally, both models (8.2) and (8.3) may be said to be *nested* within (8.1) as they constitute special cases of model (8.1).

If we want to choose between models (8.2) and (8.3) however, we have to formulate the hypotheses in a non–complementary way, so that they do not constitute together the set of all admissible values for α_1 , β_0 , and β_1. The hypotheses we want to test are:

H_1 : model (8.2) is true ,

H_2 : model (8.3) is true .

Since H_1 and H_2 do not constitute together the set of admissible hypotheses (or, in other words, neither is a special case of the other) we will call hypotheses like H_1 and H_2 *non–nested hypotheses* and the underlying models *non–nested models*. The problem of testing non–nested hypotheses is clearly different from that of testing nested hypotheses; if we treat H_1 as we treated H_0 and we reject it, it does not necessarily mean that H_2 is true. Our task is to evaluate whether model (8.2) is to be rejected in favour of (8.3) or *vice versa*, and the techniques applied will be different from those used for testing nested hypotheses.

It must be stressed that the problem of choosing between two (or more) different models can be seen in a wider context than that of selecting between 'specific' models derived from a 'general' one. For instance, (8.2) could be the result of testing Granger causality in a vector autoregressive modelling exercise, rather than a simplification of an *ADL* model. This will not change the statistical problem of selecting between (8.2) and (8.3).

A similar (and to a large extent overlapping) problem is that of the *encompassing* of econometric models. Generally, it is said that model *A encompasses* model *B* if it has the ability to account for the behaviour of model *B* or, in other words, if it can explain the behaviour of relevant characteristics of model *B* (see Mizon (1984), or Mizon and Richard (1986)). Since the 'relevant characteristics' may vary from one model to another, it is difficult to discuss encompassing in absolute terms. Instead one may speak of, for example, *variance encompassing* (where the variation of errors in model *B* can be explained by model *A*), or *forecast encompassing* (where the forecast errors from model *B* can be explained by model *A*). Although non–nested techniques are frequently used for testing hypotheses concerning encompassing (see Section 8.2 below), it does not mean that encompassing and testing non–nested hypotheses are the same. Consider, for instance, general to specific modelling. A comparison of a specific and a general model is a problem of testing nested hypotheses and therefore is not a non–nested problem. However, a specific model derived from a general model will have a larger error variance (since some of the variables have been dropped or restrictions imposed) and therefore the general model will encompass the specific one for variance. On the other hand, a specific model may encompass the general one for forecast. For instance, in the derivation of the *DHSY* model described in Chapter 3, it was the case that the forecast diagnostics for the specific model (MODEL 3.5) were superior to that of the general model (MODEL 3.6). Without any formal testing, it seems at least plausible that forecasts from the specific model may explain, to some extent, the forecast errors made by the general model.

8.2 Model Selection Tests

It was pointed out in Chapter 2 that traditional econometric criteria for selecting the 'best' model, such as the maximum R^2 (coefficient of determination) criterion, are far from being ideal especially if the model has been derived through data mining. Several other measures have been proposed, however, which aim to improve understanding of the overall characteristics of a model. The most widely used criteria for judging the goodness of fit of a particular model whilst taking into account the number of estimated parameters are:

i) The coefficient of determination, adjusted for the number of explanatory variables, $\bar{R}^2$:

$$\bar{R}^2 = 1 - \frac{T-1}{T-k} \cdot (1-R^2) \,,$$

where R^2 is the coefficient of determination, T is the number of observations and k is the number of explanatory variables (including an intercept). This measure was introduced and discussed in Chapter 2.

ii) The Akaike information criterion AIC (see for example Harvey (1990, pp. 177–178), or Judge *et al.* (1985, pp. 243–245)), computed as:

$$AIC = (-2 \cdot lnL(\bullet) + 2 \cdot k) / \ T \,,$$

where $lnL(\bullet)$ is the value of the loglikelihood function of the estimated model. The idea behind the AIC criterion is to select the model which has the minimal loss of information (that is, the smallest AIC). For models with the same number of parameters and estimated using the same sample this leads to selecting the model with the smallest residual sum of squares or, in other words, with the largest R^2 (see Maddala (1988, p.426)). For models with different number of explanatory variables the AIC and $\bar{R}^2$ criteria may differ.

iii) The Schwarz Bayesian criterion SC (see Judge *et al.* (1985, pp. 245–246)):

$$SC = \ln \hat{\sigma}^2 + \frac{k \cdot \ln T}{T} \, ,$$

where $\hat{\sigma}^2$ is an unbiased estimate of the residual variance. The formula above has been derived for the case of normally and independently distributed residuals and is the result of a Bayesian procedure of seeking the most probable (*a posteriori*) model. Model selection is on the basis of choosing the model with the smallest SC value.

iv) The Final Prediction Error FPE criterion (see Judge *et al.* (1985, pp. 243–245)):

$$FPE = \frac{T + k}{T - k} \cdot \hat{\sigma}^2 \, .$$

This, as its name implies, leads to selecting a model with the smallest *ex–post* prediction error. That is, FPE is based on forecasts made using actual rather than estimated values of explanatory variables for forecast periods and using parameter estimates for the entire sample, inclusive of the forecast period. (For a slightly different definition of *ex–post* forecasts see Klein (1971a, pp. 19–21).) Various modifications of the FPE criterion have been suggested in the literature, which are referred to in Judge *et al.* (1985, p.244).

The above criteria, as well as numerous modifications of them, are all based on the principle of minimizing the residual sum of squares as a guide for selecting the best model (see Maddala (1988, p.426)). Each criterion, however, has different underlying assumptions. The adjusted R^2 criterion assumes that a 'true' model exists and the task is in finding it, given the assumption that the 'best' model for this purpose is that which minimizes the residual sum of squares adjusted for the number of explanatory variables. The *FPE* adopts a more parsimonious position. According to this criterion, even

a 'true' model should be reduced in size if this would lead to improving the predictive quality of the model. The aim of the *AIC* and *SC* criteria is the selection of the model with the maximum information available (where 'information' is a precisely defined probability concept; see Theil (1971, pp. 636–637) and again do not concern themselves as to whether a 'true' model exists or not. The *AIC* criterion is regarded as being inconsistent in the sense that it does not select the model with maximum information with probability tending to one as $T \to \infty$. This problem seems to be overcome by the *SC* criterion, which is recommended for large samples in place of the *AIC*.

All the above statistics can be calculated for individual models and, with all the reservations described in Chapter 2, can also be used for an *ad hoc* selection between models. They do not, however, answer the question as to which of the models is better in a direct comparison with each other, that is whether one of them should be rejected in favour of the other. As was shown in Section 8.1, in principle such a selection can be made by the formulation and testing of non—nested hypotheses. Describing the structure and formal properties of tests used in evaluating such hypotheses is beyond the scope of this book. It is also not necessary to give precise formulae for computing particular statistics, since most of them are calculated by contemporary econometric computer packages.

We will discuss some simple tests for the closely related problem of testing for encompassing, however. The non-nested test described here for variance encompassing is the *J* test, proposed by Davidson and MacKinnon (1981). Suppose that the models we wish to select from are those given by the hypotheses below:

$$H_1: \quad y_t = \alpha x_t + \epsilon_{1t}, \tag{8.4a}$$

$$H_2: \quad y_t = \beta z_t + \epsilon_{2t}. \tag{8.4b}$$

The fact that the above models are linear and that each of them has only one explanatory variable is for the sake of simplification only. In practice, the models considered may well be nonlinear and/or with many explanatory variables each. The J test consists in testing the hypothesis that H_2 is true by:

1. Estimating equation (8.4b), resulting in an estimate of the parameter β which may be denoted as $\hat{\beta}$ (for a linear equation this is just the ordinary least squares estimate);

2. Adding the predicted values $\hat{\beta}z_t$ from (8.4b) to equation (8.4a) and hence estimating (8.4a) as:

$$y_t = \alpha x_t + \theta \cdot \hat{\beta} z_t + \epsilon_t. \qquad (8.5)$$

The test that (8.4b) encompasses (8.4a) for variance then simply consists of testing whether in (8.5) the *OLS* estimate of θ differs significantly from zero. This can be done, for instance, with the use of the Student–t test. When used for testing θ in an equation like (8.5), the Student–t statistic has only an asymptotic standard normal distribution and the test is not very powerful, especially for small samples.

The logical complement to the testing of whether (8.4b) encompasses (8.4a) is to test whether (8.4a) encompasses (8.4b). For this case, the test is for the null hypothesis that $\delta = 0$ in the regression equation:

$$y_t = \beta z_t + \delta \cdot \hat{\alpha} x_t + \nu_t, \qquad (8.6)$$

where $\hat{\alpha} x_t$ stands for the fitted values (predictions) from equation (8.4a). Since tests on (8.5) and (8.6) are performed independently, we cannot exclude the possibility of getting conflicting results. It may happen that in (8.5) θ is significant (so that (8.4b) encompasses (8.4a)) and, at the same time, in (8.6) δ is also significant (so that (8.4a) encompasses (8.4b)). This case is unlikely to occur except for very weak evidence. Analogously, we would not be pleased if both θ and δ appear to be insignificant, since this would mean that either both of our models are 'best', or (more likely) that both are equally bad. Ideally, we would like to have conclusive results such that if θ is significant, δ is not or *vice versa*, so that we would be able to make a clear selection of the better model.

As the J test is an asymptotic and not very powerful test, there have been numerous modifications and alternatives proposed, and one or more of these are computed by most of the specialized econometric packages. These tests include the Cox (1961) test, the adjusted Cox test (Godfrey and Pesaran (1983)), the Ericsson (1983) test, the Fisher and McAleer (1981) JA test and the 'encompassing' test (Mizon and Richard (1986); see also Maddala (1988, pp. 445–446). Whilst the J and JA tests are asymptotically equivalent, Monte Carlo studies indicate that for small samples, the J test rejects the true hypothesis more often than it should, but that the JA test is less powerful than the J test when the models being compared have very different numbers of explanatory variables (see Kmenta (1986, pp. 595–598)).

The forecast encompassing test we present here is that introduced by Chong and Hendry (1986) and developed subsequently by Ericsson (1989) and Clements and Hendry (1991). The idea of the test is quite similar to that of the J test. Suppose that the model given by (8.4a) is the 'rival' model and that given by (8.4b) is 'our' model. The question is whether our model encompasses, in terms of forecast, the 'rival' model. Suppose further that for both models, series of one—step ahead forecasts are available. These can be, for instance, forecasts made with the use of recursive least squares estimates, that is:

$$\hat{y}_t = \hat{\alpha}_{t-1} x_t ,$$

$$\tilde{y}_t = \hat{\beta}_{t-1} z_t ,$$

where $\hat{\alpha}_{t-1}$ and $\hat{\beta}_{t-1}$ are the recursive least squares estimates obtained with the use of data up to (and inclusive of) time $t-1$. Both forecasts can be pooled together to give a compound forecast $\bar{y}_t$ and compared with the observed y_t giving:

$$\bar{y}_t = (1 - \gamma) \cdot \hat{y}_t + \gamma \cdot \tilde{y}_t \, ,$$

or:

$$y_t = (1 - \gamma) \cdot \hat{y}_t + \gamma \cdot \tilde{y}_t + \bar{u}_t \, , \qquad (8.7)$$

where γ is a weight and $\bar{u}_t$ is the compound forecast error. If the 'rival' model is true and our model is not, then in (8.7) $\gamma = 0$ and $\bar{y}_t = \hat{y}_t$. This constitutes a testable hypothesis since from (8.7) we have:

$$\hat{u}_t = \gamma \cdot (\tilde{y}_t - \hat{y}_t) + \bar{u}_t \, , \qquad (8.8)$$

where $\hat{u}_t = y_t - \hat{y}_t$ and is equal to the forecast error of the 'rival' model. Hence, the procedure consists of testing for the statistical significance of γ in the regression equation (8.8).

Chong and Hendry (1986) have shown that the Student−t test for γ is a valid test, at least for large samples, provided that both forecasts are made on an *ex−ante* basis. For this analysis, the concept of an *ex−ante* forecast means that although the values of the explanatory variables may be known for the forecast period (after reading Chapter 7 we should rather say 'weakly exogenous' rather than 'explanatory' variables), the coefficients used for computing the forecasts may be estimated from data prior to the forecast period rather than known.

One of the most important features of the forecast encompassing test above is its ease of use. The models under comparison can be large nonlinear systems of equations, separately estimated, and not necessarily by recursive methods. In fact it is not even necessary for us to know the 'rival' model (full specifications of models and statistical data used for estimation are rarely published). All we need to know in order to perform the test are the 'rival' *ex—ante* forecasts.

8.3　An Empirical Encompassing Exercise

As an empirical encompassing problem we have taken the comparison of the *DHSY* consumption function with an alternative derived from the Houthakker–Taylor dynamic demand model (*HT* herewith). The Houthakker and Taylor (1966, 1970) model was especially popular in the 1960s and 1970s and has been used widely for analysing consumption and savings in a number of countries (see for example Swamy (1968) or Portes and Winter (1978, 1980)). It appears that after Taylor and Houthakker's (1990) reconsideration of their model in light of the development of cointegration theory, interest in their model has been renewed.

From various modifications and variants of the Houthakker–Taylor dynamic demand consumption model, we have chosen one which has been used for the analysis of aggregate demand and is relatively straightforward in its specification. Following the formulation of the *DHSY* model used earlier, we express the variables in the Houthakker–Taylor model in logarithms and seasonal differences. This model is then given as:

$$\Delta_4 cons_t = \alpha_1 \Delta_4 sav_{t-1} + \alpha_2 \Delta\Delta_4 inc_t + \alpha_3 \Delta_4 inc_{t-1} + \xi_t \, ,$$

where, as before, $cons_t$ stands for the logarithm of aggregate consumption of non–durables, inc_t for the logarithm of personal disposable income and $\Delta\Delta_4$ denotes first and fourth differences respectively. The new variable here is sav_{t-1}, which denotes the logarithm of personal saving (personal disposable income minus consumers' expenditure) at the end of the previous period. The Houthakker–Taylor theory suggests that α_1 should be negative, α_2 should lie between zero and one and α_3 should be equal to one. In order to impose the restriction that $\alpha_3 = 1$, we have reformulated the model by introducing a variable $\Delta_4 co_t^* in_{t-1}$ such that:

$$\Delta_4 co_t^* in_{t-1} = \Delta_4 cons_t - \Delta_4 inc_{t-1} ,$$

and the model becomes:

$$\Delta_4 co_t^* in_{t-1} = \alpha_1 \Delta_4 sav_{t-1} + \alpha_2 \Delta\Delta_4 inc_t + \xi_t . \quad (8.9)$$

The ordinary least squares estimates of (8.9) for the variables and sample period identical to that used in Chapter 3 for the estimation of the *DHSY* model are given as MODEL 8.1 in Section 8.4. The data for saving was derived from *Economic Trends, Annual Supplement,* 1981. (For simplicity, a very slight alteration to the data for one period was made to avoid a negative value for personal saving which would have precluded the use of logarithms.) In the computer output, the logarithm of saving is denoted by *ls*. In addition to the parameter estimates and the usual diagnostic statistics, also reported are the Schwarz Bayesian criterion *SC* and the final prediction error *FPE*. For comparison, for the *DHSY* model the *SC* value was −9.809 and the *FPE* value was 0.000047.

At first sight, the *HT* model looks definitely inferior to the *DHSY* model. Although the estimated coefficients are statistically significant, and have signs and magnitudes consistent with prior expectations, nevertheless the information criteria *SC* and *FPE* are not as good as those of the *DHSY* model. The Durbin–Watson statistic is very low (although greater than the R^2 coefficient and therefore consistent with the 'rule of thumb' for stationarity of the residuals — see Chapter 5). In particular, the forecasting properties of the model (Forecast χ^2 and the Chow test statistics) show that the hypothesis of the constancy of the parameters both for the period up to the end of 1971 and after that has to be rejected.

Does this mean that we have selected a 'straw man' and that without further analysis we can claim victory for the *DHSY* model over that of *HT*? Not necessarily. If we re—estimate the *HT* model by a method which explicitly accounts for the fact that the residuals display first order autocorrelation, we may note a substantial improvement in the forecasts. We have re—estimated the model by a maximum likelihood method which explicitly allows for first order autocorrelation. The properties and estimation details of this method (which is called *RALS*, for r—th order Autoregressive Least Squares) are not discussed here; details can be found in Hendry (1989, pp. 45—46). With the use of

the *RALS* estimates, the Forecast χ^2 statistic and the Chow test (reported beneath the *OLS* results for MODEL 8.1) are much improved and do not lead to the outright rejection of the hypothesis of parameter constancy. Moreover, it has to be remembered that we cannot directly compare the *DHSY* and *HT* models, since the dependent variables are not the same. The *DHSY* model explains $\Delta_4 cons_t$, while the

left—hand side variable in the *HT* model is $\Delta_4 co_t^* in_{t-1}$. Hence, further testing is needed in order to establish superiority.

We start with the *J* test for variance encompassing. As has been said already, this consists of testing the significance of the fitted values from one model when used as an additional explanatory variable in another. In our case, however, we have an additional problem, since the dependent variables in the estimated models are not the same. Before performing the *J* test, we have to transform the fitted values in order to ensure comparability. If we want to test the hypothesis that T encompasses *DHSY*, we have to re—estimate the *DHSY* model using the fitted values from the *HT* model as an additional variable. However, the fitted value from the estimated

HT model is (say) $\tilde{\Delta}_4 co_t^* in_{t-1}$, that is it corresponds to $\Delta_4 co_t^* in_{t-1}$ rather than to $\Delta_4 cons_t$. We may recompute the 'fitted' value for $\Delta_4 cons_t$ from the *HT* model as:

$$\tilde{\Delta}_4 cons_t = \tilde{\Delta}_4 co_t^* in_{t-1} + \Delta_4 inc_{t-1} \ .$$

MODEL 8.2 in Section 8.4, where the $\tilde{\Delta}_4 cons_t$ variable is denoted as *htf*, shows that the Student–t statistic on the fitted values from the *HT* model is equal to –0.595, which is not significantly different from zero at conventional levels of significance. Hence, we have no evidence that *HT* encompasses *DHSY* for variance.

MODEL 8.3 in Section 8.4 shows the *J* test regression for the hypothesis that *DHSY* encompasses *HT*. Again, the fitted value of the *DHSY* model has to be transformed for comparability, that is $\Delta_4 inc_{t-1}$ has to be subtracted from the originally computed fitted value. The variable resulting from this manipulation is denoted by *dhf* in the computer printout. It is evident that the inclusion of *dhf* substantially changes the entire model. The originally significant variables $\Delta_4 sav_{t-1}$ and $\Delta\Delta_4 inc_t$ change their signs and become insignificant. The estimated coefficient for *dhf* is close to unity and highly significant. Moreover, the Durbin–Watson statistic does not suggest a problem with autocorrelation. Hence, it seems that the *DHSY* model does encompass the *HT* model for variance. If one accepts the traditional interpretation of autocorrelation in the residuals of a fitted model as the result of model misspecification due to missing variables, it looks as if what was missing from the *HT* model was the *DHSY* component.

For the forecast encompassing test we have computed one–step ahead forecasts using the recursive least squares method. Using *PC–GIVE*, this consists of estimating the equation by *RLS*, saving one–step ahead errors (called in the

PC–GIVE menu, 'innovations') and using them for computing the forecast values. We may think of the series of
one–step ahead forecasts as a series of systematically
published one period ahead forecasts by a forecasting office,
which we wish to check against our own results. It does not
matter how large or how complicated the models are that
have been used to generate these forecasts. All we have to
know are the forecast values and realizations. Having these,
we can easily recompute the forecast errors.

In the computer output in Section 8.4, the difference
between the forecasts from the *DHSY* and *HT* models
obtained by recursive regressions are denoted respectively as
dh_ht and *ht_dh*. Analogously, the corresponding forecast
errors are denoted by *dhru* and *htru*. MODELS 8.4 and 8.5
show the computed results of the forecast encompassing test.
In MODEL 8.4, where the forecast errors of the *DHSY* model
are regressed on the differences between the forecasts *ht_dh*,
the Student–*t* ratio is insignificant. In MODEL 8.5, where
the forecast errors of the *HT* model are regressed on the
differences between the forecasts *dh_ht*, the Student–*t* ratio
is significant. We have obtained an unambiguous result.
That is we have found out that the *DHSY* model does encompass the forecasts from the *HT* model, and at the same time
the *HT* model does not encompass the *DHSY* model. Thus
both encompassing tests applied here, the variance and
forecast encompassing tests, conclusively show the superiority
of the *DHSY* model over the *HT* model.

8.4   Stylized Computer Output (*PC–GIVE*)

Initial transformation of variable
ls1   =   [LAG 1](ls)

MODEL 8.1: Modelling d4lc_li1 by OLS

The Sample is 1958 (2) to 1975 (4) less 0 Forecasts

VARI	COEF	STD ERROR	H.C.S.E.	t–VALUE
d4ls1	−.006	.00244	.00523	−2.6841
dd4li	.5432	.07877	.09061	6.89683

$R^2 = .4722$ $\sigma = .016422$ $F(2, 69) = 30.87$ $DW = .857$
$RSS = .0186092$ for 2 Variables and 71 Observations
Information Criteria: $SC = -8.126700$; $FPE = .000277$

Tests Of Parameter CONSTANCY Over   1971 1 − 1975 4

Forecast $\chi^2(20)/20$ $\qquad\qquad$ = 2.10
CHOW TEST(20, 49) $\qquad\qquad$ = 2.07

Modelling d4lc_li1 by RALS
Tests Of Parameter CONSTANCY Over   1971 1 − 1975 4

Forecast $\chi^2(20)/20$ $\qquad\qquad$ = 1.75
CHOW TEST(20, 47) $\qquad\qquad$ = 1.66

MODEL 8.2: Modelling d4lc by OLS

The Sample is 1958 (2) to 1975 (4) less 0 Forecasts

VARI	COEF	STD ERR	H.C.S.E.	t–VALUE
d4li	.5524	.10168	.10695	5.43296
dd4li	−.222	.04620	.04532	−4.8098
lc_li 4	−.090	.01432	.01362	−6.3208
inf	−.119	.02703	.02619	−4.4198
dinf	−.234	.09374	.11404	−2.4982
htf	−.077	.13005	.13864	−.59516

$\sigma = .006649$ $F(6, 65) = 189.37$ $DW = 2.144$
$RSS = .0028737$ for 6 Variables and 71 Observations
Information Criteria: $SC = -9.754587$; $FPE = .000048$

MODEL 8.3: Modelling d4lc_li1 by OLS

The Sample is 1958 (2) to 1975 (4) less 0 Forecasts

VARI	COEF	STD ERR	H.C.S.E.	t–VALUE
d4ls1	.0002	.00103	.00078	.19798
dd4li	−.001	.04216	.04214	−.0245
dhf	1.003	.05216	.04563	19.240

$\sigma =$ .006516 F(3, 68) = 254.10 DW = 2.208
RSS = .0028877 for 3 Variables and 71 Observations
Information Criteria: SC = −9.929842; FPE = .000044

MODEL 8.4 Modelling dhru by OLS

The Sample is 1965 (4) to 1975 (4) less 0 Forecasts

VARI	COEF	STD ERR	H.C.S.E.	t–VALUE
ht_dh	−.0045	.02106	.01765	−.21190

$\sigma =$ .007568 F(1, 40) = .04 DW = 2.571
RSS = .0022909 for 1 Variable and 41 Observations
Information Criteria: SC = −9.701792; FPE = .000059

MODEL 8.5: Modelling htru by OLS

The Sample is 1965 (4) to 1975 (4) less 0 Forecasts

VARI	COEF	STD ERR	H.C.S.E.	t–VALUE
dh_ht	.2665	.02799	.02411	9.52167

$\sigma =$ .010060 F(1, 40) = 90.66 DW = 2.108
RSS = .0040479 for 1 Variable and 41 Observations
Information Criteria: SC = −9.132548; FPE = .000104

8.5 Suggestions for Further Reading

The literature on non—nested hypotheses and related tests is quite abundant. Thorough discussions of the problem in an econometric context have been given by Pesaran (1974), Quandt (1974) and Pesaran and Deaton (1978). Reviews of the subject are included in MacKinnon (1983), Godfrey (1984) and McAleer and Pesaran (1986). Further developments of the *J* test can be found in Davidson and MacKinnon (1982) and, in a wider context, in Davidson and MacKinnon (1985). Godfrey (1989) reviews misspecification tests for nested models.

Not a great deal has been published on encompassing. Advanced papers on this subject are those of Mizon (1984) and Mizon and Richard (1986), where a detailed definition of encompassing is given, grounded in the concept of data generating processes (see Chapter 7). A simpler explanation and an example can be found in Hendry (1988a).

A straightforward example of an application of the Chong and Hendry forecast encompassing test is given by Charemza (1991), where the test is applied for a comparison of a large nonlinear structural model with a simple (naive) model. Holden and McGregor (1989) used encompassing tests for finding a good deflator for the *DHSY* model. The *J* test for choosing between different measures of money income was used by Cuthbertson and Taylor (1988). Various encompassing tests for analysing a model of a trade balance were applied by Ahumada (1985). An advanced empirical paper using encompassing to discriminate between a *VAR* and a structural model is that by Hendry and Mizon (1990).

A paper which considers the application of the use of encompassing for testing superexogeneity and the Lucas critique is that of Hendry (1988b). This idea has been further developed and applied to the analysis of consumption by Favero (1989).

Exercises for Discussion

Exercise 1

Two independent researchers, A and B, presented regression equations to describe a variable y. Researcher A selected her equation by choosing two explanatory variables out of 10 'candidates' x_1, x_2 ,..., x_{10} , while B selected his model with two explanatory variables out of four different 'candidates' z_1, z_2, z_3, z_4. There were 25 observations on each variable and the criteria for selecting explanatory variables to enter a model was on the basis of choosing those variables with the highest Student–t statistics. Assume that all the 'candidate' variables are orthogonal with respect to each other. The results are as follows:

$$\text{Model selected by } A: \quad y = 0.50 + 0.20x_1 + 0.70x_2 \ ,$$
$$(6.6) \quad (2.4) \quad (3.2)$$

$$\text{Model selected by } B: \quad y = 0.70 + 0.60z_1 + 0.50z_2 \ ,$$
$$(7.3) \quad (1.8) \quad (2.2)$$

where Student–t ratios are given in brackets. For the two equations above, compute the true significance levels if tests are conducted at a nominal 5% significance level. Is it possible to say which of the two results is more trustworthy?

Exercise 2

Researcher 1, while trying to evaluate a relationship explaining a variable y, regressed it on the variable x_1, and then separately on x_2, x_3 and x_4 (that is four separate simple regressions were run). This researcher selected the model with the highest Student–t on an explanatory variable, which was:

$$y = 0.25 - 5.31 \cdot x_3 + a \; residual \; ,$$
$$(2.91) \quad (4.12)$$

where the coefficient of determination $R^2 = 0.92$, and Student–t statistics for coefficients are in parentheses. Independently, researcher 2 decided to regress y on variable x_2 only, without running any other regressions. The result was:

$$y = 0.31 - 3.26 \cdot x_2 + a \; residual \; ,$$
$$(2.91) \quad (2.12)$$

with $R^2 = 0.76$. Discuss whether it is possible to decide which of the results (that is of researchers 1 and 2) is better. Would you answer differently if researcher 2 had decided to use x_3 rather than x_2 so that both researchers present the same final model? Comment on the possibility of 'Lovell bias' in these results.

Exercise 3

The estimated *DHSY* aggregate consumption model for a certain country with the use of 70 quarterly observations is the following:

$$\Delta_4 cons_t = 0.30 \cdot \Delta_4 y_t - 0.10 \cdot \Delta\Delta_4 y_t + 0.127 \cdot (cons_{t-4} - y_{t-4})$$
$$(15.3) \qquad (4.0) \qquad (2.2)$$
$$+ 0.10 \cdot \Delta_4 p_t - 0.17 \cdot \Delta\Delta_4 p_t + a \; residual$$
$$(3.2) \qquad (1.2)$$

where $cons_t$ is real aggregate consumption, y_t is total real disposable income and p_t is the price index (implicit price deflator). All variables are in natural logarithms, Student–t statistics for particular coefficients are in parentheses and Δ symbols are of the type $\Delta x_t = x_t - x_{t-1}$ and $\Delta_4 x_t = x_t - x_{t-4}$.

(i)   Comment on the possible existence of an error correction mechanism in the above model.

(*ii*)   Comment on the possible existence of Deaton's unanticipated inflation effect and (or) the 'money illusion' effect.

Exercise 4

For the general unrestricted $ADL(2)$ model, that is for:

$$y_t = a_1 y_{t-1} + a_2 y_{t-2} + b_0 x_t + b_1 x_{t-1} + b_2 x_{t-2} + an\ error,$$

formulate a set of restrictions which generate the following specific models:

(*i*)   A model in first differences with a second order error–correction mechanism, that is of the form:

$$\Delta y_t = \beta_1 \Delta x_t + \beta_2 (y_{t-1} - x_{t-1}) + \beta_3 (y_{t-2} - x_{t-2}) + an\ error.$$

(*ii*)   A specific model with two common factors, which is equivalent to a linear regression model with second-order autocorrelation in the errors, that is:

$$y_t = \alpha x_t + u_t,$$

with:

$$u_t = \rho_1 u_{t-1} + \rho_2 u_{t-2} + \epsilon_t.$$

Exercise 5

In a process of single equation modelling with the use of the 'general to specific' methodology, the autoregressive distributed lag (ADL) model:

$$y_t = \alpha_1 y_{t-1} + \alpha_2 y_{t-2} + \beta_0 x_t + \beta_1 x_{t-1} + \beta_2 x_{t-2} + an\ error,$$

has been used as a general model. During the model reduction process the following specific models have been estimated:

Model A: $y_t = \underset{(3.73)}{0.27 \cdot x_t} - \underset{(5.17)}{0.06 \cdot x_{t-1}} + a\ residual$,

Model B: $y_t = \underset{(1.33)}{0.73 \cdot y_{t-1}} + \underset{(3.34)}{0.15 \cdot \Delta x_t} + a\ residual$,

where $\Delta x_t = x_t - x_{t-1}$ and Student–t statistics for the regression coefficients are in parentheses.

(i)   Formulate restrictions on the parameters of the *ADL* model which have to be tested for the derivation of the specific models A and B.

(ii)   Describe the procedure for testing the validity of the restrictions imposed (that is, formulate the null and alternative hypotheses and describe the computations for the particular steps in testing the restrictions).

(iii)   Using the estimated models A and B evaluate, without formal testing, for which (if either) of the models the restrictions imposed on the general *ADL* model seem to be valid.

Exercise 6

Decide, using the results below, whether it makes sense to test for cointegration of the dependent and explanatory variables in models (a) and (b). What are the necessary conditions for the existence of cointegration in these models and how can they be tested?

Model (a): $y_t = \alpha_1 x_{1t} + \alpha_2 x_{2t} + u_t$,

Model (b): $y_t = \alpha_1 x_{1t} + u_t$.

The Augmented Dickey–Fuller t–ratio statistics computed for levels and first differences of particular variables, using 50 observations and without a constant term in the *ADF* regression equation, are as follows:

y_t :   −5.24 (levels)   ;   11.63 (first differences)

x_{1t} :   1.21 (levels)   ;   −4.05 (first differences)

x_{2t} :   −0.11 (levels)   ;   −7.27 (first differences)

Exercise 7

A simple wage–adjustment model is the following (w_t is a nominal wage, p_t is a price):

$$\Delta w_t = \alpha \Delta p_t + \beta(w_{t-1} - \gamma p_{t-1}) + u_t .$$

Under the hypothesis of wage homogeneity, $\gamma = 1$. The *ADF* *t*–ratio statistics (computed without a constant term) using 30 observations, for levels and first differences of w_t and p_t are as follows:

w_t : 2.18 (levels)   ; −3.37 (first differences)

p_t : −0.25 (levels)   ; −8.11 (first differences)

Under the assumption of wage homogeneity, that is where $\gamma = 1$, the cointegration of w_t and p_t was tested by the use of the ADF *t*–ratio statistic. The result was −4.97. Alternatively, where the assumption about homogeneity was dropped, w_t was regressed on p_t, with the result:

$$w_t = 1.12 p_t + v_t , \ ADF(v_t) = -0.58 , \ DW = 0.57 , \ R^2 = 0.85 ,$$
$$(2.03)$$

where $ADF(v_t)$ is the *ADF* statistic computed for the OLS residuals of the above equation, *DW* is Durbin–Watson statistic, R^2 is the coefficient of determination and the Student–*t* ratio is in brackets below the estimated coefficient.

Answer the following questions:
a) What are the levels of integration of p_t and w_t?
b) Is the necessary condition for cointegration of p_t and w_t met ?
c) Does the 'rule of thumb' for comparing R^2 and DW confirm the hypothesis about cointegration in the non-homogeneous model ?
d) Does the ADF test confirm this hypothesis in the non-homogeneous model ?
e) Are p_t and w_t cointegrated under the hypothesis of homogeneity ?
f) For estimating the wage–adjustment equation, would you prefer to use the homogeneity assumption, or to apply the Engle–Granger procedure for the non–homogeneous model?

Exercise 8.
The estimates of a static demand for money function, formulated in logarithms and based on 60 annual observations are $(m_t$ = money, y_t = nominal income, r_t = interest rate, ϵ_t = error term, Student–t values are in parentheses):

$$m_t = 1.0 + 0.22y_t - 0.70r_t + \epsilon_t$$
$$\quad\;\;(4.1)\;\;(3.3)\quad\;(-5.6)$$

$$R^2 = 0.71 \, , \; ADF(\epsilon_t) = -6.20 \, , \; DW = 2.05 \, ,$$

where R^2 is the coefficient of determination, ADF is the Augmented Dickey–Fuller statistic for the error term ϵ_t (in the form of the Student–t test) and DW is the Durbin–Watson statistic for the residuals. The Augmented Dickey–Fuller integration statistics (in the Student–t form) computed for all the variables are the following:

for m_t : 1.25 ;   for y_t : 3.11 ;   for r_t : 0.91 .

a) Comment on the results. Is there a danger of spurious regression in the model ?
b) Test and comment for the possible presence or absence of cointegration of the variables.
c) Discuss whether it is advisable to test further for the possible use of first differences of variables rather than levels and to introduce an error correction mechanism. If so, how would you proceed?

Exercise 9.
While analysing the relationship between money (m_t) and income (y_t), an econometrician estimated the following regression using ordinary least squares and 25 annual observations. (Data are in real terms, and in logarithms.)

$$m_t = 0.858 \; y_t + u_t$$
$$(5.31)$$

$$R^2 = 0.80, \quad DW = 0.75, \quad ADF(u_t) = -1.75,$$
$$ADF(m_t) = -3.22, \quad ADF(y_t) = -4.31,$$

where the Student–t statistic is given in brackets below the estimated parameter, R^2 is the coefficient of determination, DW is the Durbin–Watson statistic computed for the residuals u_t, and $ADF(-)$ is the Augmented Dickey–Fuller statistic computed for u_t, m_t and y_t respectively.

Using the results above , establish whether:
(a)   the series m_t and y_t are integrated of the same order;
(b)   the series m_t and y_t are cointegrated;
(c)   the model can sensibly be estimated in first differences, with or without the error correction mechanism.

Exercise 10

(*i*)   Describe the main differences between multi–equation structural modelling (Cowles Commission methodology) and vector autoregressive (*VAR*) modelling.

(*ii*)   In order to detect possible causality between inflation
π_t and money supply m_t the following two equation

VAR model was estimated using 80 quarterly observations:

$$\pi_t = \sum_{i=1}^{4} \alpha_{pi} \pi_{t-i} + \sum_{i=1}^{4} \beta_{pi} m_{t-i} + intercept + trend +$$

3 *seasonal dummy variables* + *an error term* ,

$$m_t = \sum_{i=1}^{4} \alpha_{mi} \pi_{t-i} + \sum_{i=1}^{4} \beta_{mi} m_{t-i} + intercept + trend +$$

3 *seasonal dummy variables* + *an error term* .

The following Lagrange Multiplier (*LMF*) statistics were
computed for testing the restrictions:

(a) $\beta_{p1} = \beta_{p2} = \beta_{p3} = \beta_{p4} = 0$: $LMF = 38.13$

(b) $\alpha_{m1} = \alpha_{m2} = \alpha_{m3} = \alpha_{m4} = 0$: $LMF = 1.16$

Determine at the 5% level of significance whether there is
a one way causal relation from inflation to money, from money to inflation, or whether there is a feedback relation
between money and inflation.   What are the appropriate
degrees of freedom for these *LMF* tests?

Exercise 11

(a)   Describe the Granger concept of causality and its
role in econometric modelling.

(b)   In order to investigate a relationship between GNP
(denoted by y_t) and government spending (g_t), a two

equation vector autoregressive (*VAR*) model was

estimated by the ordinary least squares method, using 30 annual observations. The results were as follows:

$$y_t = 0.25 + 0.66 \cdot y_{t-1} + 0.37 \cdot g_{t-1} \quad , \quad R^2 = 0.73 \quad ,$$
$$\quad (1.0) \quad (5.3) \qquad (1.3)$$

$$g_t = 0.87 + 0.18 \cdot y_{t-1} + 0.50 \cdot g_{t-1} \quad , \quad R^2 = 0.90 \quad ,$$
$$\quad (5.0) \quad (3.0) \qquad (3.2)$$

where R^2 is the coefficient of determination and Student–t statistics are given in brackets below the parameter estimates. Using the results above, can you decide in favour of the Wagnerian hypothesis that GNP is a Granger cause for government expenditure, or in favour of the Keynesian hypothesis that government expenditures are a Granger cause for GNP, or for neither hypothesis?

Appendix

Technical note for Tables 2 – 4

Tables of critical values for the Dickey–Fuller and Augmented Dickey–Fuller tests have been prepared with the use of the program *COIN* for simulating fractiles of distributions of particular data generating processes. Some details of the data generating processes used for simulation and a detailed description of some earlier results are given in Blangiewicz and Charemza (1990). Copies of the *COIN* program, written in *GAUSS*, which can also be used for computing fractiles of individually defined data generating processes (so–called *customized cointegration testing*) are available from the authors on request.

Particular percentiles have been computed for sets of 10,000 pseudo–random samples each generated for a given number of observations. For each level of significance the results were smoothed by a regression on an intercept and the inverse of the logarithm of sample size. The upper and lower bounds for the critical values were then calculated in the following way:

$$\text{upper/lower bound} = \text{fitted value} \pm 2 \times (S.R.E. + S.F.E.) \ ,$$

where $S.R.E.$ is the standard error of the regression and $S.F.E.$ is the David–Johnson estimate of the standard error of a particular percentile.

A word of caution is necessary concerning the use of Table 3 (*DF* and *ADF* tests with an intercept) for $m = 0$. Our tabulated values differ markedly from those previously published by Fuller (1976), Guilkey and Schmidt (1989) and MacKinnon (1991), which also differ substantially from each other. It is probable that these critical values are sensitive to the data generating process adopted for the computations.

Table 1: Lovell's true significance levels,

in percentages, for a 5% nominal level of significance; k - No. of selected variables, c - No. of 'candidates'

k	$c=10$	$c=15$	$c=20$	$c=25$	$c=30$	$c=35$	$c=40$	$c=45$	$c=50$
2	22.6	31.9	40.1	47.3	53.7	59.2	64.2	68.5	72.3
3	15.7	22.6	29.0	34.8	40.1	45.0	49.5	53.7	57.5
4	12.0	17.5	22.6	27.4	31.9	36.2	40.1	43.8	47.3
5	9.8	14.3	18.5	22.6	26.5	30.2	33.7	37.0	40.1
6	8.2	12.0	15.7	19.2	22.6	25.9	29.0	31.9	34.8
7	7.1	10.4	13.6	16.7	19.7	22.6	25.4	28.1	30.7
8	6.2	9.2	12.0	14.8	17.5	20.1	22.6	25.1	27.4
9	5.5	8.2	10.8	13.3	15.7	18.1	20.4	22.6	24.8
10	5.0	7.4	9.8	12.0	14.3	16.4	18.5	20.6	22.6

Table 2: Dickey-Fuller and Augmented Dickey-Fuller tests;

critical values (minus sign omitted), without intercept,
1% level of significance, $m = 0,\ldots,4$

n	m = 0 lower	m = 0 upper	m = 1 lower	m = 1 upper	m = 2 lower	m = 2 upper	m = 3 lower	m = 3 upper	m = 4 lower	m = 4 upper
15	2.86	2.54	3.84	3.38	4.25	3.83	4.62	4.27	4.90	4.59
20	2.82	2.51	3.78	3.32	4.21	3.80	4.58	4.24	4.87	4.57
25	2.80	2.48	3.74	3.29	4.19	3.78	4.56	4.22	4.85	4.55
30	2.78	2.47	3.71	3.26	4.18	3.77	4.54	4.20	4.84	4.54
40	2.76	2.44	3.67	3.23	4.16	3.75	4.52	4.18	4.82	4.53
50	2.74	2.43	3.65	3.20	4.14	3.73	4.50	4.17	4.81	4.51
75	2.72	2.40	3.61	3.16	4.12	3.71	4.48	4.15	4.79	4.50
100	2.70	2.39	3.58	3.14	4.11	3.70	4.46	4.13	4.78	4.49
150	2.68	2.37	3.56	3.11	4.09	3.69	4.45	4.12	4.77	4.48
300	2.66	2.35	3.52	3.07	4.07	3.66	4.42	4.09	4.75	4.46

Table 2: Dickey-Fuller and Augmented Dickey-Fuller tests;
critical values (minus sign omitted), without intercept,
1% level of significance, $m = 5, \ldots, 8$

n	$m = 5$		$m = 6$		$m = 7$		$m = 8$	
	lower	*upper*	*lower*	*upper*	*lower*	*upper*	*lower*	*upper*
15	5.22	4.83	5.43	5.04	5.53	5.14	5.86	5.32
20	5.20	4.82	5.41	5.03	5.54	5.17	5.86	5.34
25	5.18	4.80	5.40	5.02	5.56	5.18	5.87	5.35
30	5.17	4.79	5.39	5.02	5.56	5.19	5.88	5.36
40	5.15	4.78	5.38	5.01	5.58	5.21	5.88	5.37
50	5.14	4.77	5.38	5.00	5.58	5.22	5.89	5.38
75	5.13	4.76	5.36	4.99	5.60	5.23	5.90	5.39
100	5.12	4.75	5.36	4.99	5.60	5.24	5.90	5.40
150	5.11	4.74	5.35	4.98	5.61	5.25	5.91	5.40
300	5.09	4.72	5.34	4.97	5.63	5.26	5.92	5.41

Table 2: Dickey-Fuller and Augmented Dickey-Fuller tests;

critical values (minus sign omitted), without intercept,
5% level of significance, $m = 0,\ldots,4$

n	$m = 0$		$m = 1$		$m = 2$		$m = 3$		$m = 4$	
	lower	upper	lower	upper	lower	upper	lower	upper	lower	upper
15	1.98	1.83	2.88	2.65	3.27	3.11	3.63	3.43	4.05	3.38
20	1.98	1.84	2.88	2.65	3.29	3.13	3.67	3.46	4.14	3.48
25	1.99	1.84	2.87	2.65	3.30	3.14	3.69	3.49	4.21	3.54
30	1.99	1.85	2.87	2.65	3.31	3.15	3.71	3.50	4.26	3.59
40	2.00	1.85	2.87	2.65	3.33	3.17	3.73	3.53	4.32	3.66
50	2.00	1.86	2.87	2.65	3.33	3.18	3.75	3.54	4.36	3.70
75	2.01	1.86	2.87	2.65	3.35	3.19	3.77	3.57	4.43	3.77
100	2.01	1.86	2.87	2.64	3.36	3.20	3.78	3.58	4.47	3.81
150	2.01	1.87	2.87	2.64	3.37	3.21	3.80	3.60	4.52	3.86
300	2.02	1.87	2.87	2.64	3.38	3.22	3.82	3.62	4.59	3.93

Table 2: Dickey-Fuller and Augmented Dickey-Fuller tests; critical values (minus sign omitted), without intercept, 5% level of significance, $m = 5,\ldots,8$

n	$m = 5$		$m = 6$		$m = 7$		$m = 8$	
	lower	upper	lower	upper	lower	upper	lower	upper
15	4.10	3.93	4.30	4.12	4.43	4.23	4.57	4.37
20	4.17	4.00	4.38	4.21	4.54	4.35	4.70	4.51
25	4.22	4.05	4.44	4.27	4.62	4.43	4.78	4.60
30	4.25	4.08	4.48	4.31	4.67	4.48	4.84	4.66
40	4.30	4.13	4.54	4.37	4.74	4.56	4.93	4.75
50	4.33	4.16	4.58	4.41	4.79	4.61	4.99	4.81
75	4.38	4.21	4.64	4.47	4.87	4.68	5.08	4.90
100	4.41	4.24	4.67	4.51	4.92	4.73	5.13	4.95
150	4.44	4.28	4.72	4.55	4.98	4.79	5.20	5.02
300	4.49	4.33	4.78	4.61	5.05	4.87	5.29	5.11

Table 2: Dickey-Fuller and Augmented Dickey-Fuller tests;
critical values (minus sign omitted), without intercept,
10% level of significance, $m = 0, \ldots, 4$

n	$m = 0$		$m = 1$		$m = 2$		$m = 3$		$m = 4$	
	lower	upper	lower	upper	lower	upper	lower	upper	lower	upper
15	1.60	1.46	2.82	2.06	2.87	2.72	3.21	3.03	3.45	3.30
20	1.62	1.48	2.83	2.07	2.91	2.76	3.27	3.09	3.52	3.38
25	1.63	1.49	2.84	2.08	2.94	2.78	3.30	3.13	3.58	3.44
30	1.64	1.50	2.84	2.09	2.96	2.80	3.33	3.16	3.61	3.47
40	1.65	1.51	2.85	2.10	2.98	2.83	3.37	3.20	3.66	3.53
50	1.66	1.52	2.86	2.10	3.00	2.85	3.40	3.22	3.70	3.56
75	1.67	1.53	2.87	2.11	3.03	2.87	3.44	3.26	3.75	3.61
100	1.67	1.53	2.87	2.12	3.04	2.89	3.46	3.29	3.78	3.65
150	1.68	1.54	2.88	2.12	3.06	2.91	3.49	3.32	3.82	3.69
300	1.70	1.56	2.89	2.13	3.09	2.94	3.53	3.36	3.88	3.74

Table 2: Dickey-Fuller and Augmented Dickey-Fuller tests; critical values (minus sign omitted), without intercept, 10% level of significance, $m = 5,\ldots,8$

n	$m = 5$		$m = 6$		$m = 7$		$m = 8$	
	lower	upper	lower	upper	lower	upper	lower	upper
15	3.66	3.48	3.82	3.65	3.96	3.76	4.11	3.92
20	3.76	3.58	3.95	3.78	4.12	3.91	4.28	4.09
25	3.83	3.65	4.03	3.86	4.22	4.01	4.39	4.20
30	3.88	3.70	4.09	3.92	4.29	4.09	4.47	4.28
40	3.95	3.77	4.17	4.01	4.39	4.19	4.57	4.39
50	3.99	3.82	4.22	4.06	4.45	4.26	4.65	4.46
75	4.06	3.89	4.31	4.15	4.56	4.36	4.76	4.58
100	4.11	3.93	4.36	4.20	4.62	4.42	4.83	4.65
150	4.16	3.99	4.42	4.26	4.70	4.50	4.91	4.73
300	4.23	4.06	4.51	4.35	4.80	4.61	5.03	4.85

Table 3: Dickey-Fuller and Augmented Dickey-Fuller tests;

critical values (minus sign omitted), with intercept,
1% level of significance, $m = 0,...,4$

n	$m = 0$		$m = 1$		$m = 2$		$m = 3$		$m = 4$	
	lower	upper	lower	upper	lower	upper	lower	upper	lower	upper
15	3.76	3.13	4.22	3.95	4.55	4.27	4.92	4.57	5.17	4.75
20	3.56	2.94	4.18	3.92	4.53	4.25	4.90	4.55	5.14	4.74
25	3.43	2.81	4.16	3.90	4.51	4.23	4.88	4.53	5.13	4.73
30	3.33	2.72	4.14	3.88	4.50	4.22	4.87	4.52	5.12	4.72
40	3.20	2.60	4.12	3.86	4.48	4.21	4.85	4.51	5.11	4.71
50	3.11	2.51	4.10	3.84	4.47	4.19	4.84	4.50	5.10	4.70
75	2.98	2.38	4.08	3.82	4.45	4.18	4.82	4.48	5.08	4.68
100	2.90	2.30	4.07	3.81	4.44	4.17	4.81	4.47	5.07	4.67
150	2.79	2.20	4.05	3.79	4.43	4.16	4.80	4.46	5.06	4.67
300	2.66	2.07	4.02	3.77	4.41	4.14	4.78	4.44	5.05	4.65

Table 3: Dickey-Fuller and Augmented Dickey-Fuller tests;

critical values (minus sign omitted), with intercept,
1% level of significance, $m = 5,\ldots,8$

n	$m = 5$		$m = 6$		$m = 7$		$m = 8$	
	lower	upper	lower	upper	lower	upper	lower	upper
15	5.28	4.93	5.55	5.16	5.63	5.30	5.84	5.44
20	5.30	4.95	5.57	5.19	5.67	5.35	5.89	5.50
25	5.31	4.97	5.58	5.20	5.70	5.38	5.92	5.53
30	5.32	4.98	5.59	5.21	5.71	5.40	5.94	5.56
40	5.33	5.00	5.60	5.22	5.74	5.43	5.97	5.60
50	5.34	5.01	5.60	5.23	5.75	5.45	6.00	5.62
75	5.35	5.02	5.61	5.25	5.78	5.48	6.03	5.66
100	5.36	5.03	5.62	5.25	5.80	5.49	6.05	5.68
150	5.38	5.04	5.63	5.26	5.82	5.51	6.08	5.70
300	5.39	5.06	5.64	5.28	5.85	5.54	6.11	5.74

Table 3: Dickey-Fuller and Augmented Dickey-Fuller tests;

critical values (minus sign omitted), with intercept,
5% level of significance, $m = 0,\ldots,4$

n	$m = 0$		$m = 1$		$m = 2$		$m = 3$		$m = 4$	
	lower	upper	lower	upper	lower	upper	lower	upper	lower	upper
15	2.54	2.32	3.31	3.14	3.61	3.41	3.87	3.72	4.05	3.87
20	2.41	2.19	3.34	3.16	3.66	3.46	3.92	3.78	4.13	3.95
25	2.33	2.11	3.35	3.18	3.69	3.49	3.96	3.82	4.18	4.00
30	2.26	2.05	3.37	3.19	3.71	3.51	3.98	3.84	4.22	4.04
40	2.18	1.97	3.38	3.21	3.74	3.54	4.02	3.88	4.27	4.09
50	2.12	1.91	3.39	3.22	3.76	3.56	4.04	3.90	4.30	4.13
75	2.03	1.83	3.41	3.23	3.79	3.59	4.08	3.94	4.36	4.18
100	1.98	1.77	3.42	3.24	3.81	3.61	4.10	3.96	4.39	4.22
150	1.91	1.71	3.43	3.26	3.83	3.63	4.13	3.99	4.43	4.26
300	1.82	1.62	3.44	3.27	3.86	3.66	4.16	4.03	4.49	4.31

Table 3: Dickey-Fuller and Augmented Dickey-Fuller tests; critical values (minus sign omitted), with intercept, 5% level of significance, $m = 5,\ldots,8$

n	m = 5		m = 6		m = 7		m = 8	
	lower	upper	lower	upper	lower	upper	lower	upper
15	4.24	4.04	4.41	4.24	4.53	4.37	4.66	4.45
20	4.34	4.15	4.52	4.36	4.67	4.51	4.82	4.61
25	4.41	4.22	4.60	4.44	4.76	4.60	4.92	4.72
30	4.46	4.27	4.65	4.49	4.82	4.67	4.99	4.79
40	4.53	4.34	4.73	4.57	4.91	4.76	5.10	4.90
50	4.58	4.38	4.78	4.63	4.97	4.82	5.17	4.97
75	4.65	4.45	4.86	4.71	5.07	4.92	5.28	5.08
100	4.69	4.50	4.91	4.75	5.12	4.97	5.34	5.15
150	4.74	4.55	4.97	4.81	5.19	5.04	5.42	5.23
300	4.81	4.62	5.05	4.89	5.29	5.14	5.53	5.34

Table 3: Dickey-Fuller and Augmented Dickey-Fuller tests;

critical values (minus sign omitted), with intercept,
10% level of significance, $m = 0,\ldots,4$

n	m = 0		m = 1		m = 2		m = 3		m = 4	
	lower	upper	lower	upper	lower	upper	lower	upper	lower	upper
15	2.03	1.86	2.92	2.75	3.23	3.03	3.45	3.29	3.64	3.45
20	1.92	1.76	2.96	2.80	3.29	3.10	3.53	3.38	3.74	3.56
25	1.85	1.69	2.99	2.83	3.34	3.14	3.58	3.43	3.81	3.63
30	1.80	1.64	3.01	2.85	3.36	3.17	3.63	3.47	3.86	3.68
40	1.73	1.57	3.04	2.88	3.41	3.21	3.68	3.53	3.93	3.75
50	1.68	1.52	3.06	2.90	3.43	3.24	3.72	3.57	3.98	3.80
75	1.60	1.45	3.09	2.93	3.48	3.28	3.77	3.63	4.05	3.87
100	1.56	1.40	3.10	2.94	3.50	3.30	3.81	3.66	4.10	3.92
150	1.50	1.35	3.13	2.96	3.53	3.34	3.85	3.70	4.15	3.97
300	1.43	1.28	3.16	2.99	3.58	3.38	3.91	3.76	4.22	4.04

Table 3: Dickey-Fuller and Augmented Dickey-Fuller tests;

critical values (minus sign omitted), with intercept,
10% level of significance, $m = 5, \ldots, 8$

n	$m = 5$		$m = 6$		$m = 7$		$m = 8$	
	lower	*upper*	*lower*	*upper*	*lower*	*upper*	*lower*	*upper*
15	3.82	3.61	3.94	3.78	4.08	3.90	4.17	3.97
20	3.95	3.75	4.09	3.94	4.25	4.08	4.38	4.18
25	4.04	3.83	4.19	4.04	4.37	4.19	4.51	4.31
30	4.10	3.90	4.26	4.11	4.45	4.28	4.60	4.40
40	4.18	3.98	4.36	4.21	4.56	4.39	4.74	4.54
50	4.24	4.04	4.43	4.28	4.64	4.47	4.82	4.63
75	4.33	4.13	4.53	4.39	4.76	4.59	4.96	4.77
100	4.38	4.18	4.60	4.45	4.83	4.66	5.05	4.85
150	4.45	4.25	4.67	4.53	4.92	4.75	5.15	4.95
300	4.54	4.34	4.78	4.63	5.04	4.87	5.29	5.09

Table 4: Dickey-Fuller and Augmented Dickey-Fuller tests;

critical values (minus sign omitted), with deterministic quarterly seasonality, 1% level of significance, $m = 0, \ldots, 5$

n	m = 0 lower	m = 0 upper	m = 1 lower	m = 1 upper	m = 2 lower	m = 2 upper	m = 3 lower	m = 3 upper	m = 4 lower	m = 4 upper	m = 5 lower	m = 5 upper
15	3.86	3.50	4.16	3.99	4.55	4.18	4.81	4.39	4.90	4.52	5.14	4.50
20	3.82	3.45	4.13	3.95	4.54	4.17	4.83	4.41	4.95	4.57	5.24	4.59
25	3.79	3.42	4.11	3.93	4.54	4.17	4.84	4.42	4.98	4.61	5.30	4.65
30	3.77	3.39	4.09	3.91	4.53	4.16	4.85	4.43	5.01	4.63	5.35	4.69
40	3.74	3.37	4.07	3.89	4.53	4.16	4.86	4.44	5.04	4.67	5.41	4.76
50	3.72	3.35	4.05	3.88	4.53	4.16	4.87	4.45	5.06	4.69	5.45	4.80
75	3.69	3.32	4.03	3.86	4.52	4.15	4.88	4.46	5.10	4.73	5.51	4.86
100	3.67	3.30	4.01	3.84	4.52	4.15	4.89	4.47	5.12	4.75	5.55	4.90
150	3.65	3.28	4.00	3.82	4.51	4.15	4.90	4.47	5.14	4.77	5.60	4.95
300	3.62	3.25	3.97	3.80	4.51	4.14	4.91	4.49	5.18	4.81	5.66	5.02

Table 4: Dickey-Fuller and Augmented Dickey-Fuller tests;

critical values (minus sign omitted), with deterministic quarterly seasonality, $m = 0, \ldots, 5$ level of significance , 5% level of significance

n	m = 0 lower	m = 0 upper	m = 1 lower	m = 1 upper	m = 2 lower	m = 2 upper	m = 3 lower	m = 3 upper	m = 4 lower	m = 4 upper	m = 5 lower	m = 5 upper
15	2.98	2.83	3.37	3.19	3.69	3.39	3.87	3.57	4.06	3.60	4.22	3.64
20	2.98	2.82	3.38	3.20	3.73	3.43	3.95	3.65	4.18	3.72	4.38	3.80
25	2.97	2.81	3.39	3.21	3.76	3.46	4.01	3.70	4.26	3.80	4.49	3.90
30	2.97	2.81	3.39	3.22	3.78	3.48	4.04	3.74	4.32	3.85	4.56	3.98
40	2.96	2.81	3.40	3.22	3.80	3.50	4.10	3.80	4.39	3.93	4.67	4.08
50	2.96	2.80	3.40	3.23	3.82	3.52	4.13	3.83	4.45	3.98	4.73	4.15
75	2.96	2.80	3.41	3.24	3.85	3.55	4.19	3.89	4.52	4.07	4.84	4.26
100	2.95	2.79	3.42	3.24	3.87	3.57	4.22	3.92	5.57	4.11	4.91	4.33
150	2.95	2.79	3.42	3.25	3.89	3.59	4.26	3.96	4.63	4.17	4.99	4.40
300	2.94	2.78	3.43	3.25	3.92	3.62	4.31	4.02	4.71	4.26	5.09	4.51

Table 4: Dickey-Fuller and Augmented Dickey-Fuller tests;

critical values (minus sign omitted), with deterministic quarterly seasonality, 10% level of significance, $m = 0,\ldots,5$

n	m = 0		m = 1		m = 2		m = 3		m = 4		m = 5	
	lower	upper	lower	upper	lower	upper	lower	upper	lower	upper	lower	upper
15	2.60	2.47	2.98	2.83	3.28	3.03	3.47	3.18	3.67	3.19	3.80	3.22
20	2.61	2.48	3.01	2.86	3.34	3.09	3.57	3.28	3.81	3.33	3.99	3.40
25	2.62	2.48	3.03	2.88	3.38	3.13	3.64	3.35	3.91	3.42	4.11	3.52
30	2.62	2.49	3.04	2.89	3.41	3.16	3.69	3.40	3.97	3.49	4.20	3.61
40	2.63	2.49	3.06	2.91	3.45	3.20	3.75	3.46	4.07	3.59	4.32	3.74
50	2.63	2.50	3.07	2.92	3.47	3.22	3.79	3.51	4.13	3.65	4.40	3.82
75	2.63	2.50	3.09	2.94	3.51	3.27	3.86	3.57	4.23	3.75	4.53	3.94
100	2.64	2.51	3.10	2.95	3.54	3.29	3.90	3.62	5.29	3.81	4.61	4.02
150	2.65	2.51	3.12	2.97	3.56	3.32	3.95	3.67	4.36	3.88	4.70	4.11
300	2.65	2.52	3.14	2.99	3.61	3.36	4.02	3.73	4.46	3.97	4.83	4.24

References

Adams, F.G. and L.R. Klein (1991), 'Performance of quarterly econometric models of the United States: a new round of comparisons', in L.R.Klein (ed.) , *Comparative Performance of U.S. Econometric Models*, Oxford University Press, Oxford.

Ahumada, H.A. (1985), 'An encompassing test of two models of the balance of trade for Argentina', *Oxford Bulletin of Economics and Statistics* 47, pp. 51–70.

Aldrich, J. (1989), 'Autonomy', *Oxford Economic Papers* 41, pp. 15–34, reprinted in de Marchi, N. and C. Gilbert (eds) (1989) , *History and Methodology of Econometrics*, Oxford University Press, Oxford.

Allen, R.G.D. (1966), *Mathematical Economics*, 2nd edition, Macmillan, London.

Amemiya, T. (1985), *Advanced Econometrics*, Basil Blackwell, Oxford.

Bancroft, T.A. (1944), 'On biases in estimation due to the use of preliminary tests of significance', *Annals of Mathematical Statistics* 15, pp. 190–204.

Banerjee, A., J.J. Dolado, D.F. Hendry and G.W. Smith (1986), 'Exploring equilibrium relationships in econometrics through static models: some Monte Carlo evidence', *Oxford Bulletin of Economics and Statistics* 48, pp. 253–277.

Bernanke, B.S. (1986), 'Alternative explanations for the money–income correlation', in Brunner, K. and A. Meltzer (eds) , *Carnegie–Rochester Conference Series on Public Policy*, Volume 25, North–Holland, Amsterdam.

Berndt, E.R. and N.E. Savin (1977), 'Conflict among criteria for testing hypotheses in the multivariate regression model', *Econometrica* 45, pp. 1263–1278.

Blanchard, O. and M.W. Watson (1986), 'Are business cycles all alike?', in Gordon, R.J. (ed.), *The American Business Cycle: Continuity and Change*, University of Chicago Press, Chicago.

Blangiewicz, M. and W.W. Charemza (1990), 'Cointegration

in small samples: empirical percentiles, drifting moments and customized testing', *Oxford Bulletin of Economics and Statistics* **52**, pp. 303–315.

Bollerslev, T. and S. Hylleberg (1985), 'A note on the relation between consumers' expenditure and income in the UK', *Oxford Bulletin of Economics and Statistics* **47**, pp. 153–170.

Branson, W.H. and A.K. Klevorick (1969), 'Money illusion and the aggregate consumption function', *American Economic Review* **59**, pp. 832–849.

Brown, R.L. , J. Durbin and J.M. Evans (1975), 'Techniques for testing the constancy of regression relationships over time', *Journal of the Royal Statistical Society, Series B* **37** , pp. 149–163.

Buse, A. (1982), 'The likelihood ratio, Wald, and Lagrange multiplier tests: an expository note', *The American Statistician* **36**, pp. 153–157.

Campbell, J.Y. and N.S. Mankiw (1990), 'Permanent income, current income and consumption', *Journal of Business and Economic Statistics* **8**, pp. 269–279.

Campbell, J.Y. and N.S. Mankiw (1991), 'The response of consumption to income: a cross–country investigation', *European Economic Review* **35**, pp. 723–767.

Caudill, S.B. (1988), 'The necessity of mining data', *Atlantic Economic Review* **26**, pp. 11–18.

Charemza, W.W. (1988), 'A note on definitions of invariance and exogeneity', Discussion Paper No. 96, Department of Economics, University of Leicester.

Charemza, W.W. (1989), 'Disequilibrium modelling of consumption in the centrally planned economy', in Davis, C.M. and W.W. Charemza (eds), *Models of Disequilibrium and Shortage in Centrally Planned Economies*, Chapman and Hall, London.

Charemza, W.W. (1990a), 'The free market for foreign exchange in Poland: cointegration, speculative bubbles and error–corrections', Discussion Paper No. 133, Department of Economics, University of Leicester.

Charemza, W.W. (1990b), 'Large econometric models of an East European economy: a critique of the methodology', *Economic Modelling* **8**, pp. 45–61.

336   *New Directions in Econometric Practice*

Charemza, W.W. (1990c), 'Parallel markets, excess demand and virtual prices', *European Economic Review* **34**, pp. 331–339.

Charemza, W.W. (1991), 'Alternative paths to macroeconomic stability in Czechoslovakia', *The European Economy*, Special edition No 2, pp. 41–56.

Charemza, W.W. and S. Ghatak (1990), 'Demand for money in a dual–currency, quantity–constrained economy: Hungary and Poland, 1956–1985', *The Economic Journal* **100**, pp. 1159–1172.

Charemza, W.W. and J. Király (1990), 'Plans and exogeneity: the genetic–teleological dispute revisited', *Oxford Economic Papers* **42**, pp. 562–573.

Charemza W.W. and J. Király (1991), 'A simple test for non–random parameter variation', Department of Economics, University of Leicester (mimeo).

Chong, Y.Y. and D.F. Hendry (1986), 'Econometric evaluation of linear macro–economic models', *Review of Economic Studies* **53**, pp. 671–690.

Christ, C.F. (1966), *Econometric Models and Methods*, J. Wiley & Sons, Inc., New York.

Christ, C.F. (1975), 'Judging the performance of econometric models of the U.S. economy', *International Economic Review* **16**, pp. 54–74.

Christious, L.J., M. Eichenbaum and D. Marshall (1991), 'The permanent income hypothesis revisited', *Econometrica* **59**, pp. 397–423.

Clements, M.P. (1989), 'The estimation and testing of cointegrating vectors: a survey of recent approaches and an application to the U.K. non–durable consumption function', Applied Economics Discussion Paper No. 79, Institute of Economics and Statistics, University of Oxford, Oxford.

Clements, M.P. and D.F. Hendry (1991), 'On the invalidity of mean square error forecast comparisons in economics', Institute of Economics and Statistics and Nuffield College, Oxford University, Oxford (mimeo).

Cooley, T.F. and S.F. LeRoy (1985), 'Atheoretical macroeconomics', *Journal of Monetary Economics* **16**, pp. 283–308.

Cooper, R.L. (1972), 'The predictive performance of quarterly econometric models of the United States', in Hickman, B.G. (ed.), *Econometric Models of Cyclical Behavior*, Columbia University Press, New York.

Cox, D.R. (1961), 'Tests of separate families of hypotheses', *Proceedings of the Fourth Berkeley Symposium on Mathematical Statistics and Probability*, Volume 1, University of California Press, Berkeley.

Cryer, J.D. (1986), *Time Series Analysis*, Duxbury Press, Boston.

Cuthbertson, K. (1985), *The Supply and Demand for Money*, Basil Blackwell, Oxford.

Cuthbertson, K., S.G. Hall and M.P. Taylor (1992), *Applied Econometric Techniques*, Philip Allan, New York.

Cuthbertson, K. and M.P. Taylor (1988), 'Alternative scale variables in the U.S. demand function for narrow money; some non–nested tests', *Cyprus Journal of Economics* 1, pp. 102–110.

Darnell, A.C. (1986), 'Some observations on autoregressive distributed lag modelling', Working Paper No. 78, Department of Economics, University of Durham.

Darnell, A.C. (1988), '"General to specific" modelling: a methodological perspective', Working Paper No. 90, Department of Economics, University of Durham.

Darnell, A.C. and J.L. Evans (1990), *The Limits of Econometrics*, Edward Elgar, Aldershot.

Davidson, J.H., D.H. Hendry, F. Srba and S. Yeo (1978), 'Econometric modelling of the aggregate time–series relationship between consumers' expenditure and income in the United Kingdom', *The Economic Journal* 88, pp. 661–692.

Davidson, R. and J.G. MacKinnon (1981), 'Several tests for model specification in the presence of alternative hypotheses', *Econometrica* 49, pp. 781–793.

Davidson, R. and J.G. MacKinnon (1982), 'Some non–nested hypothesis tests and the relations among them', *Review of Economic Studies* 44, pp. 551–565.

Davidson, R. and J.G. MacKinnon (1985), 'The interpretation of test statistics', *Canadian Journal of Economics* 18, pp. 38–57.

Deadman, D. and S. Ghatak (1981), 'On the stability of the demand for money in India', *Indian Economic Journal* **29**, pp. 41–54.

Deadman, D. and S. Ghatak (1989), 'Money, prices and stabilisation policies in some developing countries', *Applied Economics* **21**, pp. 853–865.

Deaton, A.S. (1977), 'Involuntary saving through unanticipated inflation', *American Economic Review* **67**, pp. 899–910.

Denton, F.T. (1985), 'Data mining as an industry', *Review of Economics and Statistics* **67**, pp. 124–127.

Desai, M. (1976), *Applied Econometrics*, Philip Allan, Oxford.

Desai, M. (1981), *Testing Monetarism*, Frances Pinter, London.

Dhrymes, P.J. (1970a), *Econometrics: Statistical Foundations and Applications*, Harper and Row, New York.

Dhrymes, P.J. (1970b), 'On the game of maximizing $\bar{R}^2$', *Australian Economic Papers* **9**, pp. 177–185.

Dhrymes, P.J. (1978), *Introductory Econometrics*, Springer-Verlag, New York.

Dickey, D.A. and W.A. Fuller (1979), 'Distributions of the estimators for autoregressive time series with a unit root', *Journal of the American Statistical Association* **74**, pp. 427–431.

Dickey, D.A. and W.A. Fuller (1981), 'Likelihood ratio statistics for autoregressive time series with a unit root', *Econometrica* **49**, pp. 1057–1072.

Dickey, D.A., D.P. Hasza and W.A. Fuller (1984), 'Testing for unit roots in seasonal time series', *Journal of the American Statistical Association* **79**, pp. 355–367.

Dickey, D.A. and S.S. Pantula (1987), 'Determining the order of differencing in autoregressive processes', *Journal of Business and Statistics* **5**, pp. 455–461.

Doan, T., R.B. Litterman and C.A. Sims (1984), 'Forecasting and conditional projection using realistic prior distributions', *Econometric Reviews* **3**, pp. 1–100.

Duesenberry, J.S., G. Fromm, L.R. Klein and E. Kuh (eds) (1965), *The Brookings Quarterly Econometric Model of the United States*, North–Holland, Amsterdam.

Durbin, J. (1970), 'Testing for serial correlation in least squares regression when some of the regressors are lagged dependent variables', *Econometrica* **38**, pp. 410–421.

Durbin, P.T. (1988), *Dictionary of Concepts in the Philosophy of Science*, Greenwood Press, New York.

Eichenbaum, M. (1985), 'Vector autoregressions for causal inference: comment', in Brunner, K. and A.M. Meltzer (eds), *Carnegie–Rochester Conference Series on Public Policy* Volume 22, North–Holland, Amsterdam.

Engle, R.F. (1984), 'Wald, likelihood ratio and Lagrange multiplier tests in econometrics', in Griliches, Z. and M.D. Intriligator (eds), *Handbook of Econometrics*, Volume 2, North–Holland, Amsterdam.

Engle, R.F. and C.W.J. Granger (1987), 'Co–integration and error correction: representation, estimation and testing', *Econometrica* 55, pp. 251–276.

Engle, R.F. and C.W.J. Granger (eds) (1991), *Long Run Economic Relations: Readings in Cointegration*, Oxford University Press, Oxford.

Engle, R.F., C.W.J. Granger and J.J. Hallman (1989), 'Merging short– and long–run forecasts: an application of seasonal cointegration to monthly electricity sales forecasting', *Journal of Econometrics* **40**, pp. 45–62.

Engle, R.F. and D.F. Hendry (1990), 'Testing superexogeneity and invariance', Paper presented at the World Congress of the Econometric Society, Barcelona.

Engle, R.F., D.F. Hendry and J.–F. Richard (1983), 'Exogeneity', *Econometrica* 51, pp. 277–304.

Engle, R.F. and B.S. Yoo (1987), 'Forecasting and testing in cointegrated systems', *Journal of Econometrics* 35, pp. 143–159.

Epstein, R.J. (1987), *A History of Econometrics*, North-Holland, Amsterdam.

Ericsson, N.R. (1983), 'Asymptotic properties of instrumental variables statistics for testing non–nested hypotheses', *Review of Economic Studies* 50, pp. 251–276.

Ericsson, N.R. (1989), 'Mean square error and forecast encompassing', Discussion Paper, International Finance Division, Board of Governors of the Federal Reserve System.

Fair, R.C. (1988), 'VAR models as structural approximations', Working Paper No. 2495, National Bureau of Economic Research, Cambridge, Massachusetts.

Farebrother, R.W. (1980), 'The Durbin–Watson test for serial correlation when there is no intercept in the regression', *Econometrica* 48, pp. 1553–1563.

Farrell, M.J. (1959), 'The new theories of the consumption function', *The Economic Journal* 69, pp. 678–696.

Favero, C. (1989), 'The Lucas critique, feedback and feedforward mechanisms and the consumption function: an empirical study', Discussion Paper No. 73, Institute of Economics and Statistics, University of Oxford.

Ferber, R. (1962), 'Research on household behavior', *The American Economic Review* 52, pp. 19–63.

Fisher, D. and A. Serletis (1989), 'Velocity and the growth of money in the United States, 1970–1985', *Journal of Macroeconomics* 11, pp. 323–332.

Fisher, G.R. and M. McAleer (1981), 'Alternative procedures and associated tests of significance for non–nested hypotheses', *Journal of Econometrics* 16, pp. 103–119.

Flavin, M.A. (1981), 'The adjustment of consumption to changing expectations about future income', *Journal of Political Economy* 89, pp. 974–1009.

Fosu, A.K. and M.S. Huq (1988), 'Price inflation and wage inflation: a cause–effect relationship?', *Economics Letters* 27, pp. 35–40.

Franses, P.H. (1990), 'A model selection procedure for time series with seasonality', Econometric Institute, Erasmus University, Rotterdam (mimeo).

Freund, J.E. and R.E. Walpole (1987), *Mathematical Statistics*, 4th edition, Prentice Hall International, London.

Frisch, R. (1936), 'Note on the term 'econometrics'', *Econometrica* 4, p. 95.

Friedman, M. (1957), *A Theory of the Consumption Function*, Princeton University Press, Princeton.

Fuller, W.A. (1976), *Introduction to Statistical Time Series*, J. Wiley & Sons, Inc., New York.

Gapinski, J.H. (1982), *Macroeconomic Theory: Statics, Dynamics and Policy*, McGraw–Hill, London.

Geweke, J. (1984), 'Inference and causality in economic time series models', in Griliches, Z. and M.D. Intriligator (eds), *Handbook of Econometrics* Volume 2, North-Holland, Amsterdam.

Geweke, J., R. Meese and W. Dent (1983), 'Comparing alternative tests of causality in temporal systems', *Journal of Econometrics* 21, pp. 161–194.

Ghatak, S. and W.W. Charemza (1989), 'Financial dualism and virtual interest rate: the case of India', Discussion Paper No. 118, Department of Economics, University of Leicester.

Ghysels, E. (1990), 'On the economics and econometrics of seasonality', Department of Economics, University of Montreal (mimeo).

Ghysels, E. and P. Perron (1990), 'The effect of seasonal adjustment filters on tests for a unit root', Princeton University, Princeton (mimeo).

Gilbert, C.L. (1986), 'Professor Hendry's econometric methodology', *Oxford Bulletin of Economics and Statistics* 48, pp. 283–307, reprinted in Granger, C.W.J. (ed.) (1990), *Modelling Economic Series: Readings in Econometric Methodology*, Oxford University Press, Oxford.

Gilbert, C.L. (1989), 'LSE and the British approach to time series econometrics', *Oxford Economic Papers* 41, pp. 108–128, reprinted in de Marchi, N. and C. Gilbert (eds) (1989), *History and Methodology of Econometrics*, Oxford University Press, Oxford.

Godfrey, L.G. (1984), 'On the use of misspecification checks and tests of non–nested hypotheses in empirical econometrics', *Supplement to Economic Journal Conference Papers* 94, pp. 69–81.

Godfrey, L.G. (1989), *Misspecification Tests in Econometrics – Lagrange Multiplier Principle and Other Approaches*, Cambridge University Press, Cambridge.

Godfrey, L.G. and M.H. Pesaran (1983), 'Tests of non–nested regression models: small sample adjustments and Monte Carlo evidence', *Journal of Econometrics* **21**, pp. 133–154.

Goldberger, A.S. (1964), *Econometric Theory*, J. Wiley & Sons, Inc., New York.

Goldberger, A.S. (1991), '*A Course in Econometrics*', Harvard University Press, Cambridge, Massachusetts.

Granger, C.W.J. (1969), 'Investigating causal relations by econometric models and cross–spectral methods', *Econometrica* **37**, pp. 24–36.

Granger, C.W.J. (1988), 'Some recent developments in a concept of causality', *Journal of Econometrics* **39**, pp. 199–211.

Granger, C.W.J. (ed.) (1990), *Modelling Economic Series: Readings in Econometric Methodology*, Oxford University Press, Oxford.

Granger, C.W.J. and P. Newbold (1974), 'Spurious regressions in econometrics', *Journal of Econometrics* **35**, pp. 143–159.

Granger, C.W.J. and P. Newbold (1986), *Forecasting Economic Time Series*, 2nd edition, Academic Press, Inc., Orlando, Florida.

Greenberg, E. and C.E. Webster, Jr. (1983), *Advanced Econometrics: a Bridge to the Literature*, J. Wiley & Sons, Inc., New York.

Gregory, A.W. and M.R. Veall (1986), 'Wald tests of common factor restrictions', *Economics Letters* **22**, pp. 203–208.

Guilkey, D.K. and M.K. Salemi (1982), 'Small sample properties of three tests for Granger–causal ordering in a bivariate stochastic system', *Review of Economics and Statistics* **64**, pp. 668–680.

Guilkey, D.K. and P. Schmidt (1989), 'Extended tabulations for Dickey–Fuller tests', *Economics Letters* **31**, pp. 355–357.

Haavelmo, T. (1944), 'The probability approach in econometrics', Supplement to *Econometrica* **12**, pp. 1–118.

Hall, R.E. (1978), 'Stochastic implications of the life cycle –

permanent income hypothesis: theory and evidence', *Journal of Political Economy* 86, pp. 971–987.

Hall, S.G. (1989), 'Maximum likelihood estimation of cointegration vectors: an example of the Johansen procedure', *Oxford Bulletin of Economics and Statistics* 51, pp. 213–219.

Hall, S.G. and S.S.B. Henry (1988), *Macroeconomic modelling*, North–Holland, Amsterdam.

Harvey, A.C. (1989), *Forecasting, Structural Time Series Models and the Kalman Filter*, Cambridge University Press, Cambridge.

Harvey, A. C. (1990), *The Econometric Analysis of Time Series*, 2nd edition, Philip Allan, Hemel Hempstead.

Hendry, D.F. (1974), 'Stochastic specification in an aggregate demand model of the United Kingdom', *Econometrica* 42, pp. 559–578.

Hendry, D.F. (1979), 'Predictive failure and econometric modelling in macroeconomics. The transactions demand for money', in Ormerod, P. (ed.), *Modelling the Economy*, Heinemann, London.

Hendry, D.F. (1980), 'Econometrics – alchemy or science?', *Economica* 47, pp. 387–406.

Hendry, D.F. (1983), 'Econometric modelling: the "consumption function" in retrospect', *Scottish Journal of Political Economy* 30, pp. 193–220.

Hendry, D.F. (1987), 'Econometric methodology: a personal perspective', in Bewley, T.F. (ed.), *Advances in Econometrics: Fifth World Congress*, Volume 2, Cambridge University Press, Cambridge.

Hendry, D.F. (1988a), 'Encompassing', *National Institute Economic Review* No. 125, pp. 88–92.

Hendry, D.F. (1988b), 'The encompassing implications of feedback versus feedforward mechanisms in econometrics', *Oxford Economic Papers* 40, pp. 132–149.

Hendry, D.F. (1989), *PC–GIVE: An Interactive Econometric Modelling System*, Institute of Economics and Statistics, University of Oxford, Oxford.

Hendry, D.F. and N.R. Ericsson (1991), 'An econometric analysis of U.K. money demand in "Monetary trends in the United States and the United Kingdom" by Milton Friedman and Anna J.Schwartz', *American Economic Review* **81**, pp. 8–38.

Hendry, D.F. and G.E. Mizon (1978), 'Serial correlation as a convenient simplification, not a nuisance: a comment on a study of the demand for money by the Bank of England', *The Economic Journal* **88**, pp. 549–563.

Hendry, D.F. and G.E. Mizon (1990), 'Evaluating dynamic econometric models by encompassing by the VAR', Nuffield College, Oxford (mimeo).

Hendry, D.F., J.H. Muellbauer and A. Murphy (1990), 'The econometrics of DHSY', in Hey, J.D. and O. Winch (eds), *A Century of Economics*: 100 *Years of the Royal Economic Society and the Economic Journal*, Basil Blackwell, Oxford.

Hendry, D.F., A.R. Pagan and J.D. Sargan (1984), 'Dynamic specification', in Griliches, Z. and M.D. Intriligator (eds), *Handbook of Econometrics*, Volume 2, North-Holland, Amsterdam.

Hendry, D.F. and J.–F. Richard (1982), 'On the formulation of empirical models in dynamic econometrics', *Journal of Econometrics* **20**, pp. 3–33.

Hendry, D.F. and J.–F. Richard (1983), 'The econometric analysis of economic time series', *International Statistical Review* **51**, pp. 111–163.

Hendry, D.F. and T. von Ungern–Sternberg (1980), 'Liquidity and inflation effects on consumers' expenditure', in A.S. Deaton (ed.), *Essays in the Theory and Measurement of Consumers' Behaviour*, Cambridge University Press, Cambridge.

Holden, D.R. and P.G. McGregor (1989), 'The deflation of nominal magnitudes in the consumption function: a note', Discussion Paper No. 89/6, Department of Economics, University of Strathclyde, Glasgow.

Holtz–Eakin, D., W. Newey and H.S. Rosen (1988), 'Estimating vector autoregressions with panel data', *Econometrica* **56**, pp. 1371–1395.

Houthakker, H.S. and L.D. Taylor (1966, 1970), *Consumer Demand in the United States*, 1st and 2nd editions, Harvard University Press, Harvard.

Hsiao, C. (1979), 'Causality tests in econometrics', *Journal of Economic Dynamics and Control* 1, pp. 321–346.

Hsiao, C. (1981), 'Autoregressive modelling and money–income causality detection', *Journal of Monetary Economics* 7, pp. 85–106.

Hylleberg, S., R.F. Engle, C.W.J. Granger and B.S. Yoo (1990), 'Seasonal integration and cointegration', *Journal of Econometrics* 44, pp. 215–238.

Hylleberg, S. and G.E. Mizon (1989), 'Cointegration and error correction mechanisms', *The Economic Journal* 99, pp. 113–125.

Jacobs, R.L., E.E. Leamer and M.P. Ward (1979), 'Difficulties with testing for causation', *Economic Inquiry* 17, pp. 401–413.

Jacobson, T. and H. Ohlsson (1991), 'Cointegrating sectoral wages in Sweden: a maximum likelihood approach', Working Paper 1991:5, Department of Economics, Uppsala University.

Johansen, S. (1988), 'Statistical analysis of cointegration vectors', *Journal of Economic Dynamics and Control* 12, pp. 231–254.

Johansen, S. (1989), *Likelihood Based Inferences on Cointegration. Theory and Applications*, Cento Interuniversitario di Econometria (CIDE), Bologna.

Johansen, S. and K. Juselius (1990), 'Maximum likelihood estimation and inference on cointegration – with applications to the demand for money', *Oxford Bulletin of Economics and Statistics* 52, pp. 169–210.

Johnston, J. (1984), *Econometric Methods*, 3rd edition, McGraw–Hill, New York.

Judge, G.G., W.E. Griffiths, R.C. Hill, H. Lütkepohl and T.–C. Lee (1985), *The Theory and Practice of Econometrics*, 2nd edition, J. Wiley & Sons, Inc., New York.

Karni, E. and B.K. Shapiro (1980), 'Tales of horror from ivory towers', *Journal of Political Economy* 88, pp. 210–212.

Kendall, M. and J.K. Ord (1990), *Time Series*, 3rd edition, Edward Arnold, London.

Kennedy, P. (1990), *A Guide to Econometrics*, 2nd edition, Martin Robertson, Oxford.

Keynes, J.M. (1936), *The General Theory of Employment, Interest, and Money*, Macmillan, London.

Kiviet, J.F. (1986), 'On the rigour of some misspecification tests for modelling dynamic relationships', *Review of Economic Studies* **53**, pp. 241–261.

Klein, L.R. (1950), *Economic Fluctuations in the United States*, 1921–1941, J. Wiley & Sons, Inc., New York.

Klein, L.R. (1971a), *An Essay on the Theory of Economic Prediction*, Markham Publishing Company, Chicago.

Klein, L.R. (1971b), 'Whither econometrics?', *Journal of the American Statistical Association* **66**, pp. 415–421.

Klein, L.R. and A.S. Goldberger (1955), *An Econometric Model of the United States*, 1929–1952, North–Holland, Amsterdam.

Kmenta, J. (1986), *Elements of Econometrics*, 2nd edition, Macmillan, New York.

Koerts, J. and A.P.J. Abrahamse (1969), *On the Theory and Application of the General Linear Model*, Rotterdam University Press, Rotterdam.

Kramer, W., W. Ploberger and R. Alt (1988), 'Testing for structural change in dynamic models', *Econometrica* **56**, pp. 1355–1369.

Kunst, R.M (1989), 'Cointegration in macroeconomic systems: seasonality and explosive roots', Research Memorandum No. 255, Institute for Advanced Studies, Vienna.

Kunst, R.M. (1990), 'Seasonal cointegration in macroeconomic systems: case studies for small and large European countries', Research Memorandum No. 271, Institute for Advanced Studies, Vienna.

Lafontaine, F. and K.J. White (1986), 'Obtaining any Wald statistic you want', *Economics Letters* **21**, pp. 35–40.

Leamer, E.E. (1978), *Specification Searches*, J. Wiley & Sons, Inc., New York.

Leamer, E.E. (1983a), 'Let's take the con out of econometrics', *American Economic Review* **23**, pp. 31–43, reprinted in Granger, C.W.J. (ed.) (1990), *Modelling Economic Series: Readings in Econometric Methodology*, Oxford University Press, Oxford.

Leamer, E.E. (1983b), 'Model Choice and Specification Analysis', in Griliches, Z. and M.D. Intriligator (eds), *Handbook of Econometrics*, Volume 1, North–Holland, Amsterdam.

Leamer, E.E. (1985), 'Vector autoregressions for causal inference?', in Brunner, K. and A. Meltzer (eds), *Carnegie–Rochester Conference Series on Public Policy* Volume 22, North–Holland, Amsterdam.

Levačić, R. and A. Rebmann (1982), *Macro–Economics: An Introduction to Keynesian–Neoclassical Controversies*, 2nd edition, Macmillan, London.

Litterman, R.B. (1986), 'Forecasting with Bayesian vector autoregressions: five years of experience', *Journal of Business and Economic Statistics* 4, pp. 25–38.

Liu, T.C. (1960), 'Underidentification, structural estimation, and forecasting', *Econometrica* 28, pp. 855–865.

Lovell, M.C. (1983), 'Data mining', *Review of Economics and Statistics* 65, pp. 1–12.

Lubrano, M. and V. Marimotou (1988), 'Bayesian specification searches', Document de Travail No. 8803, GREQE, Marseille.

Lubrano, M., R.S. Pierse and J.–F. Richard (1986), 'Stability of a U.K. demand equation: a Bayesian approach to testing exogeneity', *Review of Economic Studies* 53, pp. 603–634.

Lucas, R.E. (1976), 'Economic policy evaluation: a critique', in Brunner, K. and A.M. Meltzer (eds), *The Phillips Curve and Labor Markets*, *Carnegie–Rochester Conference Series on Public Policy*, Volume 1, North–Holland, Amsterdam.

Lütkepohl, H. (1991), *Introduction to multiple time series analysis*, Springer–Verlag, Berlin.

MacKinnon, J.G. (1983), 'Model specification tests against non–nested alternatives', *Econometric Reviews* 2 , pp. 85–110.

MacKinnon, J.G. (1991), 'Critical values for cointegration tests', in Engle, R.F. and C.W.J. Granger (eds.), *Long–run economic relationships*, Oxford University Press, Oxford.

Maddala, G.S. (ed.) (1981), 'Model selection', *Journal of Econometrics*, **16**, (special issue).

Maddala, G.S. (1988), *Introduction to Econometrics*, Macmillan, London.

Malinvaud, E. (1981), 'Econometrics faced with the needs of macroeconomic policy', *Econometrica* **49**, pp. 1363–1375.

McAleer, M. and M.H. Pesaran (1986), 'Statistical inference in non–nested econometric models', *Applied Mathematics and Computation* **20**, pp. 271–311.

McCarthy, M.D. (1972), *The Wharton Quarterly Econometric Forecasting Model Mark III*, Wharton School of Finance and Commerce, Philadelphia.

McNees, S.K. (1979), 'The accuracy of macroeconomic models and forecasts of the U.S. economy', in Ormerod, P. (ed.) , *Economic Modelling*, Heinemann, London.

McNees, S.K. (1986), 'Forecasting accuracy of alternative techniques: a comparison of US macroeconomic forecasts', *Journal of Business and Economic Statistics* **4**, pp. 5–15.

Miller, S.M. (1988), 'Are savings and investment co–integrated ?', *Economics Letters* **27**, pp. 31–34.

Mills, T.C. (1990), *Time series techniques for economists*, Cambridge University Press, Cambridge.

Mizon, G.E. (1984), 'The encompassing approach in econometrics', in Hendry, D.F. and K.F. Wallis (eds), *Econometrics and Quantitative Economics*, Basil Blackwell, Oxford.

Mizon, G.E. and J.–F. Richard (1986), 'The encompassing principle and its application to testing non–nested hypothesis, *Econometrica* **54**, pp. 657–678.

Monfort, A. and R. Rabemanjara (1990), 'From a VAR model to a structural model, with an application to the wage–price spiral', *Journal of Applied Econometrics* **5**, pp. 203–227.

Morgan, M.S. (1990), *The History of Econometric Ideas*, Cambridge University Press, Cambridge.

Muscatelli, V.A. (1989), 'A comparison of the 'rational expectations' and 'general–to–specific' approaches to modelling the demand for M1', *Oxford Bulletin of Economics and Statistics* 51, pp. 353–375.

Muscatelli, V. and L. Papi (1988), 'Cointegration and "general to specific": an application to the demand for money in Italy', Discussion Paper No. 8804, Department of Political Economy, University of Glasgow.

Naylor, T.H., T.G. Seales and D.W. Wichern (1972), 'Box-Jenkins methods: an alternative to econometric models', *International Statistical Review* 40, pp. 123-137.

Nelson, C.R. and N. Kang (1981), 'Spurious periodicity in inappropriately detrended time series', *Econometrica* 49, pp. 741–751.

Nelson, C.R. and C.I. Plosser (1982), 'Trends and random walks in macroeconomic time series: some evidence and implications', *Journal of Monetary Economics* 10, pp. 139–162.

Nerlove, M. (1965), 'A tabular survey of macro–econometric models', *International Economic Review* 7, pp. 127—175.

Newbold, P. and N. Davies (1978), 'Error miss–specification and spurious regressions', *International Economic Review* 19, pp. 513–519.

Osborn, D.R. , A.P.L. Chui, J.P. Smith and C.R. Birchenhall (1988), 'Seasonality and the order of integration for consumption', *Oxford Bulletin of Economics and Statistics* 50, pp. 361–377.

Osterwald–Lenum, M. (1990), 'Recalculated and extended tables of the asymptotic distribution of some important maximum likelihood cointegration test statistics', Institute of Economics, University of Copenhagen (mimeo).

Pagan, A.R. (1987), 'Three econometric methodologies: a critical appraisal', *Journal of Economic Surveys* 1, pp. 3–24, reprinted in Granger, C.W.J. (ed.) (1990), *Modelling Economic Series: Readings in Econometric Methodology*, Oxford University Press, Oxford..

Park, J.Y. and P.C.B. Phillips (1988), 'Statistical inference in regressions with integrated processes: Part I', *Econometric Theory* 4, pp. 468–498.

Park, J.Y. and P.C.B. Phillips (1989), 'Statistical inference in regressions with integrated processes: Part II', *Econometric Theory* 5, pp. 95–131.

Patterson, K.D. (1986), 'The stability of some annual consumption functions', *Oxford Economic Papers*, **38**, pp. 1–30.

Perron, P. (1989), 'The great crash, the oil price shock and the unit root hypothesis', *Econometrica* 57, pp. 1361-1401.

Pesaran, M.H. (1974), 'On the general problem of model selection', *Review of Economic Studies* 41, pp. 153–171

Pesaran, M.H. and A.S. Deaton (1978), 'Testing non–nested nonlinear regression models', *Econometrica* **46**, pp. 677–694.

Pesaran, M.H. and R. Smith (1990), 'A unified approach to estimation and orthogonality tests in linear single equation econometric models', *Journal of Econometrics* 44, pp. 41–66.

Pesaran, M.H., R.P. Smith and J.S. Yeo (1985), 'Testing for structural stability and predictive failure: a review', *Manchester School* 53, pp. 280–295.

Phillips, P.C.B. (1986), 'Understanding spurious regressions in econometrics', *Journal of Econometrics* **33**, pp. 311–340.

Phillips, P.C.B. (1988a), 'Reflections on econometric methodology', *The Economic Record*, **64**, pp. 344–359.

Phillips, P.C.B. (1988b), 'Regression theory for near–integrated time series', *Econometrica* 56, pp. 1021–1043.

Phillips, P.C.B. and M. Loretan, 'Estimating long–run economic equilibria', *Review of Economic Studies* 5, pp. 407–436.

Phillips, P.C.B. and S. Ouliaris (1990), 'Asymptotic properties of residual based tests for cointegration', *Econometrica* 58, pp. 165–193.

Pindyck, R.S. and D.L. Rubinfeld (1991), *Econometric Models and Economic Forecasts*, 3rd edition, McGraw-Hill, New York.

Podvinsky, J. (1990), 'Testing misspecified cointegrating vectors', Working Paper No. 19/90, Department of Econometrics, Monash University.

Pokorny, M. (1987), *An Introduction to Econometrics*, Basil Blackwell, Oxford.

Portes, R. and D. Winter (1978), 'The demand for money and for consumption goods in centrally planned economies', *Review of Economics and Statistics* 60, pp. 8–18.

Portes, R. and D. Winter (1980), 'Disequilibrium estimates for consumption goods markets in centrally planned economies', *Review of Economic Studies* 47, pp. 137-159.

Pratt, J.W. and R. Schlaifer (1984) 'On the nature and discovery of structure', *Journal of the American Statistical Association* 79, pp. 9–21.

Quandt, R.E. (1974), 'A comparison of methods for testing non–nested hypotheses', *Review of Economics and Statistics* 56, pp. 92–99.

Runckle, D.E. (1987), 'Vector autoregressions and reality', *Journal of Business and Economic Statistics* 5, pp. 437–442 (also comments pp. 443–454).

Said, S.E. and D.A. Dickey (1984), 'Testing for unit roots in autoregressive moving average models of unknown order', *Biometrika* 71, pp. 599–607.

Sargan, J.D. and A. Bhargava (1983), 'Testing residuals from least squares regression for being generated by the Gaussian random walk', *Econometrica* 51, pp. 153–174.

Sargent, T.J. (1976), 'A classical macroeconomic model for the United States', *Journal of Political Economy* 84, pp. 207–238.

Shannon, R. and M.S. Wallace (1985–86), 'Wages and inflation: an investigation into causality', *Journal of Post Keynesian Economics* 8, pp. 182–191.

Sims, C.A. (1972), 'Money income and causality', *American Economic Review* 62, pp. 540–552.

Sims, C.A. (1980), 'Macroeconomics and reality', *Econometrica* 48, pp. 1–48.

Sims, C.A. (1982), 'Policy analysis with econometric models', *Brookings Papers on Economic Activity* 1, pp. 107—152.

Singh, B. and B.S. Sahni (1984), 'Causality between public expenditure and national income', *Review of Economics and Statistics* 66, pp. 630–644.

Spanos, A. (1986), *Statistical Foundations of Econometric Modelling*, Cambridge University Press, Cambridge.

Spanos, A. (1988), 'Towards a unifying methodological framework for econometric modelling', *Economic Notes* No.1, pp. 1–28, reprinted in Granger C.W.J. (ed.) (1990), *Modelling economic series*, Oxford University Press, Oxford.

Spanos, A. (1989), 'Early empirical findings on the consumption function, stylized facts or fiction: a retrospective view', *Oxford Economic Papers* 41, pp. 150–169, reprinted in de Marchi, N. and C. Gilbert (eds) (1989), *History and Methodology of Econometrics*, Oxford University Press, Oxford.

Spohn, W. (1984), 'Probabilistic causality: from Hume via Suppes to Granger', in Galavotti, M.C. and G. Gambetta (eds), *Causalita e modelli probabilistica*, Clueb Editrica, Bologna.

Steel, M.F.J. (1987), 'Testing for exogeneity: an application to consumption behaviour', *European Economic Review* 31, pp. 1443–1463.

Steel, M.F.J. (1989), 'Weak exogeneity in misspecified sequential models', Discussion Paper No. 8942, CentER, Tilburg University.

Steel, M.F.J. and J.–F. Richard (1989), 'Bayesian multivariate exogeneity analysis; an application to a UK money demand equation', Discussion Paper No. 8929, CentER, Tilburg University.

Stewart, M.B. and K.F. Wallis (1981), *Introductory Econometrics*, 2nd edition, Basil Blackwell, Oxford.

Stock, J.H. and M.W. Watson (1988), 'Testing for common trends', *Journal of the American Statistical Association* 83, pp. 1097–1107.

Stock, J.H. and M.W. Watson (1989), 'Interpreting the evidence on money–income causality', *Journal of Econometrics* 40, pp. 161–181.

Swamy, S. (1968), 'A dynamic personal savings function and its long–run implications', *Review of Economics and Statistics* 50, pp. 111–116.

Taylor, L.D. and H.S. Houthakker (1990), 'Co–integration and habit formation: a reformulation of the dynamics of the Houthakker–Taylor models', Paper presented at the 6th World Congress of the Econometric Society, Barcelona.

Taylor, M.P. (1988), 'An empirical examination of long–run purchasing power parity using cointegration techniques', *Applied Economics* 20, pp. 1369–1381.

Theil, H. (1971), *Principles of Econometrics*, North–Holland, Amsterdam.

Thomas, J.J. (1989), 'The early econometric history of the consumption function', *Oxford Economic Papers* 41, pp. 131–149, reprinted in de Marchi, N. and C. Gilbert (eds) , *History and Methodology of Econometrics*, Oxford University Press, Oxford.

Tinbergen, J. (1951), *Econometrics*, George Allen & Unwin Ltd., London.

Tinbergen, J. (1959), *Selected Papers*, edited by Klaassen, L.H., L.M. Koyck and J.H. Witteveen, North–Holland, Amsterdam.

Tintner, G. (1952), *Econometrics*, J. Wiley & Sons, Inc., New York.

Todd, R.M. (1990), 'Improving economic forecasting with Bayesian vector autoregression', in Granger, C.W.J. (ed.), *Modelling Economic Series: Readings in Econometric Methodology*, Oxford University Press, Oxford.

Urbain, J.–P. (1991), 'On weak exogeneity in error correction models', Research Paper No. 9103, C.R.E.D.E.L., University of Liège.

Vandaele, W. (1983), *Applied Time Series and Box–Jenkins Models*, Academic Press, Orlando.

Wallace, T.D. (1977), 'Pretest estimation in regression: a survey', *American Journal of Agriculture Economics* 95, pp. 431–443.

Wallace, T.D. and Ashar, V.G. (1972), 'Sequential methods in model construction', *Review of Economics and Statistics* **54**, pp. 172–178.

Wallis, K.F. (1974), 'Seasonal adjustment and relations between variables', *Journal of the American Statistical Association* **69**, pp. 18–31.

Wallis, K.F. (1989), 'Macroeconomic forecasting: a survey', *Economic Journal* **99**, pp. 28–61.

West, K.D. (1988), 'Asymptotic normality, when regressors have a unit root', *Econometrica* **56**, pp. 1397–1417.

White, H. (1980), 'A heteroscedasticity–consistent covariance matrix estimator and a direct test for heteroscedasticity', *Econometrica* **48**, pp. 817–838.

Wickens, M.R. and T.S. Breusch (1988), 'Dynamic specification, the long–run and the estimation of transformed regression models', *The Economic Journal* **98** (Supplement), pp. 189–205.

Williams, D., C.A.E. Goodhart and D.H Gowland (1976), 'Money, income and causality: the UK experience', *American Economic Review* **66**, pp. 417–423.

Wold, H. (1954), 'Causality and econometrics', *Econometrica* **22**, pp. 162–177.

Worswick, G.D.N. (1972), 'Is progress in economic science possible?', *The Economic Journal* **82**, pp. 73–86.

Wu, D.–M. (1983), 'Tests of causality, predeterminess and exogeneity', *International Economic Review* **24**, pp. 547–558.

Wynn, R.F. and Holden, K. (1974), *An Introduction to Applied Econometric Analysis*, Macmillan, London.

Zellner, A. (1979), 'Causality and econometrics', in Brunner, K. and A. Meltzer (eds), *Carnegie–Rochester Conference Series on Public Policy*, Volume 10, North–Holland, Amsterdam.

Author Index

Subject Index

A

Absolute Income Hypothesis
  defined, 2, 32—34, 172
  estimation of, 38—41, 45—46,
    48—49
Adaptive expectations, 35—36
Additive seasonality, *see* Seasona-
  lity
ADF test, *see* Dickey—Fuller
ADFSI test, *see* Dickey—Fuller

Adjusted R^2 ($\overline{R}^2$), 17, 293
Adjustment (feedback) matrix,
  200
Admissible
  forecasts, 204
  intervention, 271, 279
  model, 176
  values, 291
Aggregation, 33
Akaike's criteria (*AIC*), 293, 295
A priori restrictions and tests
  exclusion (zero), 6, 22—23,
    29, 107, 180—182,
    210—213, 239
  linear, 80, 84, 87—92
  nonlinear, 80, 86, 88—95
Atheoretical macroeconomics, 182
Augmented Dickey—Fuller
  (*ADF*) test, *see* Dickey—
  Fuller

Autocorrelation
  caused by omitted varia-
    bles, 55, 103
  Durbin—Watson test, 42,
    160
  LM test, 103—104
  and *VAR*, 186, 195, 200
Autoregressive distributed lag
  (*ADL*) models
  and cointegration, 157—158
  general, 80—83
  specific, 83—86, 96
Autoregressive (*AR*) processes
  $AR(1)$, 42, 84—86,
    130—131, 280, 290
  $AR(m)$, 103—104
  stability condition for
    $AR(1)$, 131
Average propensity to consume,
  2, 33—34, 37, 60

B

Bayesian inference, 114, 184,
  236, 287, 294
Binomial distribution, 23—24
Bivariate normal distribution,
  242—243, 246—247,
  256—258, 272
'Bottom up' modelling, 65,
  108—109, 115
Brookings models, 10